Digital Dawn in Adland

Drawing on a unique study of Australian advertising agencies at the dawn of the digital era, this book provides a hitherto unexplored study of the advertising industry at a point of its disruption. By exploring the dynamic interaction between this established but complacent industry, and a radically new communication medium, this book reveals how advertising agencies were forced to change fundamentally, yet as an industry helped shape the digital economy, and the platforms that dominate it.

Based on contemporary reports, company archives, personal archives, and over 50 interviews with past and current advertising practitioners across the range of agency departments, this unique historical narrative reveals how power shifts between agencies, advertisers, and other media platforms forged the current models of advertiser-funded digital media.

For scholars of marketing, media, communication, and contemporary history, this is an illuminating perspective on the early impact of the digital revolution and its relevance to the media landscape today.

Robert Crawford is a Professor of Advertising and Associate Dean of Research and Innovation in the School of Media and Communication at RMIT University in Melbourne, Australia. His research has focused on the growth and development of the advertising, marketing and public relations industries across Australia, Oceania, and South East Asia.

Routledge Studies in the History of Marketing
Edited by **Mark Tadajewski** and **Brian D. G. Jones**

It is increasingly acknowledged that an awareness of marketing history and the history of marketing thought is relevant for all levels of marketing teaching and scholarship. Marketing history includes, but is not limited to, the histories of advertising, retailing, channels of distribution, product design and branding, pricing strategies, and consumption behaviour—all studied from the perspective of companies, industries, or even whole economies. The history of marketing thought examines marketing ideas, concepts, theories, and schools of marketing thought including the lives and times of marketing thinkers.

This series aims to be the central location for the publication of historical studies of marketing theory, thought, and practice and welcomes contributions from scholars from all disciplines that seek to explore some facet of marketing and consumer practice in a rigorous and scholarly fashion. It will also consider historical contributions that are conceptually and theoretically well-conceived, that engage with marketing theory and practice, in any time period, in any country.

For more information about this series, please visit: www.routledge.com/Routledge-Studies-in-the-History-of-Marketing/book-series/RSHM

Digital Dawn in Adland

Transforming Australian Agencies

Robert Crawford

Routledge
Taylor & Francis Group
LONDON AND NEW YORK

First published 2021
by Routledge
2 Park Square, Milton Park, Abingdon, Oxon OX14 4RN

and by Routledge
605 Third Avenue, New York, NY 10158

Routledge is an imprint of the Taylor & Francis Group, an informa business

© 2021 Robert Crawford

British Library Cataloguing-in-Publication Data
A catalogue record for this book is available from the British Library

Library of Congress Cataloging-in-Publication Data
Names: Crawford, Robert, 1975- author.
Title: Digital dawn in adland : transforming Australian agencies / Robert Crawford.
Description: Milton Park, Abingdon, Oxon ; New York, NY : Routledge, 2021.
| Includes bibliographical references and index.
Identifiers: LCCN 2020056445 (print) | LCCN 2020056446 (ebook)
Subjects: LCSH: Advertising agencies--Australia--History.
Classification: LCC HF5813.A8 C74 2021 (print) | LCC HF5813.A8 (ebook) |
DDC 659.1/1250994--dc23
LC record available at https://lccn.loc.gov/2020056445
LC ebook record available at https://lccn.loc.gov/2020056446

ISBN: 978-1-138-39388-2 (hbk)
ISBN: 978-1-032-01663-4 (pbk)
ISBN: 978-0-429-40149-7 (ebk)

Typeset in Bembo
by SPi Global, India

For Emily

Contents

Acknowledgements

This book would not have been possible without the support of many people and institutions.

I would firstly like to thank the interviewees, who generously provided their insights, enthusiasm, and time to the project. Michael Abdel, Jhonnie Blampied, Ed Brice, Sean Cummins, Matt Donovan, David Fouvy, Nick Garrett, Michael Godwin, John Grono, Tony Hale, Phil Hayden, Kate Henley, Imogen Hewitt, Simon Lawson, Gavin Macmillan, Victor Maree, Michael McEwen, Paul McMillan, Ricci Meldrum, Bob Miller, Anthony Moss, Tom Moult, Peter Murphy, Dominic Pearman, John Sintras, Nicole Taylor, Jane Walshe, Kimberlee Wells, Martin Williams, Colin Wilson-Brown, and Mike Zeederberg were all wonderful, insightful, and gracious interviewees. Their accounts and experiences not only offered unique perspectives that were absent from the official records, they were also enlightening in their own right. Collectively and individually, they underscore the power and significance of oral history to business history.

This book grew out of the work conducted as part of the Research Council Discovery grant DP120100777 Globalising the Magic System: A History of Advertising Industry Practices in Australia 1959–1989, which was funded 2012–2014. The interviews conducted as part of that project were essential to the central ideas in this book and, in particular, Chapter 1. That project also enabled me to work with Jackie Dickenson. Jackie's contribution to this book has been nothing short of profound. In addition to providing one of the best sounding boards for ideas, she provided enormous help with research. Jackie also provided frank and fearless feedback on all chapters—and was right every time. Without Jackie's razor-sharp insights on both the advertising industry and historical approaches, not to mention her humour and friendship, this book would not have been possible.

Lastly, I would like to thank my family. I remain particularly grateful for the support that my wife Rebecca has given me throughout this project. Despite being confronted with yet another book on advertising history, she has continued to share her love, generosity, patience, and good humour with me. And, finally, I would like to thank my dearest Emily, who arrived just as I started to write the first words of this book. In addition to granting me slithers of time to complete this book, she has also filled my world with smiles and wonder.

Acti labores jucundi!

Robert Crawford,
Melbourne, 2021

Notes on the author

Professor Crawford's research books include *Behind Glass Doors: The World of Australian Advertising Agencies 1959–89* (2016, co-authored with Jackie Dickenson) and *But Wait There's More…: A History of Australian Advertising, 1900–2000* (2008). His edited various collections include *Decoding Coca-Cola: A Biography of a Global Brand* (Routledge, 2021, co-edited with Linda Brennan and Susie Khamis), *Global Advertising Practice in a Borderless World* (Routledge, 2017, co-edited with Linda Brennan and Lukas Parker), and *Consumer Australia: Historical Perspectives* (2010, co-edited with Judith Smart and Kim Humphery). He is also the author of over 80 book chapters, journal articles, and encyclopaedia entries.

Introduction

Certainty and the digital dawn

INTERVIEWER: Do you remember the internet arriving at all?

JHONNIE BLAMPIED: Oh, I so do. Yes. Oh yes, and so much fear about it and uncertainty about how it would be used.[1]

***

NICOLE TAYLOR: I think … the digital transformation time was so confusing to so many people and so it created so much fear as a consequence about "Am I on top of this from a marketing perspective?" and agency to some degree, but agencies would always wing it, right.[2]

***

INTERVIEWER: To what degree do you think the agencies were ahead of the client [in terms of digital]?

JANE WALSHE: Not much. Everyone was finding out together … it's just my opinion, but I feel like it was a constant anxiety for agencies to appear that they were ahead of the game.[3]

***

TOM MOULT: The best description that I think I've ever heard of … advertising is, "advertising agencies turn what the client wants to say into what the customer wants to hear". And it still is that in essence, but we used to do that by understanding the hopes, fears, needs of the clients, of the consumer, better than the client did. But now that's—I mean, data has changed all that…[4]

***

As the opening four quotes demonstrate, the period spanning the 1990s through to the mid-2000s was a time of uncertainty for the advertising industry. It was also a time of profound change. To this end, the anxieties recalled by these advertising agency professionals reflect the fears and concerns about the arrival of the internet and its impact on their work and, indeed, their industry more generally—from the agency to the client and on to the consumer. Not surprisingly, few were willing to risk their careers at the time by publicly making such candid observations about the industry's anxieties, not to mention its struggle to comprehend the new medium. In true advertising style, they understood the need to present themselves and their industry as being leaders or, at the very least, active contributors in the digital space. However, as this study will demonstrate, fear and hope were both constituent parts of the uncertainty that underpinned the advertising industry's outlook and activities throughout this period.

In 1977, economist John Kenneth Galbraith's *The Age of Uncertainty* was published as a book and broadcast as a television documentary on the BBC. Commenting on the title, Galbraith mused: 'It sounded well; it did not confine thought; and it suggested the basic theme: we would contrast the great certainties in economic thought in the last century with the great uncertainty with which problems are faced in in our time'.[5] A similar description can be levelled at the advertising industry at the turn of the century. Over the previous decades, the advertising industry operated with great certainty—advertisers wanted the agencies' creative skills and marketing insights, media wanted the advertisements they created and the budgets they handled, and audiences wanted the products or services they were selling. It was both a comfortable and lucrative space to occupy, and the advertising industry took full advantage of it. However, the digital revolution would progressively disrupt, challenge, and ultimately dismantle each of these three certainties. While the rise of Google and the advent of the iPhone and Facebook profoundly changed the advertising industry and generated great uncertainty in the process, the roots of these changes and attitudes were to be found in the preceding fifteen years.

In *Behind Glass Doors*, Jackie Dickenson and I examined the growth and development of advertising agencies in Australia from the 1960s through to the 1980s. We argued that the Australian advertising agencies profited enormously from the combination of a booming economy, the arrival of multinational advertisers, and the emergence of television as an advertising medium, and that their capacity to position 'themselves as glamorous partners rather than mere service-providers to their clients all combined to create a "golden age" for Australian advertising agencies'.[6] In both form and content, the narrative in *Behind Glass Doors* reflects advertising historiography's overarching emphasis on documenting and accounting for the expansion of the advertising industry, along with its concurrent increase in power across the social, cultural, economic, and political domains.[7] The trajectory presented is largely uniform: advertising, and the industry responsible for it, steadily increase in size, scale, and scope. It is also strongly linked to the emergence of mass media platforms, which provided an important vehicle for reaching mass audiences and, indeed, for advertising agencies to demonstrate the effectiveness of their work. Such conditions served to foster a strong degree of certainty about the advertising industry and its future. While some historians have used the industry's quest for legitimacy to question the progressivist assumptions underpinning the conventional expansion narrative,[8] the seemingly irrepressible growth of advertising, advertising budgets, and the advertising industry business effectively reconfirmed the established narrative and enhanced certainty, whilst leaving little scope for alternative interpretations. However, more recent accounts have undertaken closer readings of this growth and revealed some of its constituent parts. In unpacking the structures underpinning advertising's 'golden age' in Australia, *Behind Glass Doors* suggested that the industry's power and status was the product of a unique set of circumstances, and, as such, its growth was neither assured nor sustainable: 'Advertising's glory days were fleeting'.[9] This book, then, takes up this story to demonstrate how the advertising industry's 'golden age' gave way to an 'age of uncertainty' over the 1990s and early 2000s.

As the following chapters will demonstrate, the abiding sense of uncertainty that permeated this period grew out of the social, cultural, economic and technological changes sweeping through the industry, as well as their impact on the infrastructure that had created and maintained the 'golden age'. These developments must also be viewed as part of the broader embrace of neoliberalism occurring at both national and international levels. Premised on the assumption that society 'can best be advanced by liberating individual entrepreneurial freedoms and skills within an institutional framework characterized by strong private property rights, free markets, and free trade', neoliberalism certainly found a receptive audience in the advertising industry.[10] It is hardly surprising then that neoliberal ideas and values would play a key role in informing and driving many of the major shifts and developments that swept through the advertising industry over the 1990s and early 2000s. However, the certainty that adherents to neoliberalism ascribed to their ideology would be counterbalanced by the uncertainty that stemmed from the implementation of neoliberal practices—particularly in terms of the reorganisation of power relationships within the advertising industry. Such tensions are therefore integral to understanding this age of uncertainty.

Although the internet has been used as an advertising medium for over quarter of a century, it appears few advertising and marketing historians feel that sufficient time has elapsed to warrant any historical analysis of this period. Journalists have had little qualm in filling this void—an unsurprising development given the maxim that holds that journalism is the first draft of history. Mark Tungate's *Adland: A Global History of Advertising* thus describes aspects of the industry's increasing engagement with the new medium, but offers little coherent examination of such activities, let alone their broader significance.[11] In *Frenemies*, Ken Auletta limits himself to the advertising industry's experiences of the twenty-first century. Focusing on the disruptions or 'assaults' experienced by the advertising agencies during this time, Auletta argues that the 'comfortable agency business is now assailed by frenemies, companies that both compete and cooperate with them'.[12] While Auletta develops a more cohesive narrative that identifies many of the key themes and developments, his survey similarly eschews critical analysis for descriptive accounts. Not surprisingly, researchers working on contemporary advertising and marketing trends and developments have paid close attention to the growing impact of the internet. However, their emphasis has largely been on the immediate experiences (often experienced at the local or national levels) rather than locating them within their broader contexts. While a handful of recent overviews of contemporary advertising have attempted to contextualise current trends against past practices, their analysis of the past all too frequently opts for generalities rather than nuance.[13]

It has been media scholars who have led the way in critically examining and contextualising the nature of change within advertising industry in the digital age. In its examination of the growing impact of data on marketing, media, and society more generally, *Niche Envy* by Joseph Turow situates current developments against their historical precedents to demonstrate that the current advertising practices do not exist or operate in a vacuum.[14] John Sinclair's *Advertising, the Media and Globalisation* offers a succinct yet insightful account of the ways that digital media not only challenged the advertising industry's standard practices but also forced it to respond. Demonstrating how old business models were failing and audiences were fragmenting, Sinclair contends that this was a time of crisis—both economically and culturally—for the advertising industry.[15] However, this description is principally based on the developments that occurred post-2006, notably the rise of Google and Facebook and the invention of the iPhone, rather than the mid-90s to mid-2000s period. Significantly, Sinclair recognises that this earlier period differs from the latter insofar as the advertising industry was initially 'sluggish in recognising the potential of the internet as an advertising medium' and that those forays into the digital realm were small in scale and largely 'experimental' in nature.[16] It is hardly surprising then that this period would be overshadowed by the new digital age wrought by Google, Facebook, and the iPhone. However, the developments and changes that affected the advertising industry over 1990s and early 2000s are not only integral to providing a more nuanced understanding of what happened next, they also constitute an important historical period in its own right—to wit, the dawn of the digital age.

The selection of Australia as the focus of this study is deliberate. While it has long been my area of interest, Australia also occupies a unique and significant place in the global advertising industry. Despite its distance from major centres and, indeed, its middle-sized population, Australia has regularly been ranked one of the top ten markets internationally in terms of advertising expenditure.[17] Australian agencies have similarly fared well in international awards, such as the Cannes Lions.[18] Not surprisingly, Australian advertising professionals take great delight in asserting (and often reasserting) that 'Australia punches above its weight' in the advertising world.[19] Australia's advertising industry also occupies an important space in terms of the globalisation of the advertising industry and advertising practices. Its size and location often drove innovation—whether this was on account of necessity or the result of agencies and/or clients deliberately using Australia as a convenient test market. However, this is not to say that Australians had *carte blanche* when it came to creating or producing campaigns. In the main, local branches of multinational operations had little scope to deviate too far from the missives received from headquarters located in other parts of the world. As the Australian experience was deeply informed by global developments, it offers an important and revealing case study for developing a deeper understanding of the early digital age. Significantly, the local aspects of the Australian advertising industry also add important perspective to this narrative. In the early 1990s, Australia's advertising industry stood out from those in most other major markets insofar as it was regulated. It had also suffered badly during the early 1990s Recession. By 2006, the economy was strong, such structures had long since been dismantled, and Australia's advertising industry now operated under the same conditions as elsewhere. To this end, this book illustrates the importance of adopting glocal perspectives in order to identify and, indeed, reassess various factors that were integral to the dawn digital age.

The source materials for this study are twofold. Firstly, it makes significant use of the local trade press, notably *AdNews* and *B&T*. Both document the developments taking place in the local advertising industry, as well as the issues affecting them. Such publications also played a key role in building a community by connecting local advertising professionals with international developments via regular updates, interviews with practitioners with international experience, and the reprinting of articles from overseas. However, the intense competition between the two publications meant that they needed to provide the most up to date news as well as a distinct point of difference. As independent media agency head Dominic Pearman subsequently reflects, this meant that some stories were given greater attention than they warranted, resulting in somewhat skewed coverage:

> And I think [it is] only now that businesses really understand the role of digital, whereas before it was … driven by the media. If you look at the trade press, it would be interesting to look at … how much exposure is or was given to digital media versus the traditional, TV, radio, print. … yeah, they've also managed to give TV, radio, print the 'correct' name—they're calling it the legacy media. So, I think it was probably driven by the likes of *AdNews*, *Mumbrella*, *B&T*, in the media industry to basically give digital a greater importance than probably what it deserved.[20]

In order to ameliorate this issue, this book makes significant use of oral history testimony. As Carl Ryant notes, oral history's capacity to 'customize evidence by the careful crafting of questions' as well as its ability to elicit evidence from a broad range of eyewitnesses means that 'is well suited to the study of business history through investigation of corporate culture'.[21] Rob Perks similarly advocates the importance of oral history for business historians as it enables them 'to "people" and demystify the little-understood and complex processes of business and economic activity, and to calibrate "big" ideas such as globalisation … by introducing historical context and individual agency'.[22] In terms of this study, oral history's strength is its capacity to access and document the everyday experience of working in the advertising industry, which is seldom reported in the trade press. Of course, oral history is not without its own shortcomings. Details can be hazy, distorted, or even incorrect. Moreover, recollections can be based on hearsay rather than actual experience. A more unique problem, particularly in an industry like advertising, is self-aggrandisement, where interviewees reinterpret their actions with the benefit of hindsight. Such issues notwithstanding, oral history's capacity to complement and challenge the dominant narrative (in this case the trade press) nevertheless expands the historical record.

As part of this project, I conducted interviews with 30 individuals in Melbourne and Sydney who had worked in advertising in the 1990s and early 2000s—either in creative agencies or media agencies, or as clients. Some were just starting out during this period, others were already in mid-level positions. At the time of the interviews, most had reached the senior echelons. In addition, I was able to draw on a further 20 interviews conducted as part of the *Behind Glass Doors* project. The aim of the new interviews was straightforward: to invite respondents to reflect on their experiences in the advertising industry and to identify the ways that the internet affected their work over the course of the 1990s and early 2000s. Underscoring Perks' point as well as the strength of oral history, each interviewee confirmed many of the major themes identified in the trade press while offering further individual accounts that often challenged them or were simply absent from them. Collectively, they tell the story of the advertising industry at the dawn of the digital age, along with the uncertainties that pervaded it and continue to inform its practice through to the present day.

Chapter 1 traces the roots of uncertainty back to the Recession of the early 1990s. Within the global context, Australia was hit hard by the economic downturn, and the local advertising industry was one of the worst affected areas. While the advertising industry had certainly experienced economic downturns in the past, the Recession was particularly harsh as clients dramatically reduced budgets forcing agencies to slash their staffing sizes. After years of comfortable growth, the industry experienced its first major contraction. The realisation that advertising budgets were not guaranteed was an unwelcome if sobering lesson. The economic crisis would set in motion a series of developments that not only changed advertising practices and agency operations, but also set the foundations for a new hierarchical order that would emerge over the coming decades.

One of the major causes of uncertainty that grew out of the Recession (but was not necessarily caused by it) was the realignment of the power relationship between the agency and the client. Chapter 2 follows this epoch-defining shift, demonstrating how clients exploited the Recession to demand more of their agencies while paying less. With a greater understanding of marketing practices and theory, they also demanded greater accountability—something that the agencies had hitherto evaded. As agencies were demoted from being marketing partners to mere service providers, their status in the client's eyes began to diminish, which, in turn, meant that advertising budgets could be further cut.

The status of the advertising agency was further threatened by the emergence of the media agency. As Chapter 3 demonstrates, the media agencies grew out of the advertising agencies' media departments before becoming advertising giants in their own right. Their power was reflected in their active role in ending the advertising (creative) agencies' most lucrative income streams as well as the media accreditation system that supported it. The dramatic rise of the media agency was not only a response to the client's need for greater accountability, it also reflected an awareness of the increasingly complex media ecosystem and the need to navigate it—something that would become even more pronounced with the internet.

Chapter 4 examines the advertising industry's uncertain embrace of new information technology systems and equipment in the early 1990s. Beginning in the 1960s, the first computers in agencies were used by the media department and the agency's administrative team. By the early 1990s, the personal computers (usually Apple Macs) were being used by the other departments, changing the ways that they operated at a day-to-day level. While the personal computer effectively ended the careers of the agencies' secretaries, the savings they wrought in terms of costs and time enabled agencies to ride out the downturn in advertising expenditure. Significantly, the new information technology firms not only emerged as highly profitable clients, they also helped their agencies' entry into the digital age.

The advertising industry's uncertain entry into the Information Superhighway is covered in Chapter 5. While many have criticised the advertising industry's failure to embrace new media quickly or wholeheartedly, this chapter examines the deeper reasons for its torpid response. Costs and the primitive state of technology effectively inhibited the realisation of the internet's promises. These were compounded by structural issues and pragmatic concerns. The rising power of clients and media agencies had severely weakened the creative agencies' standing. In the face of further uncertainty, creative agencies deemed that it was safer to stick to their area of expertise than to risk too much time, money, and effort on a new medium that was untried and did not seem particularly well suited to their needs.

Chapter 6 examines the rise of the consumer. While consumers have always been an integral part of the advertising business, they have largely been viewed as passive audiences waiting to be motivated by the right creative appeal. However, ideas about audiences over the 1990s and early 2000s would be fundamentally reshaped by media and audience fragmentation, audience autonomy, new audience information systems, and the blurring of the division between content providers and audiences. The advertising industry's discussions about audiences and consumers were equally informed by technology-related factors as much as their own needs, challenges, and ongoing anxieties. Although the relationship between the advertising industry and the consumer was symbiotic, this chapter reveals that it was a dynamic and, indeed, uneven relationship.

In Chapter 7 we follow the creative agencies' efforts to re-examine and re-invent themselves and their work in the face of the digital disruption of the early 2000s. Still wary of the new medium but aware of its growing importance for clients and consumers, the creative agencies found themselves conscripted into the digital age. While the Dotcom Boom and its subsequent bust did little to quell the industry's deep-seated uncertainty, it nevertheless compelled the agencies—both creative and media—to pay more serious attention to the internet and to recalibrate their services and operations accordingly. As the realities concerning the medium's functionality became clearer, the advertising industry adopted a more hard-headed perspective of new media and the ways that it affected their work and, indeed, their status.

★★★

The advertising industry in 1990 appeared to be a world away from the industry in 2005. As the following chapters demonstrate, advertising agencies would progressively become smaller, less profitable, and more fragmented as they sought to connect with increasingly disparate audiences across an expanding range of media outlets. Their relationships with clients, consumers, and, of course, media outlets underwent a radical transformation, with advertising agencies forced to cede power each time. As a result, the advertising agencies, as well as the advertising industry more generally, would become less confident of their place in the marketing and media ecosystems, as well as the work they were charged with creating. For the advertising industry then, it was this uncertainty rather than the emergence of new technologies that would ultimately emerge as the defining aspect of its experience of the dawn of the new digital era.

Notes

1 Jhonnie Blampied, interview by author, July 31, 2019.
2 Nicole Taylor, interview by author, February 1, 2019.
3 Jane Walshe, interview by author, October 17, 2018.
4 Tom Moult, interview by author, May 11, 2020.
5 John Kenneth Galbraith, *The Age of Uncertainty* (London: British Broadcasting Corporation/Andre Deutsch, 1977), 7.
6 Robert Crawford and Jackie Dickenson, *Behind Glass Doors: Inside the World of Australian Advertising Agencies, 1959–1989* (Crawley, WA: UWA Publishing, 2016), 3.
7 See Stephen Fox, *The Mirror Makers: A History of American Advertising and its Creators* (Urbana, Ill.: University of Illinois Press, 1997); Juliann Sivulka, *Soap, Sex, and Cigarettes: A Cultural History of American Advertising*, 2nd ed. (Belmont, CL: Wadsworth, 2012).
8 Jackson Lears, *Fables of Abundance: A Cultural History of Advertising in America* (New York, NY: Basic Books, 1994); Robert Crawford, *But Wait, There's More… : A History of Advertising in Australia, 1900–2000*, (Parkville, Vic.: University of Melbourne Press, 2008).
9 Crawford and Dickenson, *Behind Glass Doors*, 5.
10 David Harvey, *A Brief History of Neoliberalism*, (Oxford: Oxford University Press, 2007), 2.
11 Mark Tungate, *Ad Land: A Global History of Advertising* (London and Philadelphia: Kogan Page, 2007).
12 Ken Auletta, *Frenemies* (New York: Penguin Books, 2019), 4.
13 See Iain MacRury, 'What is an Advertising Agency in the Twenty-First Century', in *The Advertising Handbook,* 4th edition, ed. Helen Powell, Jonathan Hardy and Iain MacRury (Abingdon, Oxon. and New York Routledge, 2018), 18–43; Nicholas Holm, *Advertising and Consumer Society: A Critical Introduction* (London, Palgrave, 2017), 14–32.
14 Joseph Turow, *Niche Envy: Marketing Discrimination in the Digital Age* (Cambridge, Mass. and London, MIT Press, 2008).
15 John Sinclair, *Advertising, the Media and Globalisation: A World in Motion* (Abingdon, Oxon. and New York Routledge, 2012), 49–50.
16 Ibid., 55–6.
17 See 'Advertising Prospects for 2002', *AdNews*, 18 January 2002, https://www.adnews.com.au/yafNews/F2839001-D278-40DC-9F4FE14B1B974346.
18 See David Blight, 'Australia Dominates Awards Circuit in 2012', *AdNews*, 1 February 2013, https://www.adnews.com.au/adnews/australia-dominates-awards-circuit-in-2012.
19 See Michael Stocks, 'Cannes Young Lions: Marketers Take on the Challenge', *AdNews*, 4 July 2017, https://www.adnews.com.au/opinion/cannes-young-lions-marketers-take-on-the-challenge. 'Buying Success', *AdNews*, 28 July 2006, https://www.adnews.com.au/yafNews/791DE883-68CD-44A7-BAEA057810D250C0.
20 Dominic Pearman, interview by Robert Crawford, May 18, 2020.
21 Carl Ryant, 'Oral History and Business History', *The Journal of American History* 75, no. 2 (1988): 560.
22 Rob Perks, 'Corporations are People too!: Business and Corporate Oral History in Britain', *Oral History* 38 no. 1 (Spring 2010): 49.

1 The end of certainty

On 29 November 1990, Australia's Treasurer, Paul Keating, formally announced that the national economy was in recession. It was grim news. Keating, however, saw things differently, stating: 'The most important thing about that is that this is a recession that Australia had to have'.[1] Having played an instrumental role in deregulating and liberalising Australia's economy over the past seven years, Keating considered the recession to be an unfortunate development, albeit a necessary one that would ultimately benefit the nation. His choice of words, however, did not go down well. Over the following months, Australia's GDP shrank, the Australian dollar fell to record lows, unemployment rapidly increased, interest rates skyrocketed, and a series of lending institutions collapsed. For those who had lost their jobs and their homes, the phrase 'the recession we had to have' rang hollow. In his survey of this 'decisive transformation' of Australia's economy along with its impact on the nation, Paul Kelly concludes that a fundamental change had occurred—Australians in the early 1990s 'had reached the end of certainty'.[2] Frank Bongiorno offers a more circumspect interpretation, writing that Australia's 1980s had been 'a magic mirror in which the legacies of the past and the crises of the present were seen with greater clarity than before, and the possibilities of the future made faintly visible'.[3] Similar claims could also be directed at Australia's advertising industry.

From the 1950s through the 1980s, Australia's advertising agencies enjoyed what Robert Crawford and Jackie Dickenson describe as a 'golden age'.[4] Their success was built on increasing advertising budgets, generous media commissions, and the insatiable appetite of the affluent consumer. By positioning themselves at the centre of this lucrative triangle, the advertising agencies succeeded in presenting themselves as an indispensable part of modern business. However, the advertising industry's success was not entirely premised on firm foundations. Its growth was more dependent on economic stability rather than ingenuity on its own behalf. As long as consumption levels were growing, there was little need for marketers to question the agencies and their practices. The 1990s recession fundamentally disrupted this convenient arrangement in Australia and, indeed elsewhere—yet its significance has been ignored by studies of the industry's development.[5] With consumption levels falling and advertising expenditure shrinking, advertising and the advertising industry faced serious questions. While the advertising agencies took active steps to deal with the crisis, they assumed that stability would return, along with a resumption of the 'golden age' conditions. Such hopes, however, would ultimately be dashed. As Andrew Killey, the co-founder and creative director at KWP in Adelaide, recalls: 'the Recession just stopped everything'.[6] Although few in the advertising industry could see it at the time, the 1990s recession would prove to be the defining moment that the advertising industry 'had to have' if it was to break from the past. The economic crises of the late 1980s and, in particular, the early 1990s set in motion a series of developments that not only changed advertising practices and agency operations, but it also lay the groundwork for a new hierarchical order within the advertising industry itself.

A stumble before the fall

When Black Monday wiped 23 per cent off American stocks on 19 October 1987, the world held its breath. Any hopes that Australia might avoid a similar fate were quickly dashed. By the time the time the Australian stock market closed on Tuesday, it had suffered 25 per cent loss. Australian observers were alarmed, but cautioned against comparisons with 1929. Days later, *Sydney Morning Herald*'s economics commentator Ross Gittins described the situation 'serious, but … not the end of the world'.[7] While he felt it was still too early to comment on the crash's impact on Australia's economy, Gittins nevertheless warned that 'psychological damage' wrought by the crash could undermine 'the confidence of consumers and inves-tors' and that a 'severe dent to confidence will bring recession on earlier'.

As fear swept through the international business sector, companies considered ways of safeguarding their existence. Some three weeks after the collapse, the Business Council of Australia reported that 'the risk of a slide into recession' had prompted a third of the nation's major companies to pay closer attention to discre-tionary costs, including overtime, staff recruitment, investment, and advertising expenditure.[8] While the prospect of shrinking advertising budgets was a certainly worrying development for the advertising industry, its leaders expressed a more sanguine view when speaking publicly. Malcolm Spry, the chairman of the Mojo-MDA group, Australia's only publicly owned agency, presented an upbeat analysis of the agency's fortunes. In addition to assuring audiences that Mojo-MDA's finances were in order and that its global expansion strategy was profitable, Spry declared that the agency's key clients were 'market leaders dealing in basic com-modities which, on past experience, are more immune from the effects of a reces-sion'.[9] Similar sentiments were expressed by other leading figures. At the Outlook for the Media conference in New York, John Perriss, worldwide media director of Saatchi & Saatchi, noted that past economic downturns had in fact resulted in advertising expenditure being increased. Explaining 'I'm not suggesting that reces-sion is good for advertising … but if recession makes its way in in 1989, advertising may not fare as badly as some may fear', Perris sought to reassure his audience. However, such efforts hint at the insecurity that lurked just below the surface.[10]

Almost a year after the markets crashed, it seemed that the advertising industry's positive predictions were proving correct. In his weekly column for *Business Review Weekly*, Neil Shoebridge observed that the 'talk of a recession' had not necessarily 'depressed' the marketing community—advertising expenditure at end of 1989 was predicted to be 'no less than $5.13 billion, a substantial rise over last year's

$4.43 billion'.[11] Television stations confidently increased advertising rates.[12] However, a report in the *Financial Review* painted a more complicated picture. It revealed that '[a]dvertisers are becoming increasingly pessimistic about the economic outlook' and that the 'impact of the slump in confidence is showing up patchily and seems to be restricted to print and radio at the moment'. Further investigation revealed that television advertising was bound to suffer. While advertising space on the medium was 'still fairly solidly booked until the end of the year', the report predicted that television was 'likely to be hit in 1990 because many 1989–90 advertising budgets have been held at 1988–89 levels'.[13] Such warnings, however, had little outward impact on the agencies. With advertising expenditure continuing its decades-long increase, many saw the current economic downturn as a blip and assumed that business would simply continue as usual.

The collapse

When Brisbane agency LGO&M shut its doors in March 1990, it was described as 'the first agency casualty'.[14] A solid middle-to-large sized agency, LGO&M's reliance on tourism and property-related clients made it vulnerable to a downturn in the economy. By mid-1990, it was clear that Australia's economy was worsening and that LGO&M would not be the only agency forced to take drastic action. Declaring that the '[c]hampagne days at advertising agencies are fading fast', the *Sydney Morning Herald* reported that 'since January, 200 people have been retrenched from Sydney's advertising agencies' and that '[e]ven more are believed still to be working out the three months' notice to find another job'.[15] When speaking to trade press newspaper *Ad News* in July 1990, agency executives maintained a positive outlook. Richard Whitington, the managing director of Chiat/Day/Mojo's Sydney office, thus explained that the agency's decision to retrench 15 staff was not necessarily a bad thing for the agency: 'We have now put ourselves into the sort of shape where, if things stay this bad, or get any worse, we'll be in a better condition to emerge from it. We'll be in a position of strength'.[16] While such comments were certainly an attempt to put a positive spin on a difficult situation, they nevertheless revealed an abiding confidence borne of decades of sustained growth. Such confidence appeared genuine, at least to the journalist at *Ad News*, who was led to conclude that '[t]he economic turn-around will be slow and clients will be treading very carefully. The worst is over, but it's going to be tough for agencies until at least the end of the year'.[17] By the end of the year, it was clear that the worst was far from over. Over 1990, Australia's top 50 agencies had cut their workforce by 10 per cent, which amounted to 502 jobs.[18] Almost a third of Australia's biggest agencies saw declining incomes.[19] In his prediction for the year ahead, the outspoken advertising executive John Singleton bluntly outlined what was in store for Australia's agencies in 1991: 'The law of the jungle will apply; survival of the fittest and the slaughter of the fattest'.[20]

The Recession's impact on the advertising industry would become unmistakable in 1991.[21] In the US, advertising expenditure fell by 1.5 per cent, 'the worst year for [American] advertising since the Second World War'.[22] Advertising expenditure across the UK, France, and Japan was all in decline. Figures tabled at the

Advertising Federation of Australia's annual general meeting in May revealed an industry in crisis. The past year had seen the most dramatic decrease in advertising expenditure since 1943, staff levels would drop by some 15 per cent, and bad debts to the tune of $4 million had contributed to the closure of 20 accredited agencies.[23] And the bad news continued. In July, the trade newspaper *B&T* announced: 'It's official—for the first time since figures were collated, advertising expenditure in main media has dropped' by 2 per cent.[24] On top of a 30 per cent reduction in billings, this decrease in advertising expenditure unceremoniously marked the end of the advertising agencies' age of unfettered growth. In his assessment of the year, John Singleton Advertising's managing director, Russell Tate, reiterated this view, declaring: '1991 was the year which really exposed in the industry some glaring structural weaknesses, poor management, laziness, and the unwillingness or inability of many agencies and people to accept that the "good old days" of advertising have been gone for some time'.[25]

As the industry entered 1992, the outlook was grim. The horror stories concerning Australian advertising agencies continued to appear in the local trade publications. Published in the trade press in February, Table 1.1 shows the dramatic decreases in agency billings over 1990 and 1991. In the accompanying report, agency executives once again put on a brave face. 'We are perfectly poised when the economy turns, and it will, to take advantage of it', declared Alex Hamill, the Chief Executive Officer of Australia's largest agency, George Patterson.[26] While George Patterson's percentage decline was modest in comparison to others, the loss of $40 million in billings nevertheless overshadowed those of its competitors. Jeff Reeves, the managing director of Young & Rubicam's Sydney office, tried to explain that the agency's downturn could be attributed to the loss of a single account, KFC. While Young & Rubicam had suffered a 10.7 per cent loss in billings that equated to $30.05 million, he confidently explained that this was 'a setback but it is not a long term trend' before adding that '[t]he gloom and doom attitude is starting to clear and we're looking forwards to a bright time in the next six months'.[27] Such confidence, however, was not entirely misplaced. There were signs of improvement. Over the course of 1992, metropolitan television revenue grew by 10 per cent.[28] After declining by 2 per cent in 1990 and 3.5 per cent in 1991, advertising expenditure finally grew by 5.7 per cent in 1992.[29] However, the industry was not out of the woods yet. Reports from Madison Avenue noted another round of retrenchments in December 1992 owing to declining advertising expenditure.[30]

Discussion of post-Recession strategies began to appear in local and international trade publications in 1992.[31] In May 1993, *Ad News'* survey of agencies and clients revealed that 55 per cent of respondents believed that there had been a turnaround in advertising expenditure, while 43 per cent 'believed the industry is yet to experience the worst of the recession'.[32] By the end of 1993, advertisers were predicting further growth in marketing budgets and media budgets.[33] Despite the promising signs, the impact of the last three years had resulted in an uncharacteristically subdued outlook among agency heads. In December 1993, *B&T* thus reported:

Table 1.1 Australian agency billings and staffing in 1991

Agency	Billings (AU$m)		Staff	
	1991	*Increase on 1990*	*1991*	*Increase on 1990*
George Patterson	640	−40	428	−32
Clemenger/BBDO	396.9	−9	n/a	n/a
Mattingly & Partners	272.1	12.9	301	−45
DDB Needham	250.2	6.6	274	12
Young & Rubicam	249.7	−30.5	302	−56
Chiat/Day/Mojo	208.8	−32.1	182	−26
Lintas	151.7	33.4	163	21
Leo Burnett Connaghan & May	144.2	48.1	175	28
Saatchi & Saatchi	141.5	−12	105	−17
McCann Erickson	140	−27.2	142	−84
J. Walter Thompson	133	−2	152	−5
Foote Cone & Belding	125.9	0.1	107	1
Neville Jeffress	120.8	−25.6	326	−36
D'Arcy Masius Benton & Bowles	94	2.7	77	18
Ogilvy & Mather	83.6	−38.2	86	−48

Table adapted from *Ad News*, 28 February 1992, p. 25.

Now, at the end of 1993, the mood is slightly more optimistic—but this doesn't mean that 1994 will herald the beginning of the end for the recession. Opinion is that it won't even come close. Advertising and marketing leaders maintain Australia's economic woes are far from over, although they predict recovery is not too far off. Speculation ranges widely: some pick the 1995/96 period as the one to look forward to; others point to the Year 2000 and beyond. But the fact that Australia continues to be loaded down by a hefty foreign debt, high unemployment and a shell-socked corporate sector must be a considerable burden on the minds of even the most confident of pundits[34].

Over 1994, Australia's economic recovery was reflected in the agencies' improving fortunes. Of the top 50 agencies in Australia, only seven reported a decrease in gross income for 1994.[35] Staff numbers were also increasing. With billings going from $420 million in 1993 to $450 million in 1994, George Patterson was able to put on some 50 new staff.[36] Confidence was duly returning to Australian agencies, and by the beginning of 1995, senior figures were unanimously talking about growth.

Russell Tate thus observed: 'There are signs across the industry generally that advertisers are starting to find those extra dollars in the bottom drawer ... There's more confidence and enthusiasm about the future than before'.[37] Although the economic outlook was positive, the agencies' expectation that things would simply return to normal was highly problematic—it failed to appreciate the scale of the devastation within the agency ranks as well as its impact on the broader advertising ecosystem.

Fighting in the trenches

For agency staff, the defining feature of the Recession was the loss of jobs. Accounting for some 70 per cent of agency expenses, staff costs were the first to come under the microscope when clients began to reduce their advertising bud-gets. While agency executives adopted a confident air in public, their concerns about staffing were already evident from the very early days of the economic crisis. In January 1990, *Ad News* featured an article on recruitment consultants, which observed: 'As agencies inch their way into the year of "gloom and doom" and slashed clients budgets, finding, and keeping high-calibre staff is going to be of paramount importance'.[38] By the end of the year, almost 895 workers from the nation's top 300 agencies were without a job—a loss of 11 per cent, which was worse than the national average that same year.[39]

Redundancies came in all shapes and forms. In April, D'Arcy Masius Benton & Bowles closed its retail operations in Sydney, while McCann Erickson closed its Adelaide office.[40] On 7 June 1991, McCann Erickson was in trouble again, announc-ing the closure of its head office division, which principally affected finance and administration staff.[41] A week later came the news that J. Walter Thompson was retrenching four of its creatives.[42] The following month Saatchi & Saatchi, which had been 'previously unscathed by widespread retrenchments', informed the trade press that 10 per cent of its staff would be cut across the board.[43] Expensive middle managers were the first target, but it was not long before junior staff were also hit.[44]

The experience of redundancy was a sobering one. Responding to the growing number of unemployed advertising men and women, *Ad News* ran an article 'How to Cope with Redundancy'. While it reported that 'redundancy has always been a possibility in the hot-today-cold-tomorrow adworld', the article noted that 'when it actually happens it casts the person concerned into a period of terrible trauma'.[45] Rob Palmer was one such case. In 1989, Palmer was an account manager at Mojo-MDA, Australia's largest locally owned agency. Looking back on his early days with the agency, he recalled how management was 'spending way too much money on everything: salaries, office fit outs, cars, Porsches, you name it'. But the good times came to an abrupt halt:

> The Recession hits, thanks to Paul Keating, in ... late 1989. All of a sudden, we're in strife. All of a sudden one Tuesday—pink slips to 80 staff. It was hideous. And I'm one of the 80. Out of a job. Here I am, nice big, fat mortgage, three kids at private school, happy marriage ... nice house in Hunter's Hill. Jobless for the first time. Humiliating blow to the ego because I had always been a bit of a

wonderchild. I'd always been the guy who'd had the jobs offered to him. ... And then—bing-bang-bong—out of a job. And as I put my CV together and started doing the rounds, every other agency was kind of in the same boat. ... I just couldn't get a job. I was one of thousands of guys just out of work....[46]

Others faced a more drawn-out situation. At D'Arcy Masius Benton & Bowles, creative director Tony Stewart had to implement a raft of redundancies. Rather than moving immediately to dismiss staff, Stewart opted to give staff a two-month warning: 'I gave the opportunity to perform well in that two months' period to avoid the chop. But I'm not sure if that was a good thing to do. I think it may have made 15 people nervous rather than make a couple of people better'.[47]

Victor Maree had recently arrived in Australia from South Africa and was not sure whether he wanted to take up a position straightaway. In 1990, he joined the account department of Box Emery, a mid-sized agency in Melbourne. It would be a wise decision:

All I can say is that when things started tightening up, they tightened up really quickly for us. Vulcan ... had been a big client of Box Emery. ... They literally stopped spending, because people weren't buying the right goods, they weren't buying air conditioners, heaters, et cetera. So that business literally went from expenditure to no expenditure. ... We had to reduce our staff numbers and that—I know at the time, you know, it was really difficult for [principal] Mike Emery ... we knew that if somebody lost their job, there was a very good chance that they wouldn't get another job.[48]

While Maree managed to keep his job, he and his colleagues at Box Emery had to make some sacrifices:

I think where it really ..., hit home for me as well was probably for the first time in that agency's history, they had to encourage people to take leave. You had to drop your leave balance down. ... [T]he other thing is that we ended up taking 10 per cent salary cuts ... the feeling was rather than dropping another 10 per cent of people because we were down—maybe we were down by then to about 20 people. ... You know, and I think it was good because even though it was hard, you never felt, you know, this agency isn't going to be here tomorrow. It really felt like everybody was trying. And also, we were pitching regularly. We probably started pretty much as it is happening now, probably taking on smaller clients. All of that sort of stuff.

Colin Wilson-Brown, head of client service and director at the independent agency Magnus, Nankervis and Curl, recalled a similar situation. 'We were perhaps in the fortunate position of then owning our own business', he explains, and this meant doing the 'right things' for clients and the staff. So when the Recession hit, 'we were in a position to say "Well tough, we won't to get a dividend this year", but we all got our jobs ... The focus was really on trying to protect the people and the work, rather than actually kind of the making draconian cuts'.[49]

Retrenchments coupled with the fact that departed staff could not be replaced meant that those that managed to keep their job found themselves working harder and longer hours than before. Some found themselves promoted on account of being 'the last man standing'.[50] Everyday practices also changed. Jhonnie Blampied notes that in the '80s it was difficult to 'find anyone in an agency on a Friday afternoon, because they were all out getting hammered and lunches were long and … often turned into dinners'. The Recession caused a discernible shift that would continue on: 'the creatives used to actually start having lunch at their desk as opposed to going out for lunch … lunchtime meetings with clients would be sandwiches'. These changes, Blampied observes, were emblematic of a broader shift that saw advertising evolve 'from an entertainment business into a business that was business-like'.[51] Many more had to make even greater sacrifices than lunch. Maree thus recalled the experiences of those who were less fortunate than he had been:

> There were people that I knew who were finding jobs in Sydney and com-muting. You know, like literally living in a studio apartment in Sydney and coming back to Melbourne on a weekend to be with the wives and that. And they were taking any job. … But it was a very tough time and I don't know how many people contacted me for a job, for instance. You know, I mean, there was nothing that one could do. But even friends … would be saying "Jeez, is there anything that's around?"

Others, however, recounted a somewhat different experience. Tony Hale, the prin-cipal of the independent agency Hale & Collins, only had hazy memories of the Recession: 'I can certainly remember there being a recession. But I can't really remember anybody taking it too seriously. … I can't recall there being swathes of people being let go'.[52] Such memories stem from two sources. On the one hand, they illustrate his own agency's experience: 'As far as we were concerned, we weren't big enough to worry about any recession. And, if anything, it probably made us a little bit more agile or it made clients look around for a bit more value'.[53] On the other, such comments offer a counterpoint to more recent developments: 'Most agencies were making good margins. They weren't the skinny organisations they are today … So they probably had a little bit of fat to ride it out'.[54] Others offered different explanations for why the Recession left them relatively unscathed. Sean Cummins, a creative at Mojo's Melbourne office, explained that the Recession did not really have a major impact on him or his work:

> Look, it would seem like we were blissfully unaware, but … if you've got cli-ents over a number of categories … they know when to spend, and other clients are sheepish and may pull their horns in. But some clients are better in a time of economic drought than they are in a time of feast. … So no, it was the swings and roundabouts.[55]

Bob Miller, the marketing director at Toyota Australia, provides a different per-spective. Not only was his marketing budget devised in Japan, it was also informed by Japanese cultural norms which held that the firm would also remain true to its agency. For Miller then 'it was business as usual'.[56] However, this did not mean that he left his agency alone. 'Don't screw us around', he told them, 'What we want is to be more powerful in the marketplace. We don't want to stand still. We want 20, then later 25 per cent market share'.[57]

Cummins noted that the management of some agencies were also able to take advantage of the situation: 'These sorts of economic circumstances were often opportunities for agencies to clean house a little bit'. This observation was supported by Jhonnie Blampied, a senior executive at DDB's Sydney office, who recalled that 'you could manage staff quite well, because there is a natural level of attrition and you could restructure around that to just not replace people and get other people to do more work for the same money'.[58]

Although the actual experience of the Recession varied from position to position and agency to agency, the fears and concerns surrounding retrenchment were deep and would not be forgotten quickly. These anxieties and memories would continue to have an impact on all aspects of the agency business—even after the economy had improved.

The changing face of advertising

Speaking at a conference on the future of creativity organised by the Advertising Federation of Australia (AFA) in 1991, Frank De Vito, Lintas New York President and Chief Creative Officer for the Americas, outlined the situation facing advertising agencies across the globe:

> The economy is bad and we are all hurting. Advertising is depressed and the creative work is not looking good. It's hard to create great ads when your friends are being fired or clients are cutting back. As budgets are pulled back and agency resources tightened, it stops free thinking and stops creative thinking. Business is in a downturn right now and the long-term effect will be on the nature of the business and the creative work.[59]

Such comments were not just industry hyperbole—advertisements were changing. Advertisements created during the Recession were shorter (and aired more frequently), cheaper, more product-oriented, and more likely to use rational appeals.[60] They were also less creative. Such trends were discernible at the 1992 Cannes Advertising Film Festival where the quality of work was described as 'patchy' and 'workman-like ... with the odd flare of outstanding creative'. Attending the festival as a judge, George Patterson's creative director John Fawcett was equally underwhelmed by the standard of work submitted by his fellow Australians: 'We're sticking to the tried and true. There are no really brave ideas there. In fact, the look was very parochial'.[61] Interviewed decades later, Kevin Luscombe, who headed his own agency at the time, expressed similar sentiments, noting that Recession-era advertisements were 'so conservative and dumbed down that they lacked sparkle and ideas'.[62]

The shift to a more conservative approach was not simply the result of less money flowing through the agencies. Social researcher Hugh Mackay claimed that social changes over the 1970s and 1980s—from changing patterns of work to the use of technologies in the home—had left consumers anxious well before the full force of the Recession hit home. Speaking at a conference on cost-effective advertising in Sydney, Mackay explained that consumers had embraced three strategies to reduce anxieties: escapism, values revolution, and retribalisation. The result, he argued, was a more conservative consumer and the advertising industry would need to tailor its messages to these shifts.[63] A few months later, Vicki Arbes, another social researcher observed that consumers were becoming more sceptical. Labelling them 'the Sensible Consumers', she claimed that they placed 'little priority on (routine) shopping', were interested in '"value" (though not necessarily a cheaper price)' and considered themselves to be 'smarter than the marketer and advertiser and capable of seeing though the glitz and flummery'.[64] With consumers and advertisers alike adopting a more conservative outlook, advertising agencies were left with little choice with their work—creativity and innovation had to run second to appeals that were safe and solid.

A more fundamental challenge to the appearance, the appeals, and the sound of Australian advertising stemmed from the move to overturn the regulations that restricted the use of foreign advertisements on commercial television. Since the 1950s, government regulations mandated that Australian television commercials contain no less than 80 per cent Australian content. Such regulations had their basis in the early days of radio, when many expressed fears about the negative impact of overseas (American) material on Australian audiences. In addition to addressing abiding concerns about dubious imports, the regulations for Australian television would also function as something of 'a protective tariff that saw the advertising industry become an important producer of Australian content on television'.[65] The regulations were also instrumental in drawing overseas agencies into the Australian market. Unable to export advertisements to Australia, agencies with multinational clients needed a local branch to create advertisements (or simply re-create overseas advertisements) for Australian television.[66] By the early 1990s, the need for such regulations was beginning to be questioned by major advertisers and the US Government, which considered the regulations to be 'unfair trading practices'.[67]

In 1989, the Australian Broadcast Tribunal commenced a review of foreign content on Australian television. By 1990, it had brought television commercials into its remit. The Tribunal's 'Preliminary View on Foreign Content' in 1991 signalled that it supported a move away from the strict limits on overseas content although it was also of the view that a 'clear majority of advertisements seen on Australian television remain Australian'.[68] It recommended that 80 per cent of all advertisements broadcast on television be locally made. The advertising industry was divided—advertisers and larger multinational agencies supported the move, while small local agencies and production houses were against it. In November 1991, the Tribunal formally published its findings, which reconfirmed its earlier stance but added that the period spanning 6 pm to midnight would be unregulated and that any materials from New Zealand would be counted as Australian.[69]

The new system commenced on 1 January 1992. Over the first two weeks of the new year, foreign advertisements only made up 1.4 per cent of the total number of commercials accepted for television broadcast.[70] A spokesman for the Association of Australian National Advertisers (AANA), which had strongly fought against the foreign content regulations, was unsurprised by the low number: 'an advertiser would have to make sure the brand name, packaging, positioning and product formulation was the same in the foreign and Australian markets before it could use a foreign ad here'.[71] Advertising agencies were still not sure what the fallout would be for them. While David Blackley, Clemenger BBDO's creative director, felt that the new regulations were unlikely to reduce the size of any agency's creative department, 'the growth rate of Australian-created advertising could slow, particularly in global product categories such as soft drinks and airlines'.[72] Wayne Wood, managing director of Box Emery & Partners, was more critical: 'Some multinationals will use the same boring, brain-numbing commercials that don't work overseas here, because it will save money on production'.[73] Others saw a deeper problem. Richard White-Smith, managing director of The Ball Partnership, felt that the move seriously undermined the agency's creative role: 'Clients will question what is the value of the motional and strategic agency–client partnership. No advertiser would be prepared to pay full whack for full service fee unless input is substantial'.[74]

By the end of 1992, the AANA happily reported that the number of foreign advertisements broadcast on Australian television peaked at 5 per cent—significantly less than the 20 per cent quota.[75] In June 1993, the ongoing low number of foreign advertisements being broadcast led the Australian Broadcasting Authority, the Tribunal's successor, to deem the topic a 'non issue'.[76] The announcement in April 1994, that the Ten Network, which targeted the youth demographic, was nearing the 20 per cent figure indicated that advertisers were becoming less dependent on their agencies.[77] While this development appeared to be yet another blow for local agencies and creativity in general, few registered it at the time. With Australia's improving economy placing agency billings back on to an upward trajectory, agencies ignored these shifts and blithely assumed that everything was at last headed back to normal.

Defending advertising's image

In the early 1990s, the satirical comedy programme *Fast Forward* was broadcast on Australian national television. One of the recurring sketches featured two sleazy, fast-talking executives of the fictional agency, Brent Smyth & Barry, who pitched ridiculous campaign ideas to their clients. Steve Vizard, who played Brent Smyth, recalled that industry's excesses made it a perfect target for comedians. Vizard recalls that he and 'Barry' (played by Peter Moon) were 'even approached by several large clients … to create advertisements for them based on the fact that we had created parody ads for *Fast Forward* that had cost the advertisers hundreds of thousands (and more) to make through the traditional advertising process'![78] While popular culture had long used advertising and advertising agencies as a vehicle for critiquing consumption,[79] the fact that some marketers felt that comedians might produce better work than advertising professionals reveals that the industry had a very real reputational problem.

When the advertising industry encountered a serious threat to its livelihood, it launched campaigns to generate awareness of advertising's social and economic contribution and to improve its public perception.[80] In March 1991, the UK's Institute of Practitioners in Advertising launched a campaign to persuade senior businesspeople of the need to maintain their advertising in a recession, but critics noted that the campaign's efforts to highlight advertising's effectiveness might well have an adverse impact on the way that agencies were remunerated.[81] A few months later, the American Association of Advertising Agencies sought to reach a similar market with its optimistic booklet *Advertising in a Recession*, which was also advertised to Australian agencies.[82] The following year saw the International Advertising Association launch a global campaign to demonstrate to consumers the need for advertising. Two variations were created. In advanced markets such as the US and Australia, the tagline was 'Advertising. The Right to Choose', while the tagline in developing markets such as Russia and China stated 'Advertising. That's the way it works for you'.[83] While the campaigns made the creators feel they were using their skills to protect their livelihoods, the reality was that such campaigns did little to change broader opinions about advertising and those responsible for it.

In 1994, the AFA effectively acknowledged that such campaigns were struggling. A review of advertising's image among clients revealed that the industry had an image problem. Bev Dyke, the federal director of the AFA, thus explained that '[t]he perception that agencies make super profits is inaccurate and a challenge for me to correct'.[84] The retrenchments and the reduced marketing budgets over the past years had evidently done little to change client perceptions. Stating that the AFA's main goal was to improve the advertising industry's standing among consumers and with business, the AFA's federal chairman, Max Gosling, also took aim at the efforts to advertise advertising: 'We can only improve (the industry's) standing by our actions and deeds, not by words. It is not something that can be achieved in the next year or two'.[85] As Gosling conceded, the task of overturning negative stereotypes could not be done quickly or simply left to a forgettable advertising campaign—it would require advertising agencies to think more seriously about themselves, their work, their relationships with clients and the public, and their future.

Training and the next generation

In 1991, *B&T* reported that the 'marketing and advertising fraternity is going back to the classroom. Training has become a buzzword in an industry where jobs are tight, agencies are running lean and employees are expected to perform from day one'.[86] While advertising had long prided itself as a meritocracy that did not place too much emphasis on formal education, the reality was that things had been changing since the 1970s.[87] A growing number of agency staff had university degrees, causing a slow but steady 'arms race' across the industry. The push was also coming from outside. Calling for the advertising industry to embrace tertiary education, McSpedden Carey executive director Bani McSpedden criticised 'the industry for lagging behind its marketing client in attracting academically and professionally qualified applicants, who instead are gravitating towards other industries'.[88] If the advertising did not pay serious attention to training its current and future staff, it risked becoming irrelevant in the modern marketing matrix.

The Recession would place an even greater premium on education and advanced training. Agency staff now looked to upskill in order to maintain their current position, or to enhance their chances of securing another in the event they received a dreaded pink slip. To meet demand, various industry organisations (such as the Australian Marketing Institute and the AFA) as well as universities and other tertiary education institutions created a range of courses. Interest in education was also driven by the Federal Government's Training Guarantee Act, which sought to make a more resilient workforce by placing a training level on all companies with a payroll of $200,000. While some smaller agencies struggled to pay, many agencies readily enrolled staff in training programs in the hope of improving their competitiveness in a cut-throat market.[89]

Entry into Australia's advertising agencies had traditionally been through the dispatch department, where young men and, later, women, served an apprenticeship cycling through the agency's different departments, while undertaking some formal study in the evenings.[90] Driven in part by the Government's training levy, the AFA sought to establish a more formalised system in 1991 with the formation of Ad School.[91] Trainees who made it through the strict selection schemes were placed in an agency for nine months, where they would circulate through the different departments and be paid.[92] Interest waned in the following year with a significant drop in applications from prospective trainees. Course coordinator Gawen Rudder offered a curious if rather convenient explanation: 'People have said this is extremely tough to get into and my gut feeling is some of them have said this year "It's too hard, I won't bother"'.[93] Rudder, it seems, was desperately hoping that no one would notice the elephant in the room—in this economic climate, very few graduates would successfully land at a job at the end of their studies. In 1994, the number of positions went from twenty down to six, revealing that the agencies were still feeling under pressure even though the economy was displaying clear signs of improvement.[94]

With fewer jobs, longer hours, and lower pay, it seems that the advertising agency of the early 1990s had lost much of the glamour and appeal that it had enjoyed over the last decades. Although *Marketing* predicted that further training and education would benefit agencies and marketers in the long term,[95] the reality in Australia was that only a small number would be in a position to benefit—those who had kept their jobs and the handful of young stars whose talent had enabled them to defy the odds of landing a job.

★★★

'In the end it all comes down to confidence', declared the British trade journal *Marketing* in mid-1993, 'It is not surprising that confidence took a severe knock in the past two years, there was not much for anyone to feel confident about'.[96] As the world's economies showed signs of improvement, confidence began to return to agencies across the globe. Australian agencies, however, remained a little more wary than their counterparts in other markets. Looking at 1995, Mal Wilcock, managing director of Clemenger Brisbane, mused that 'growth is imminent' before adding that 'I don't think we will hit the halcyon days of the '80s'.[97]

Such caution underscored the dramatic impact of the last four years on Australia's advertising agencies. While the Recession affected agencies in most markets across the world, Australia's experience was particularly damaging. The number of people employed in agencies had decreased by a third through the closure of agencies and branch offices, the rationalisation of staff numbers, and the agencies' reluctance to take on untrained, entry-level staff.[98] (By comparison, Britain, which had also fared badly during the Recession, saw a quarter of agency staff lose their jobs.[99]) The spectre of unemployment haunted those who managed to keep their jobs, driving them to work under harsher conditions than before. 'In the '90s everyone has had to work harder for their dollars and agency and agency executives are now getting used to it', reported *Ad News* in 1994.[100] As agencies learnt how to do business with fewer staff, it was clear that the majority of those who lost their jobs would never be returning to the industry. Although there was always room for new creative talent, the agencies' preference for proven experience over potential revealed that they were more interested in addressing immediate problems rather than developing long-term strategies. By 1994, it seemed that the agencies' responses had worked. Agency efficiency ratings (based on staff numbers per million dollars spent on advertising) went from 1.59 staff per million dollars in 1990 to 1.15 per million in 1993.[101] With billings on their way up and healthy profits returning to agency bottom lines, it seemed that agencies in Australia and, indeed, internationally, would remain leaner and meaner for the foreseeable future.[102]

The impact of the Recession could also be seen on the work being produced by the agencies. Creativity took a back seat to the job of selling as advertisements became blander and appeals drier. The pervasiveness of such approaches would even inform the industry's own efforts to advertise itself. While the advertising styles and approaches would inevitably change, there was no going back on the process of dismantling of the local content regulations. The number of foreign commercials on Australian television may have initially been small, but their very presence marked a deeper and more profound shift in agency–client relationships that served to diminish the agency's marketing role in the client's eyes. Looking back on the period, Peter Murphy, a creative at Mojo-MDA's Melbourne office observed that this shift was part of a broader change in the balance of power that emerged when clients reduced their advertising budgets: 'I remember distinctly you would quite often have a conversation that [went] "well, if you look after us, we'll look after you, you know, when things get better," which of course they never do'.[103] But in late 1994, the significance of this development did not really appear to register—billings were finally climbing and agencies rediscovering their confidence and profitability. However, it would soon become apparent that clients had no desire to relinquish their dominance in the post-Recession world. A new advertising order had emerged across the world, and it was the agencies that had lost out.

Notes

1 'Transcript of the Treasurer, The Hon. Paul Keating MP, Press Conference Re September Quarter National Accounts, November 291990', https://parlinfo.aph.gov.au/parlInfo/download/media/pressrel/HPR08019363/upload_binary/HPR08019363.pdf;fileType = application%2Fpdf#search = %22media/pressrel/HPR08019363%22, accessed 11 June 2019.

2 Paul Kelly, *The End of Certainty: The Story of the 1980s* (Sydney: Allen & Unwin, 1992), 686.

3 Frank Bongiorno, *The Eighties: The Decade that Transformed Australia* (Collingwood: Black Inc., 2015), 306.
4 Robert Crawford and Jackie Dickenson, *Behind Glass Doors: The World of Australian Advertising Agencies, 1959–1989* (Crawley, WA: UWA Publishing, 2016), 3.
5 For example, see Mark Tungate, *A Global History of Advertising* (London, Philadelphia, PA: Kogan Page, 2007).
6 Andrew Killey, interview by author, December 13, 2013, Title No: 1489016, National Film and Sound Archive (NFSA), Canberra, ACT.
7 Ross Gittins, 'It's Serious, but We are not in for a Great Depression', *Sydney Morning Herald*, October 21, 1987, 19.
8 Matthew Moore, 'Big Firms Tighten Belts after Crash', *Sydney Morning Herald*, November 12, 1987, 3.
9 Lea Wright, 'Mojo gives Priority to Offshore Growth', *Sydney Morning Herald*, November 13, 1987, 27.
10 'Advertising will not be Badly Hurt by Recession', *Sydney Morning Herald*, December 10, 1987, 32.
11 Neil Shoebridge, 'Who Spends Most of Advertising in Australia', *Business Review Weekly*, September 1, 1989, 88.
12 Neil Shoebridge, 'Shoebridge', *Business Review Weekly*, August 18, 1989, 91.
13 Louise Boylen, 'Ad Spending on the Decline as Clients Batten Down for Recession', *Financial Review*, September 5, 1989, 38.
14 Chris De Bono, 'LGO&M: The First Agency Casualty', *Ad News*, May 4, 1990, 24.
15 Lea Wright, 'Cold Wind blows through Adland', *Sydney Morning Herald*, July 12, 1990, 32.
16 Amanda Ritchie, 'Agencies Roll up their Sleeves as the Hard Times Really Bite', *Ad News*, July 27, 1990, 17.
17 Ibid.
18 Mark Phillips, Billings of Woes', *Ad News*, 22 February, 1991, 3.
19 Neil Shoebridge, 'Agencies feel the Pain of a "Year of Sobriety"', *Business Review Weekly*, 58.
20 '1991: Blood, Sweat, and Tears', *Ad News*, December 14, 1990, 36.
21 Pat Gillespie, 'Ad Megatrends Identified', *Ad News*, May 17, 1991, 3.
22 Neil Blackley, 'Prospects for the Industry: Rummaging through the Ashes for Phoenix', *Admap Magazine*, January 1992, WARC Database.
23 Andy Biziorek, 'Agency Profits Slide', *B&T*, May 3, 1991, 2.
24 Mark Miller, 'Ad Spend hits the Wall–CEASA', *B&T*, July 19, 1991, 1.
25 'Highs and Lows', *B&T*, December 13, 1991, 12.
26 Andy Biziorek, 'Recession Digs in Across the Board', *B&T*, February 21, 1992, 47.
27 Ibid.
28 Pat Gillespie, 'Industry Faces Marginal Growth', *B&T*, December 4, 1992, 12.
29 Neil Shoebridge, 'Ad Agencies Celebrate a Brighter Year', *Business Review Weekly*, February 14, 1994, 74.
30 'Layoffs Stalking Madison Ave', *B&T*, December 4, 1992, 29.
31 'After the Recession', *Ad News*, August 27, 1993, 32; 'Marketing without the Tears: Beyond the Recession', Marketing, September 17, 1992, 22.
32 Penny Warneford, 'Recovery Is On, But Only Just', *Ad News*, May 21, 1993, 10.
33 Martin O'Shannessy and Minna Keso, 'Budgets to Grow as Stability Returns', *Ad News*, November 5, 1993, 24; Melissa Pearce, 'New Directions Predicted in 1994', *B&T*, December 17, 1993, 14.
34 'Mind Change for the Better', *B&T*, December 17, 1993, 18.
35 'Top Agencies–National 1–50', *Ad News*, February 24, 1995, 24.
36 Ibid.
37 'Crystal Gazing–1995', *B&T*, January 6, 1995, 10.
38 Marise Donnolley, 'Headhunting in a Shrinking Market', *Ad News*, January 25, 1990, 10.
39 Neil Shoebridge, 'Agencies feel the Pain of a "Year of Sobriety"', *Business Review Weekly*, 58.
40 'Retail Closure', *B&T*, April 5, 1991, 1; Mark Miller, 'McCann Pulls Out of Adelaide', *B&T*, April 19, 1991, 4.

41 Rochelle Burbury, 'McCann Cuts 12', *B&T*, June 7, 1991, 1.
42 'JWT Sheds Creatives', *Ad News*, June 14, 1991, 3.
43 Rochelle Burbury, 'Saatchi Cuts', *B&T*, July 12, 1991, 1.
44 Ellen McArthur, 'Agencies Move into the Nervous '90s', *B&T*, July 19, 1991, 16.
45 Delia Rothnie-Jones, 'How to Cope with Redundancy', *Ad News*, 20 September 1991, 15.
46 Rob Palmer, interview by author, November 23, 2012, Title No: 1489216, National Film & Sound Archive, ACT.
47 Brian Boyd, 'Coping with the Axe Man', *B&T*, February 14, 1992, 18.
48 Victor Maree, interview by author, July 23, 2019.
49 Colin Wilson-Brown, interview by author, May 6, 2020.
50 Michael Ritchie, interview by author, 18 April 2013, Title No: 1489298, National Film & Sound Archive, ACT.
51 Jhonnie Blampied, interview by author, 31 July 2019.
52 Tony Hale, interview by author, May 13, 2019.
53 Ibid.
54 Ibid.
55 Sean Cummins, interview by author, May 29, 2019.
56 Bob Miller, interview by author, May 7, 2019.
57 Ibid.
58 Jhonnie Blampied, interview by author, July 31, 2019.
59 Lea Wright, 'Cost-cutting killing Spark of Creativity', *Sydney Morning Herald*, October 10, 1991, 26.
60 'How to Advertise in a Recession', *Ad News*, July 2, 1993, 43.
61 Lynda Gray, 'Recession shows at Cannes', *Ad News*, July 17, 1992, 24.
62 Kevin Luscombe, interview by Rosemary Francis, November 28, 2012, Title No: 1489035, National Film & Sound Archive, ACT.
63 'Consumer Anxiety Epidemic to Impact on Ad Industry', *Ad News*, March 22, 1991, 3.
64 Vicki Arbes, 'The Birth of the "Sensible" Consumer', *B&T*, June 7, 1991, 28.
65 Robert Crawford, 'Changing the Face of Advertising: Australia's Advertising Industry in the Early Days of Television', *Media International Australia*, no.121 (November 2006): 115.
66 Crawford and Dickenson, *Behind Glass Doors,* 36.
67 'Foreign Content Trial mooted for July start', *Ad News*, 3 May 1991, 4.
68 Ibid., 55.
69 Australian Broadcasting Tribunal, 'Australian Content in Advertising: Decision and Reasons', IP/86/11, November 1991.
70 Penny Warneford, 'Foreign Ads well within New ABT Quota–so far', *Ad News*, January 17, 1992, 6.
71 Ibid.
72 Pat Gillespie, 'Foreign Ads Frighten Agencies', *Ad News*, February 28, 1992, 16.
73 Ibid.
74 Ibid.
75 'Foreign Content—Where is it going?', *Ad News*, December 4, 1992, 53.
76 Ian Muir, 'Foreign Ads: A Bane on Society', *B&T*, June 4, 1993, 34.
77 Jacqueline Nunan, 'Foreign Ad Blow-out', *Ad News*, April 22, 1994, 1.
78 Steve Vizard, email to author, 4 May 2020.
79 See Susan Smulyan, *Popular Ideologies: Mass Culture at Mid-Century* (Philadelphia, University of Pennsylvania Press, 2007), 115–56; Jackie Dickenson, *Australian Women in Advertising in the Twentieth Century* (Houndmills Basingstoke: Palgrave Macmillan, 2016), 14–18.
80 See Robert Crawford, 'The Quest for Legitimacy: The Growth and Development of the Australian Advertising Industry, 1900–1969', *Australian Historical Studies* 36, no.124 (2004): 365–71.
81 Alan Mitchell & Mat Toor, 'IPA Campaign First Seeks to Push Advertising Harder', *Marketing*, March 7, 1991, 11.

82 Simon Broadbent, 'Adspend in a Recession: US Optimism Contains Some Practical Lessons', *Admap Magazine*, June 1991, WARC Database; 'In a Recession, the Best Defence is a Good Offense', *Ad News*, October 18, 1991, 17.

83 Sue Lecky, 'Campaign Promotes Selling to Consumers', *Sydney Morning Herald*, October 8, 1992, 36.

84 Jan Chesterfield-Evans, 'Ad Industry to boost Image', Financial Review, 5 April 1994, 40.

85 Neil Shoebridge, 'Ad Industry goes on Offensive to restore a Tarnished Image', Business Review Weekly, 15 August 1994, 82.

86 'Learning New Lessons', *B&T*, November 1, 1991, 24.

87 Crawford and Dickenson, *Behind Glass Doors*, 266.

88 Mark Farrell, 'Training from Top to Bottom', *B&T*, November 1, 1991, 25.

89 Lea Wright, 'Training Levy a Heavy Cost to Small Players', *Sydney Morning Herald*, June 20, 1991, 28.

90 Crawford and Dickenson, *Behind Glass Doors*, 158–59.

91 'Ad School Student call', *Ad News*, May 17, 1991, 39.

92 David Jackson, 'It's Tough to get into Agencies', *Sydney Morning Herald*, September 28, 1991, 77.

93 Mark Miller, 'AFA Trainee Program faces Uncertain Future', *B&T*, January 10, 1992, 2.

94 Rochelle Burbury, 'Crucial to invest in Young People', *Sydney Morning Herald*, February 17, 1994, 34.

95 David Pearson, 'Training: Why Recession can be a Useful Experience', *Marketing*, January 28, 1993, 16.

96 Confidence: When It's not a Trick', *Marketing*, June 24, 1993, 20.

97 'Crystal Gazing–1995', *B&T*, January 6, 1995, 10.

98 Neil Shoebridge, 'Ad Agencies Celebrate a Brighter Year', *Business Review Weekly*, February 14, 1994, 74.

99 Nick Phillips, 'Getting Ad Agencies Ready for the Future', *Admap Magazine*, September 1994, WARC Database.

100 Angela Jackson, 'Consultants see the Light Despite Staff Cuts', *Ad News*, January 14, 1994, 17.

101 Louise Boylen, 'Agencies Mauled by Fee Discounts', *Australian Financial Review*, April 23, 1993, 12.

102 Ian Buchanan, 'Time to Look at Your Interns', *Marketing*, June 3, 1993, 22.

103 Peter Murphy, interview by author, August 2, 2019.

2 The new ascendancy

Writing in *Admap* in 1994, Chris Powell, the CEO of BMP DDB Needham Worldwide, offered a pithy account of the changing relationship between advertising agencies and their clients over the past three decades: 'Agencies found out how to do better work in the 1970s, overdid things (clients were sold some pups) in the 1980s, and got clobbered in the recessionary early 1990s'. Today, he continued, the 'relationship has become adversarial, and at a bad time'.[1] In many ways, this trajectory reflects the nature of agency–client relationships outlined by Lucy Henke. Drawing on interviews conducted in the early 1990s, Henke found that creativity was a crucial determinant in marketers' selection of an agency. However, over time, creativity becomes less important than the nature of the agency–client relationship. Significantly, this relationship also sees a shift in the balance of power where the 'agency-as-Star (how well the agency has done for its other accounts) gives way to client-as-Star (how well the agency will do for us, now)'.[2] The shift in power from the agency to the client would become a defining feature of the advertising industry of the 1990s and would continue to exert a direct influence into the 2000s.

As the Australian experience closely followed the trajectory outlined by Powell, it is unsurprising that Australian agencies would find themselves in a similarly adversarial relationship with marketers in the early 1990s. The Recession provided a rude awakening for agencies, as clients slashed their advertising budgets. Clients also began to ask more questions and place greater demands on their agencies. The severely depleted agencies were hardly able to resist. Although the advertising budgets returned, marketers would not give up their newfound status as 'the industry's most powerful player, taking every opportunity to press their advantage home'.[3] The rise of the marketer was not just an economic by-product of the Recession, it was also the result of clients' upskilling and developing a more sophisticated understanding of marketing knowledge and practices, and advertising's place in them. At a broader level, it could similarly be seen as a reflection of the neoliberal age's abiding belief in letting the market determine relationships. While the balance of power appeared to have shifted irrevocably in the client's favour, issues with marketing practice coupled with the emergence of a new medium enabled the advertising agencies to reclaim some of the territory they had lost in the early 1990s.

From cosy to accountable

Over the decades spanning the 1940s to the 1980s, advertising agencies and their clients had developed a comfortable relationship. Advertising agencies had established themselves as something of a glamorous partner for their clients. They were the magicians who created the advertisements that would make the client's product or service famous. The agencies also had better offices, drove better cars, and ate lunch at better restaurants than their clients. Of course, clients were actively invited to participate in the latter. Agencies also succeeded in identifying themselves as the custodians of the client's brand. They undertook research on the client's behalf and proclaimed to have a better understanding of the clients' market than the clients themselves. For their part, clients appeared to accept this arrangement. As client CEOs saw themselves in the business of manufacturing cars or servicing bank accounts, they did not yet consider advertising or marketing to be part of their core business. Client marketing departments, if they had them, were relatively small and often staffed by individuals with some retail or advertising experience but no formal marketing education. And even if they wanted to create their own television commercials, media accreditation regulations prevented them from being able to broadcast them. Their lack of marketing knowledge meant they were highly dependent on their agency. As the executive director of the Association of Australian National Advertisers (AANA) recalled, the status quo was a very 'cosy' one for the agencies.[4] However, this entire situation would be fundamentally and irreversibly upended by the Recession.

As it became apparent that 1990 was going to be a difficult year, agencies and clients alike began to pay closer attention to advertising budget along with the agency–client relationship. Writing on the 'inexact science of ad budgets' in *Ad News* in May 1990, Quentin Munro, the managing director of the agency Addyman Coles Munro, urged his fellow agency professionals to pay greater attention to client expectations:

> Every so often, it is worthwhile reminding ourselves what clients expect from their advertising investment. Yes, they expect awareness, attitude shifts, performance dimension associations, positioning and a few other market research buzz words. But they also expect sales. They expect their sales to go up, to at least hold or halt or slow down a downward trend. In other words, they expect some type of causal relationship between sales and advertising dollars invest.[5]

As Munro rightly points out, clients valued sales more than creative advertisements—especially in the midst of an economic recession. 'There was then a lot of talk about, obviously, cutbacks in advertising expenditure', recalls Kate Henley, executive director of the AANA. This, she explains, stimulated 'the first real demands for advertising accountability'.[6] With the economy weakening, advertisers' calls for greater accountability in their advertisements and, indeed, their relationship with advertising agencies became louder and more insistent. The theme of the 1990 convention of the AANA was 'Accountable Advertising'—and it would be a theme that would continue long after the Recession had receded into the past.[7]

In a shrinking market, the decisions being made by marketers assumed a greater importance for the advertising agencies. Not surprisingly, the industry press was keen to gain an insight into the clients' mindset. Their reports would prove to be sobering reading for agencies.

A mid-1991 survey conducted by industry consultant and former chairman of Foote Cone & Belding chairman Wayne Wood found that many marketers had little knowledge of the advertising agency business and harboured a 'very pessimistic' outlook on most advertising agencies.[8] Around the same time, a survey of marketers undertaken by *B&T* indicated that 30 per cent had changed agencies. It was a significant figure given that marketers had traditionally been loyal to their agencies. The reasons cited for ending their relationship included 'Cost too much and provide too little'; 'Ad hoc, cheap and nasty, inconsistent and non-coherent'; and 'Creative and commercial arrogant'.[9] Not surprisingly, similar comments were expressed in another survey of marketers conducted just weeks later.[10] Academic studies found similar results. In his survey of 95 Australian marketers who had recently changed agencies, Grahame Dowling found that 'the two most important reasons were, first, the need for new creative ideas; and second, the need for a new marketing approach', followed by 'poor account service, and senior agency staff not giving sufficient attention to the client'.[11] While these comments and findings could have been directed at any agency at any other point in time, they nevertheless collectively point to a growing frustration among advertisers. The results of a 1992 survey of marketers conducted for the *Australian Business Monthly* did not offer better news. It found that 20 per cent of marketers were dissatisfied 'with their agency's knowledge of market trends and needs' while another 40 per cent were undecided. However, the finding that 69 per cent of respondents noted that the Recession 'had a direct impact on their advertising budget for the current year' revealed that the broader economic context was integral to the marketers' changing views.[12]

Frustrations with agencies combined with a growing understanding of their economic power emboldened marketers to challenge established practices and conventions. One of their first steps was to review their agency. Although agency reviews had long been a standard business practice, the frequency and the nature of such reviews were different. The growing number of agency reviews being implemented by clients not only prompted such dramatic headlines as 'Recession leads to Market Promiscuity',[13] they also led the AANA to publish practical advice on the reviews process in its monthly newsletter.[14] It soon became apparent to agencies that being under review was a euphemism for being sacked. A 1993 survey of reviews thus found that 'the chances of an incumbent keeping the business in a review are miniscule' and that 'if you're the incumbent and you're not prepared to totally rebuild an agency to hold on to the account, forget it'.[15]

While those under review rued the clients' decision to exert greater autonomy over their marketing strategies and approaches, others relished the opportunity to snare a new account. Competition within the already cut-throat agency world intensified, as agencies invested even more time, money, and effort in developing their pitches to potential clients.[16] In 1992, it was estimated that Australian agencies had spent $9.5 on new business pitches—a significant amount given the parlous state of advertising expenditure.[17] By 1993, some agencies were beginning to complain about the impact of regular pitches for new business. Writing in *Ad News*, DDB Needham managing director Darryl Lindberg complained that some pitches could cost anything up to $100,000 when the costs of research, staff hours, and pitch consultant fees were all taken into consideration.[18] There were also other costs too: 'You can walk out having won $10 million and lost $5 million through the companies you ignore'.[19] Lindberg also complained about those responsible for these costs: 'Many times clients don't know what they're getting into and how seriously we take them (pitches). Once they decide to do it—they have this Godzilla thing that grows'.[20] Others took aim at the clients for providing 'vague briefs' as well as their reluctance to provide 'reliable information' to agencies vying for their account.[21] While the agencies' peak body, the Advertising Federation of Australia (AFA), developed pitching guidelines, the increased level of competition among agencies meant that they had little impact.[22] By 1994, the AFA was complaining of a culture of exploitation. AFA executive director Bev Dyke thus explained that '[i]n recent years we have seen some advertisers seeking credentials submissions from ten, even up to 15 agencies with short-lists as high as six'. Dyke went on to claim that '[t]he only explanation must be that some advertisers play an unethical game of gathering as many ideas and insight into their business as they can find'.[23] The AFA consequently called for agencies to receive appropriate remuneration for their pitching efforts. Although the AANA's Kate Henley agreed that a level remuneration for the time and effort spent on client pitches was warranted, she reminded the agencies that they were far from the hapless victims they made themselves out to be:

> One-upmanship, it seems, is the name of the game, and that's largely why pitching has become 'discount city'. ... Agencies should budget for new business and manage that budget. Too often agencies will pitch for practically any new business that comes along. Whatever happened to being selective? Client lists too long? Don't pitch then ... We don't need regulations or a fixed fee, just some common sense.[24]

The Recession also prompted marketers to take a closer at the fees that agencies were charging them. For decades, the standard remuneration rate charged by all Australian advertising agencies was 10 per cent media commission plus 7.5 per cent service fee. However, a growing number of anxious and desperate clients were willing to reconsider their service fee to secure a client. The annual survey of AANA members found that in 1992, 60 per cent were paying the 7.5 per cent service fee—a year later this percentage had dropped to 44 per cent. AANA members were opting for more flexible payment options, notably performance-based and sliding-scale approaches.[25] In the same year, the small Sydney agency Cooke Collins Advertising announced that it was removing its service fee altogether and would be deriving its income solely from media commissions. The agency's director, Bill Cooke, explained that the move 'was because our clients are hurting in the recession'.[26] Other agency principals dismissed the move. Gordon Alexander of Marketforce labelled it 'suicide', arguing that '[n]o agency's structure can work on the 10% media commission. The profit margins are not enough', while Jeff Reeves, the managing director of Young & Rubicam's Sydney office, expressed concerns about agency work being devalued in that it 'pushes the industry for a service into a supplier mode'. By 1994, the AANA found that the 7.5 per cent service fee was 'no longer the norm' with 5 per cent being more common. Marketers and agencies also developed a range of other payment options, including head hours, monthly fees, and project fees.[27] In contrast, the 10 per cent commission remained stubbornly unchanged—for the time being. Responding to these findings, the AFA commissioned its own report which offered a very different perspective. The AFA's confidential report found that 90 per cent of members worked on the traditional remuneration model. 'Perceptions on agency remuneration have been fuelled by media reporting, agency paranoia and client tactics to browbeat suppliers', noted AFA Chairman Max Gosling in the report's preface, before taking a swipe at those who had the temerity to question the long-standing agency–client accord: 'My concern is that clients do not generally fully appreciate the contribution we [agencies] make to their business'.[28]

While the agencies were smarting from the marketers' increased belligerence, many agency leaders understood the importance of demonstrating accountability to their clients. Agencies established their credentials in different ways. Richard Sauerman observed that many agencies sought to impress their clients by embracing their processes and their methodical approach to business. This, he claimed, was particularly prevalent in the account service department which:

> seems to be more intent on conforming than differentiating. There's the standard Powerpoint presentation—standard agency font ... There are standard research methodologies. The standard 'proprietary' planning tools. The standard market data and knowledge the standard 'consumer insights'. There's even a standard way of dressing for a client meeting. More and more, our world is home to a sea of sameness. People and organisations conforming to requirements, not to greatness. Products, services, strategies and ads that are flawless .... But far from dazzling.[29]

For others, being accountable was not a constraint on advertising—it was in fact an essential part of advertising. When Hugh Spencer was elected Chairman of AFA in 1990, he was concerned about the agency's lack of credibility.[30] He used his first speech to argue 'how we had to be held accountable for the effectiveness of what we did, not the creativity—I don't give a toss about creativity. Creativity's a means to an end'.[31] Industry commentator Neil Shoebridge applauded Spencer's stance, particularly in the current economic climate, noting: 'His calls should not be ignored. If the advertising industry is to prosper, it must prove it is an essential business tool. ... If they fail ... advertising's importance and its share of marketing dollars will dwindle'.[32] Spencer succeeded in creating the AFA Advertising Effectiveness Awards, which were first held in 1990. Of course, such awards were hardly unique—the Effie Awards had been operating in the United States since 1968, while the UK's Institute of Practitioners in Advertising implemented its Effectiveness Awards in 1980.

The Australians' relatively late recognition of effectiveness hints at a level of ambivalence towards accountability among agencies. This would become more apparent in the mid-1990s, just as the economic crisis was beginning to pass. In 1995, Shoebridge observed that the AFA's Effectiveness Awards were 'a valiant attempt to prove the value of advertising, but they are not widely known, not widely publicised and are not enough'. If the agencies failed to impress their worth to clients, he warned, the value of advertising and advertising agencies 'will continue to diminish'.[33] Such concerns were not unfounded. A survey of marketers' views of the advertising industry conducted a few months earlier found that 'agencies had become less self-indulgent, more cost conscious and more responsible during the past five years'. However, clients still wanted more with over half of respondents stating that they 'would like to see their agency taking a broader role in their business than it currently does'.[34]

Ian Alwill had seen some of the agency's problematic accountability practices first-hand. So when Alwill moved from his role as director at McCann Erickson-Hakuhodo to take up a marketing position with Nestlé, one of his first moves was to implement an audit of all of the agencies—'McCann was the first'.[35] As the age of accountability set in, the days of cosy relationships between agencies and marketers increasingly seemed a world away.

The marketing push

Although marketing practices can be traced back to antiquity, the rise of marketing as a managerial practice across the globe was a 20th-century phenomenon.[36] In Australia, it was the post-war economic boom coupled with the increasing presence of multi-national firms that stimulated a growing interest in marketing practice and theory.[37] This Long Boom saw businesses establishing their own marketing departments, while universities were seeking to fill them with graduates who had completed their newly created marketing degrees. This growing interest in marketing would have a direct impact on the advertising agencies. As Robert Crawford and Jackie Dickenson observe, the embrace of marketing from the 1960s to the 1980s resulted in 'a gradual shift away from the personal relationships that had been at the heart of the agency–client relationship towards a more businesslike, professional arrange-ment'.[38] Continuing through the 1990s and into the early 2000s, these processes not only underpinned marketing's rise, they also precipitated advertising's decline.

Client marketing departments of the 1970s and early 1980s were often ad hoc affairs. At the National Australia Bank, staff in the marketing department had no formal marketing training—they were experienced bank managers whose appointment to the marketing department was, as Tony Hale recalls, 'almost a reward for loyal service'. Hale, who worked for the bank's agency, adds that 'you wouldn't call them sophisticated marketers but they were very good people. They took advice of agencies by-and-large, they were smart enough to ask piercing questions'. Reflecting on the coming changes that would envelop the sector, Hale observes 'I think over the course of the next three or four decades the sophistication of the marketing people increased dramatically but necessarily to the betterment of the work that was being generated'.[39] The sophistication that Hale noticed would accelerate over the 1990s. At this time, the young marketing graduates of 1970s and 1980s were beginning to enter the upper echelons of many businesses—including agencies themselves. Wayne Kingston, who had completed an MBA while working as the marketing manager for Tooheys brewery in the early 1970s, was one such graduate. Although his time in marketing was relatively short in comparison to his time in the agencies, Kingston's elevation to the CEO of DDB's Australian operations in 1990 nevertheless revealed marketing's growing reach. Comparing the 1980s to the 1990s, Kingston echoes Hale's sentiments: 'Clients became a lot more educated in dealing with the agencies. Over this period in time, you get agencies dominating the process to clients dominating the process'.[40] The AANA's board similarly reflected this shift, as an older generation of marketers gave way to a new generation of hard-nosed professionals with deeper and more sophisticated understanding of the theory and practice of marketing.[41]

While advertising agency principals could see that marketing was becoming an essential part of their clients' communication management strategies, they did not foresee the full impact of this development on their business until it was too late. Dennis Merchant had established one of Australia's first independent media agencies in 1974. He would eventually sell his agency to Interpublic in 1990 and would remain with the firm for most of the decade. Over this period, he saw a major shift in client perceptions as well as the type of person that advertising and media agencies were now dealing with:

> Suddenly they more concerned with what the financial analysts and market analysts were saying. And so they relegated this function to this new breed of university graduates, marketing graduates, and left them in control without any authority. … [Agencies] put forward a concept, a recommendation and it would be "I don't know, let's put it into research" or "I don't know the boss won't like that" … But what these clowns up the top didn't understand is that these people might have been trained in marketing *per se*, but the advertising world went to a different school. They might be marketing experts, whatever that entails, they're not advertising experts! … It was a thing that went right across every spectrum of the industry, this introduction of the so-called marketing graduate, product managers … that whole side of the industry was controlled by accountants and bean counters.[42]

Merchant claims that the marketing-driven emphasis on costs and finances led clients to treat advertising as a cost and not investment, and it was shared by other agency principals.[43] As noted in Chapter 1, the hallmarks of Recession era advertising—shorter ads with lower production values—certainly bear testament to this claim.

Alex Hamill, who headed George Patterson Bates, Australia's largest agency, expresses similar concerns about the growing impact of product managers and their detrimental impact on the agency relationship. Hamill adopted a more nuanced view of marketing and its impact on the advertising agency business, however. Noting that that those marketers who made the effort to learn 'a bit about the agency business' were in fact 'a bit more intelligent'. Consequently, 'they lifted the intelligence of the agency to some degree towards the end of the nineties or the middle of the nineties'. The impact, according to Hamill was twofold: 'They were starting to be better clients. Better clients generally mean better advertising but often mean tougher, tougher decisions'. In outlining this improvement, however, Hamill also identified a more problematic shift. Clients may well have started to make tougher decisions, but they were increasingly the result of a more protracted, hierarchical process, which he labels the 'ladder of OKs':

> The ladder of OKs is always difficult. Whereas I could generally go to the chairman or managing director and have an ad approved, if I had to, but now you had to go up this bloody ladder to get there because he or she wouldn't get involved with the product manager. So, the ladder of OKs got longer, not so much destructive, but you could feel the impact more. The clients were having much more impact on the [creative] work, much more.[44]

While David Mattingly recounts a similar story, he also identifies another key development. As the head of the retail-focused agency Y&R Mattingly, Mattingly had spent much of the 1970s and 1980s working directly with retail store owners. In the late 1980s and early 1990s, many of these retailers became public companies with new hierarchies and a greater emphasis on driving profits above all else. Despite his long-standing relationships and abiding understanding of the retail industry, Mattingly found himself on unfamiliar terrain: suddenly the managing director wasn't interested in advertising, he was only interested in analysts. And that's where the whole advertising industry changed dramatically because suddenly we were dealing with marketing managers, or whatever they called themselves, instead of the owner of the business.[45] It was a significant change that underscored advertising's changing status.

For the agencies then, the marketing tide was moving things in the wrong direction. As they became more distant from the key decision makers in the client ranks, agencies found themselves 'drifting downstream'.[46] This not only required them to work with less experienced junior staff who had little understanding of or interest in advertising, it also restricted their access to the client's marketing budget.

The shrinking slice of the marketing pie

Advertising's diminishing share of the marketing budget reflected broader changes and developments within the marketing industry. Specifically, the increasing complexity of the marketing matrix as well as the growing number of activities and approaches that now constituted marketing practice meant that advertising was fast becoming just another tool in the marketer's arsenal. Horst Stipp, a researcher at NBC Universal, also observed another factor: 'Many advertisers think advertising does not work as well as it used to and they have reduced advertising budgets, often in favor of promotion and other marketing strategies. In other words, there is a *crisis of confidence* in advertising'.[47]

With its promise of providing accurate and measurable insights, market research had become an increasingly indispensable part of marketing practice. Although the first documented example of formal market research being conducted by an advertising agency dates back to 1879, it was only in the mid-twentieth century that it became a standard part of marketing practice, with advertising agencies and independent market research consultancies both undertaking the bulk of the research.[48] Australia's post-war economic boom stimulated consumption and, with it, competition between marketers.[49] During this time, market researchers functioned as mediators who 'translated consumer preferences and marketers spent much energy (and money) telling consumers that they knew what they wanted and needed'.[50] While marketers often undertook some rudimentary market research training,[51] the growing size, scope, and complexity of market research necessitated the employment of university-trained staff to undertake these studies and interpret them.[52]

During the tight recession years, market research's promise of delivering greater accuracy and accountability struck a chord with marketers. In a 1990 interview with *Ad News*, John Clark, the marketing services manager of L&K: Rexona at Unilever, provided an insight into the ways that marketers currently saw and understood the role of market research:

> At the onset of hard times, I think management becomes more risk averse. Seeking security in numbers we see qualitative suffering relative to quantitative because financial executives and accountants do take a greater interest in research and numbers are what they're happiest working with … Market research is not an invention technique, it's an assessment technique. In hard times, there is no less enthusiasm for creativity and innovation but there is greater concern for more thorough evaluation of new ideas before implementation … It has two tasks to perform: identification and explanation. A good research company should help identify where the focus of investigation should be … After identification, the research company's job is to offer explanations about what marketing activities will work in those core markets.[53]

However, the claim that market research was simply an evaluation tool was increasingly questioned by many in the advertising agencies. Although the advertising agencies had been key proponents of market research, they now found themselves and their work being subjected to greater levels of market research evaluation. Specifically, it was the timing and changing nature of such research that troubled them. Rick Osborn, the general manager of George Patterson's Sydney office, thus railed against the propensity for clients to make the sudden decision at the tail end of campaign development that market research needed to be undertaken: 'The money is spent. The research must be done before the big money is spent, to develop the concept, not destroy the finished object. Any finding other than that the package is terrific will result in additional cost, waste, and dented egos'.[54]

Agency creative departments were particularly aggrieved with the intrusion of market research into their space. For them, the testing of commercials was frustrating but understandable. However, the clients' decision to subject creative concepts to market research was altogether insulting. Noting that the value of market research was undone 'by the success of many great campaign that research predicted would fail', Stephen Fisher, the creative director at Thomson White FCB, argued that 'concept pre-testing is not the "science" that it's portrayed to be, but is simply a constantly evolving skill'.[55] Mike Daniels, senior strategy planner at DDB Needham Sydney, agreed: 'when it comes to creative development and the interaction of creative ideas and the research process ... we run into problems. ... Research becomes a suppressing and conservative force, even a destructive one. It can kill the new and the different, it can make the interesting ordinary'.[56] Some market researchers agreed with such claims, noting that the problem lay in the misuse of market research rather than the practice of market research.[57] Again, the finger of blame was pointed at the client, specifically, 'young product managers looking for every backstop in case a campaign goes wrong'.[58]

The claim that market research was beginning to dominate every part of the marketing communications process was not necessarily shared by market researchers themselves. Brian Fine, managing director of AMR: Quantum and the president of Market Research Society of Australia identified a series of issues affecting the market research, from the public's reluctance to divulge private information to the emergence of telemarketers whose annoying sales pitches were undermining the public's confidence in the cold calling strategies that were the cornerstone of market research practice. [59] Significantly, the Recession had also decimated the market research industry's management ranks—a shortfall in staff trained in qualitative methods also meant that many firms were using 'interviewers and researchers with only minimal training, partly in an effort to cut costs'. [60] Such observations indicate that market research was not necessarily the all-pervasive presence that many in the advertising agencies claimed.

With Australia's economy improving, Fine observed that marketers were again investing more in market research and that market researchers needed to reposition themselves accordingly: 'There's more information to absorb and less time to do it in. So we have to move ourselves to the wavelength of marketers we have to become more than researchers. We have to become part of the marketing team'.[61] Current trends certainly indicated that market research would assume a greater presence in all marketing decisions. Malcolm Spry thus declared that the 'whole field of marketing is being revolutionised and the impetus is the rapid development in technology that is changing both research methods and the industry itself'. [62] A former advertising agency executive who had moved across to market research giant AGB McNair, Spry predicted that technology would deliver larger and larger datasets on consumer attitudes, habits, and lifestyles that would necessitate a greater reliance on the skillset of the market researcher. While market researchers would be integral, Spry claimed that 'traditional market research departments will disappear', replaced by:

> new information units headed by 'chief information officers' and information technology will no longer be exclusive territory for the few. It will become more accessible and more vital, and it will be necessary for chief executives to become directly involved and to fully understand all aspects of information collection. ... There will be an arrival of new players in the market. Not traditional research companies, but organisation with access to new information technology and skills.[63]

Spry's vision of marketing's future resonated with practitioners engaging in the small but increasingly important field of direct marketing.

Direct marketing was a more recent addition to the marketing mix. It has been defined as 'a relational marketing process of prospecting, conversion, and maintenance that involves information feedback and control at the individual level by using direct response advertising with tracking codes'.[64] Direct marketing included such channels as mailouts, telemarketing, and insert media. While the term direct marketing was first used in 1961, it was Lester Wunderman who emerged as the 'father of direct marketing'. Wunderman's principles of direct marketing were clear: direct marketing was a strategy rather than a tactic; the consumer was the hero, not the product; communicate with customers individually; create relationships; be accessible to the consumer; media is a contact strategy.[65]

A handful of small direct marketing firms were operating in Australia in the 1970s and the 1980s. Luella Copeland-Smith worked briefly with one of these direct marketing firm before moving across to the direct marketing departments at Young & Rubicam and then Ogilvy & Mather. While Copeland-Smith's appointment indicated that the agencies were already taking a great interest in direct marketing prior to the 1990s, their commitment to it was still lukewarm. Significantly, they were not the only ones. Of her clients, Copeland-Smith thus recalls that a 'lot of them were actually directed by their American owners ... because direct marketing was very, very much more established in the [United] States than it was here'. This outlook also reflected the direct marketing's image problem. Copeland-Smith thus notes that 'I always got the impression that they [CEOs] passed anything to do with direct marketing down the line to somebody else ... they didn't want to get in involved, they wanted the more glamorous end in advertising not direct marketing'.[66] This dowdy image also reflected the backgrounds of many of those in direct marketing who had started out working in the printing trade rather than the newer and more exciting communications fields.[67]

By the 1990s, Copeland-Smith observed a discernible shift: 'When it became obvious that direct marketing was very much something that they had to do, people started to take a lot more interest at the top, whereas before it was middle management area really'.[68] Unlike advertising, direct marketing was able to show a direct relationship between their marketing efforts and consumer response. Martin Williams, principal of the direct marketing agency Cartwright-Williams, recalls that the Recession led clients to direct marketing as 'they were looking for more return on investment so ... stuff they could measure was becoming increasingly sexy'.[69] The AANA's 1993 survey of members reflected this shift, with 73 per cent stating that they used 'direct marketing in one form or another. Of these, all used direct mail, 94 per cent used catalogues and 91 per cent used database marketing'. The survey also found that 'advertisers are not treating DM as a separate function, but as a part of a more integrated marketing approach', adding that 'it appears highly likely that the roles of and approaches to direct marketing in the overall mix will become undistinguishable from main media advertising'.[70] Recruitment specialists observed a similar trend, noting that creatives with direct marketing experience were now in 'high demand' and well paid, and that the image of direct response as 'the "poor man's" advertising was changing'.[71]

While client perceptions were changing, agencies remained sceptical. Tom Moult, a creative director who would go on to become CEO of Euro RSCG in Australia, recalls that a strict 'pecking order' operated in the advertising agencies. The direct marketing department was 'where the B class people operated, and that was known to the rest of us, the glamour boys ... as "shit that folds"'.[72] Matt Donovan, a strategic planner at FCB and Euro RSCG, similarly remembers a senior agency figure dismissively referring to direct marketers as 'the stamp lickers' (a reference to their direct mail activities).[73] Stating that 'reported swing to below the line is not welcomed by agency chiefs who argue that non media promotions produce only short term bursts and undermine the product's "long term brand franchise"', *B&T* underscored the agency's sense of hierarchy.[74] Such concerns, however, ran deeper. At Cartwright Williams, Williams worked alongside leading creative agencies on major accounts such as Apple and found that the agencies' outlook was informed by two separate but connected factors. Firstly, the media commission system (see Chapter 3) meant that advertising agencies simply had little interest in pursuing direct marketing in any major way. Williams thus observes that advertising agencies 'didn't get it [direct marketing] because they were earning too much money really from the media. It didn't pay them to get it'.[75] Secondly, he found that advertising agencies remained fundamentally concerned about maintaining their slice of the marketing pie:

> They didn't really like direct marketing very much and advertising agencies were very wary of it all. So they used to employ us to work alongside a client, but also tried to keep us at a suitable distance because they didn't want us taking all of their money.[76]

At the turn of the century, direct marketing still occupied ambiguous space. On the one hand, its place in the marketing mix was assured. The 2001 survey of AANA members found that 7 per cent had used direct marketing in 1999, 10 per cent in 2000, and an estimated 11 per cent for 2001.[77] While the figure was growing, it still constituted a relatively small percentage of the client 'adspend'. In 2002, direct marketing spend was estimated to be $17.4 million, a 6 per cent increase on the previous year—a solid improvement but hardly an earth-shattering one.[78] Rather than seeing the rise of direct marketing in its own right, observers claimed that it was being subsumed by new communication strategies. 'Done properly, it should be impossible to separate DM from mainstream media', noted Douglas Nichol, general manager of George Patterson, adding: 'In the long term, DM and above-the-line should be seamless'.[79] Joel Norton, group business director at iLeo, saw a similar shift: 'We are seeing more combined campaigns and more sophisticated multimedia integrated campaigns'. However, Norton also identified another important development: 'the big change has been that more and more DM teams are allowed to be involved in client business and DM has been recognised as a valid part of that business'.[80]

Marketing's growing sophistication over the 1990s and early 2000s similarly saw the growth of other approaches which enhanced the marketers' capacity to reach their specific target audiences and, indeed, to deliver a verifiable return on investment. Marketers' growing interest in point-of-sale marketing was not only driven by the desire to find new touchpoints for connecting with the consumer, they were also premised on the view that 'traditional media [was] beginning to fall by the wayside as a result of modern society's burgeoning literacy in regards to communications and technology'.[81] Declaring that '[s]hoppers are demanding more and more information, and they want information in an entertaining and non-pressured way', Alan Holroyd, the national advertising manager of Woolworth's, a national supermarket chain, similarly sounded an ominous marketing message for the advertising agencies.[82] With marketers eager to utilise any marketing strategy that would enable them to reach their desired market in the most cost-effective way, the advertising industry found itself in an increasingly challenging battle to win a piece of the shrinking marketing pie.

Re-branding the brand

With marketers exercising greater sway over marketing strategies, it was inevitable that they would also pay greater attention to branding and revisit the advertising agency's role in its development. Looking back on the relationship between advertising agencies and client brands, Tony Hale recalled that 'in the '70s and '80s, it was very, very much a relationship-building industry. The agencies were very much what they used to be called the holders of the brands—the custodians of the brand'.[83] Advertising agencies, as Tom Moult observes, occupied a unique space and served an important function for clients: 'There was a total separation between the advertised brand and the consumer, and advertising people ... filled that gap with clever advertising'.[84] Over the 1990s and 2000s, the advertising agency's role in maintaining the client's brand would come under increasing pressure—both from within and without.

As part of their review of marketing strategies and practices during the Recession, marketers began to pay closer attention to their brands and the process of branding. Speaking at the 'Maintaining Brand Supremacy' conference in 1991, Stephen Dillon, the sales and marketing director for Uncle Toby's oat products, revealed the way that the marketers' desire for accountability was informing the way that they now viewed the brand: 'The intrinsic worth of a brand is now being carefully measured to determine its dollars and cents value'.[85] Here again, advertising agencies were coming under pressure, as marketers were 'abandoning brand building activities, such as advertising, in favour of tactics, especially price promotions, which aim to increase market-share quickly'.[86] Advertising agencies inevitably sought to protect their territory. In an article for *B&T*, Jhonnie Blampied argued that during the Recession marketers could not afford to undermine their brand by pursuing a low-cost strategy. Warning that 'consumers do not equate value for money with price alone', Blampied mounted a defence of advertising: 'A tough economic climate is undoubtedly an important motivation to deliver better value for money. But it is brands that use advertising to add value rather than trade with it, that will be more successful in the long run'.[87]

The advertising agencies' 'custodianship' of the brand would also come under further pressure from a somewhat paradoxical source—non-branded or generic products sold by retailers. A 1994 survey found that 38 per cent of Australian consumers felt that generic products were as good as their branded equivalent. While this figure paled in comparison to the 82 per cent of British consumers who expressed a similar outlook, it was nevertheless a worrying development for the advertising agencies. Explanations for this development varied. Some attributed it to marketing's evolution, whereby 'most products are now reliable' and that 'service is becoming standardised at a highly acceptable level'.[88] Others pointed to socio-economic factors, such as improving education levels, along with the retail sector's growing sophistication in terms of operations and marketing strategies.[89] However, the fears of generic products dominating the marketplace would be allayed by a 1994 Nielsen report on grocery trends, which found that branded products were in fact regaining some of the ground that they had lost during the darkest days of the Recession.[90] A 1995 US poll that found that brand loyalty was still strong among consumers similarly offered hope to the agencies (and, indeed, their clients).[91]

The rise of the generic signalled in no uncertain terms that the relationship between advertising and the brand was changing. For marketing consultant, David Kieg, the issues were clear:

> Why is it then that after almost 40 years of brands being supported heavily through television and other media are now looking at a situation in which brands, quite simply, don't look as strong and secure as they used to? The truth is that the marketing and advertising environment has changed enormously over the past few decades; this change has recently accelerated markedly.... All too often, however, the advertising industry has chosen to see these changes in terms of a diversion of funds to below-the-line activities and has agreed this dilution of above-the-line funds is a major factor in the erosion of brand values. [92]

Writing almost a decade later, Stephen Byrne, the principal of a branding and communications consultancy, similarly attributed the growing disconnect between advertising and branding to the advertising agencies' lack of agility as well as their flawed approach to advertising strategy.[93] However, many agencies were unwilling to accept that they were to blame. Reg Bryson, CEO of one of Australia's most eminent creative agencies The Campaign Palace, pointed his finger in an altogether different direction. Declaring that the 'brand is simply not working any more', Bryson claimed that there had been 'a breakdown in brand differentiation, brand impact, brand loyalty, brand value, band reliance, brand position'. These issues, he argued, had emerged at a time when 'brands began to be treated as commodities and became less relevant'.[94] In short, Bryson was taking a swing at the marketers who had sought to demystify the brand by removing it from the agency orbit and reducing it down to the quantifiable sum of its equal parts.

In 1996, brand expert David Aaker observed that 'CEOs are seeing that developing a brand strategy intertwined with developing a business strategy'.[95] By the 2000s, branding was accepted as an essential part of business. Writing in *AdNews* in 2004, Tim Heberden of the Brand Finance Institute underscored the growing importance attributed to the brand:

> Gone are the days when brands were the exclusive domains of advertising agencies and marketing departments. (And, of course, consumers.) These days finance directors, investment bankers, venture capitalists, intellectual property lawyers and risk mangers all have a particular interest in brands, and some have gone so far as to add the term 'brand equity' to their repertoire of business jargon. ... In many instances agencies have seen their role as brand guardian usurped by clients' own beefed-up marketing departments or external advisers.[96]

Marketers were not the only ones displaying a greater interest in brands at the turn of the century. Consumers were also looking to brands in new ways. 'In a world where everything changes minute by minute, often monstrously, humans need to be able to identify solid reference points', claimed online branding expert Martin Lindstrom, adding that '[b]rands need to communicate every possible signal of solidity. Brands must be here to stay—able to offer consumer familiarity and permanence'.[97] Grey Worldwide's 2005 *Eye on Australia* report echoed these claims, noting that 'Australians feel abandoned by the corporate and government world, and are turning to brands they trust in record numbers. ... Australians believe first and foremost that great brands are those that they can trust'.[98] The fact that this need could not be satisfied by generic products indicated that all was not lost for the advertising agencies.

The role of advertising in brand development was also being affected by the emergence of 'new' media. While advertising agencies were coming to grips with the ways that digital media operated and what it meant for their own practice (see Chapters 4–7), the other stakeholders in the brand were also exploring what it meant for them. In their 1997 study of banner advertisements, Rex Briggs and Nigel Hollis from Millward Brown International found that online media was already having an impact on brand marketing strategies, reminding people of a brand's existence, stimulating latent or dormant brand associations, and causing people to change their attitudes towards the brand.[99] Briggs and Hollis thus conclude that '[t]he unique marketing power of the on-line environment and the established communication benefits of traditional advertising combine to make the Web a powerful new advertising medium with real potential for brand building'.[100] A decade later, the medium's potential had become much clearer. Rosie Gray-Spencer, the general manager of Brand and Communications for the telecommunications firm Vodafone Australia, thus explained that 'I love traditional media but for us to be true to our brand it's about doing things differently and having a conversation with our customers' before adding 'we need to use different media in different ways to achieve that'.[101] Consumers were developing new relationships with brands through digital media. As Daryl Nelson, an information and communication technology analyst at market research firm Frost & Sullivan, observed, this trend was creating a deepening chasm between marketers and consumers: 'Online citizens are almost entirely cynical of old-school marketing techniques. ... For those who have been advertising in a certain way and are comfortable with that ... then I'd say this is probably extremely frightening'.[102]

Of course, the sense that the all-conquering marketer had successfully wrested control of the brand from the hapless advertising agency was not true. Agencies still had a role to play. Ironically, it involved going 'back to the future' insofar as it saw them filling the gaps in the emerging hierarchy. Michael Abdel, founder and principal of The Sphere Agency, observes that the new 'kings'—the brand managers and the marketing managers—seldom remained with a brand for long. This churn, Abdel argues, left the brand in a vulnerable position (and the agency with it):

> [A] new marketing manager or brand manager will come on board and want to overhaul with their rubber stamp, leave their mark on the brand—that generally starts at good agency reviews. ... you [agencies] would invest time and resource on building the relationship and you'd go over and above to make sure that the relationship is set and you'd expect that that marketing person would probably hang around for four/five years. But we've come to a point right now where across the board it's a revolving door. So, unless you're building the relationship with the founder or the CEO, it makes it very difficult to get the security you need as an agency to invest in resource and invest in the relationship ...[103]

Sean Cummins, creative director and founder of creative agency Cummins & Partners, recounts a similar experience. Clients, he notes, 'have got egos' and they 'want to make a mark, and because their time and their "stick-outedness" was getting a lot shorter, they needed to make an impact within a given advertising cycle; maybe a couple of years'.[104] Cummins argues that the ensuing result was 'the discontinuity of a brand' as 'brands started to become a lot more indefinite in their direction, a lot more chopped and changed, a lot more inconsistent in their tone'.[105] Significantly, this situation provided an opportunity for the advertising agency to reassert themselves and to reclaim their role as brand custodians. Cummins recalls that:

> I remember it dawned on me one day when I heard one client leave ... I realised that after a certain point of time the agency became the corporate memory of the brand, and it was a really interesting shift of power. Then what would happen was new clients would come in. You'd almost be telling the client that, look, we do it like this, or the brand stands for this. ... trusted brands are very hard things to build, and you do it over a long period of time with relentless consistency because, all things said and done, people pick the brand that they're most familiar with. They do their own little emotional inventory about what a brand stands for, and if they feel that the brand's been there for a long time, it works in the brand's favour.[106]

Despite the rise of the marketing, the emergence of new media and the changing consumer attitudes, it seems that agencies still had a role in connecting the 'advertised brand and the consumer'—even if they were no longer the sole point of connection between them.

Although the capacity to understand brands and deliver creative solutions to client problems was increasingly identified as the advertising agency's unique selling proposition, the agency's capacity to dominate this role was being undercut by another marketing-led issue. If the Recession had given clients the confidence to question their agency, the seemingly irrepressible rise of marketing values across the entire sector gave clients the confidence to challenge another advertising shibboleth. 'One of the notable trends around clients' quest for greater creativity seems to be an inclination and an openness to add multiple creative resources to their agency rosters', observed Catherine Benson from agency search consultancy Select Resources International, 'Whereas several years ago it would have been inconceivable for major marketers to openly go outside of their core agency relationships for creative work, today this has become more common'.[107] For clients, this move made marketing sense, reflecting the growing scope and sophistication of marketing practices over the last decades. For the agencies, this additional split in the marketing expenditure was perhaps less galling than the fact that some clients now held the view that an individual agency was no longer up to the task of generating creative ideas on their own.

★★★

Some three decades after he published *Madison Avenue, USA*, Martin Mayer published *Whatever Happened to Madison Avenue?* The industry he found at the beginning of the 1990s was shadow of its former self. Mayer quotes Hal Riney's claim that advertising had by this time become 'a business run by businessmen [sic] who have no real interest in advertising. They think they do, but they don't ... I don't think any of them cares about long-term brand images. They don't sell advertising, they sell services. They're MBAs'.[108] Over the coming decade, similar claims would be levelled at the advertising industry across the globe. By the early 2000s, it had become a fact of advertising agency life. Writing on 'How an Agency evaluates a Client' in the *ANA Magazine* in 2005, Bob Isherwood and Kevin Roberts of Saatchi & Saatchi presented a heartfelt plea to clients: 'We want to be included at the highest levels of your strategy development and implementation. ... We want to be your partner, not your supplier. ... It's not a master-servant relationship, it's a marriage of equals'.[109] The appeal revealed the new state of play in the advertising industry, where clients happily ruled the roost. Of course, the relationship between agencies and their clients had always been a complicated one. Bob Miller, who had worked in agencies before moving over to the client side, recalls that the problem went both ways:

> [O]n the client side there was a certain contempt for the agencies because the agencies always send you a bloody great bill once a month. And if they took you to lunch that was buried away in miscellaneous. And there was a certain cultural attitude on the client side that didn't seem to show adequate respect for the amount of sweat, blood and tears, quite apart from all the other things, that the ad agencies would put into developing campaigns.[110]

However, it was the Recession of the early 1990s that tipped the balance of power away from the agency. Clients had become more sophisticated in their understanding of advertising and where it sat in the broader marketing mix. Agencies, as Henley recalls, were being held accountable for their actions: 'They were being questioned on how they were measuring it. They were being questioned about how expensive things were, and it really did put advertising costs in focus'.[111] In this context, clients saw 'advertising as cost on the balance sheet' and duly developed a more transactional account of advertising and their relationship with the advertising agency.[112] The emphasis on accountability and the marketer's need to show a return on investment meant that the agencies no longer had anywhere to hide. Agencies increasingly needed to show their worth to marketers and the marketing mix if they were to survive. And there was no turning back—marketing was here to stay. In 2003, marketing psychologist Max Sutherland mused 'Have you noticed people don't ask what marketing is anymore?' before explaining that 'marketing is much more intrinsic to people's thinking … It doesn't have the same need to be forcibly grafted onto organisations in the form of a speciality department … virtually all business occupations get exposed to it'.[113]

Marketing's emphasis on methodical processes that would guarantee a positive return was something of an anathema to the creative departments in the advertising agencies. They watched on forlornly as marketers were now paying greater attention (along with a greater proportion of the marketing budget) to what they perceived to be the dull, uncreative, and constricting work undertaken by the market research nerds and the direct marketing 'stamp lickers'. With marketers demanding accountability across all aspects of the agency practice, advertisements and the creative departments responsible for them collectively became more cautious in their creative approach. The erosion of the agencies' custodianship of the brand was yet another blow to their egos and, indeed, bottom line. Significantly, the agencies did not altogether lose their grip of the brand or the branding process, nor were they crushed to oblivion by their new marketing overlords. Their diminished role meant that they would need to be more attentive to changes affecting their industry and, indeed, be more proactive in the ways that they met them. Such awareness and agility would become integral as the advertising agencies found themselves dealing with a new competitor that had emerged from their very own backyard—the media agency.

Notes

1 Chris Powell, 'The Client-Agency' Relationship', *Admap Magazine*, January 1994, WARC Database.

2 Lucy L. Henke, 'A Longitudinal Analysis of Ad Agency-Client Relationship: Predictions of an Agency Switch, *Journal of Advertising Research* 35, no. 2 (March/April 1995): 29.

3 Robert Crawford, *But Wait, There's More…: A History of Australian Advertising, 1900–2000* (Carlton, VIC, Melbourne University Press, 2008), 253.

4 Kate Henley, interview with author, May 15, 2020.

5 Quentin Munro, 'The Inexact Science of Ad Budgets', *Ad News*, May 18, 1990, 24.

6 Kate Henley.

7 'Accountable Advertising–Convention Programme', *Ad News*, 7 September 1990, 37.

8 Pat Gillespie, 'Survey Shock of Agencies', *Ad News*, July 12, 1991, 3.

9 'As Budgets get the Nod, Agencies get the Flick', *B&T*, July 26, 1991, 33.

10 Mark Miller, 'Clients Call Tune', *B&T*, August 23, 1991, 1.

11 Grahame Dowling, 'Searching for a New Advertising Agency: A Client Perspective', *International Journal of Advertising* 13, no. 3, 1994, 231.

12 Melissa Pearce, 'Clients Unsure with Agencies', *B&T*, September 4, 1992, 8.

13 Rochelle Burbury and Chris Pearson, 'Recession Leads to Market Promiscuity', *B&T*, July 26, 1991, 1.

14 'Accountability in Client-Agency Relations', 'National Advertiser' Supplement, *Ad News*, July 31, 1992, 18.

15 'Big Advertisers review more – Survey', *Ad News*, 3 December 1993, p.24

16 Pat Gillespie, 'To Pitch or not to Pitch: But Who Pays, Who Gains and Who Loses', *Ad News*, December 14, 1990, 12.

17 Rochelle Burbury, 'Self-Discipline Key to Agency Pitch Problems', *Sydney Morning Herald*, August 5, 1993, 32.

18 Katrina O'Brien, 'Pitching Boom Bleeds Agencies Dry', *Ad News*, December 3, 1993, 21.

19 Ibid., 24.

20 Ibid., 21.

21 Ibid., 22.

22 Katrina O'Brien, 'Pitching Boom Bleeds Agencies Dry', *Ad News*, December 3, 1993, 22.

23 Jacqueline Nunan, 'Agencies Act on "Climate of Abuse" Surrounding Pitching', *Ad News*, April 22, 1994, 13.

24 Kate Henley, 'AANA hits back over Pitch Complaints', *Ad News*, May 6, 1994, 9.

25 'Service Fee abandoned', 'National Advertiser, *Ad News*, November 5, 1993, 28.

26 '"Suicide" Agency drops its Fees', *Ad News*, May 22, 1992, 6.

27 'Remuneration Systems—Signs of Change', 'National Advertiser', *Ad News*, February 25, 1994, 41.

28 Paul McIntyre, 'Agency Commissions thriving', *Australian Financial Review*, September 6, 1994, 42.

29 Richard Sauerman, 'The Differentiator as Agent Provocateur', *Ad News*, February 24, 1994, 24.

30 Neil Shoebridge, 'Why Ad Chief fears for Industry', *BRW*, May 11, 1990, 103.

31 Hugh Spencer, interview by author, May 5 2013, Title No: 1489316, National Film and Sound Archive (NFSA), Canberra, ACT.

32 Neil Shoebridge, 'Shoebridge Column', *BRW*, July 27, 1990, 65.

33 Neil Shoebridge, 'Shoebridge', *BRW*, May 1, 1995, 67.

34 Scott Morton, 'We Want More, Say Advertisers', *B&T*, February 24, 1995, 3.

35 Ian Alwill, interview by author, April 15, 2013, Title No: 1485205, NFSA.

36 See Eric H. Shaw, 'Ancient and Medieval Marketing', in *The Routledge Companion to Marketing History*, ed. Brian Jones and Mark Tadjewski (Abingdon, Oxon.: Routledge, 2016), 23–40.

37 Amanda McLeod, *Abundance: Buying and Selling in Postwar Australia* (Melbourne: Australian Scholarly Press, 2007); Robert Crawford, 'More than Froth and Bubble: Marketing in Australia, 1788–1969', in *The Routledge Companion to Marketing History*, ed. Brian Jones and Mark Tadjewski (Abingdon, Oxon: Routledge, 2016), 297–314.

38 Robert Crawford and Jackie Dickenson, *Behind Glass Doors: The World of Australian Advertising Agencies, 1959–1989* (Crawley, WA: UWA Publishing, 2016), 178.

39 Tony Hale, interview by author, May 13, 2020.

40 Wayne Kingston, interview by author, Title No: 1489018, 6 February 2013, NFSA.

41 Kate Henley, interview by author, May 15, 2020.

42 Dennis Merchant, interview by author, January 15, 2013, Title No: 1489192, NFSA.

43 Andrew Killey, interview by author, December 13, 2013, Title No: 1489016, NFSA.

44 Alex Hamill, interview by author, April 12, 2013, Title No: 1488984, NFSA.

45 David Mattingly, interview by Rosemary Francis, September 17, 2013, Title No: 1489176, NFSA.

46 Tom Moult, interview by author, March 11, 2020.

47 Horst Stipp, 'Crisis in Advertising?', *Marketing Research*, March 1992, 39.
48 Stefan Schwarzkopf, 'In Search of the Consumer: The History of Market Research from 1890 to 1960', in *The Routledge Companion to Marketing History*, ed. Brian Jones and Mark Tadjewski (Abingdon, Oxon: Routledge, 2016), 67–74.
49 Crawford, 'More than Froth and Bubble'.
50 McLeod, *Abundance*, 21.
51 David Fouvy, interview with author, February 21, 2019.
52 Crawford and Dickenson, *Behind Glass Doors*, 213.
53 'The Role of Marketing Research in Hard Times: An Inside Story', *Ad News*, October 19, 1990, 30–32.
54 Rick Osborn, 'What Research Buyers Really Want', *Ad News*, October 19, 1990, 31.
55 Stephen Fisher, 'Pre-Testing Ads can take the Edge off Creative, say CDs', *Ad News*, October 8, 1993, 22.
56 Mike Daniels, 'Why Today's Research Depresses Creatives', *Ad News*, October 7, 1994, 25.
57 Lynne Hughes, 'Does Research Stifle Creativity?', *Ad News*, September 22, 1995, 21.
58 Kirsty Needham, 'So, is Research Killing Creative', *Ad News*, February 28, 1997, 16.
59 Tony Burrett, 'Fine: Where Market Research is Headed', *Ad News*, October 7, 1994, 24.
60 Ibid.
61 Ibid.
62 Malcolm Spry, 'Keeping Pace with Research's Revolution', *Ad News*, October 8, 1993, 25.
63 Ibid.
64 Connie L. Bauer & John Miglautsch, 'A Conceptual Definition of Direct Marketing', *Journal of Direct Marketing* 6, no. 2 (1992): 10.
65 'The Father of DM Speaks', *Ad News*, November 5, 1999, 19.
66 Luella Copeland-Smith, interview with author, February 15, 2013, Title No: 1488629, NFSA.
67 Martin Williams.
68 Luella Copeland-Smith.
69 Martin Williams.
70 Minna Keso, 'Direct Marketing builds Brands', *Ad News*, November 5, 1993, 30.
71 Katrina O'Brien, 'Direct Creatives in Hot Demand', *Ad News*, October 7, 1994, 1.
72 Tom Moult.
73 Matt Donovan, interview by author, May 29, 2020.
74 Ellen McArthur, 'Agencies Move into the Nervous '90s', *B&T*, July 19, 1991, 16.
75 Martin Williams.
76 Ibid.
77 'The Mood for 2001', *AdNews*, December 15, 2001, 25.
78 Danielle Long, 'From Steak Knives to Brand Business, *AdNews*, July 18, 2003, 35.
79 Ibid.
80 Ibid., 36.
81 'Supermarket Marketing', *B&T*, March 4, 1994, 16.
82 Emily Carr, 'In-store Marketing–The Final Link in the Marketing Chain', *B&T Weekly*, August 29, 1997, 25.
83 Tony Hale, interview with author, May 13, 2020.
84 Tom Moult.
85 Stephen Dillon, 'Brands Under Threat', *B&T*, December 6, 1991, 14.
86 Ibid.
87 Jhonnie Blampied, '"Feel Good" Brands a Value Asset in Recessionary Times', *B&T*, June 11, 1993, 20–1.
88 Richard Wilson, 'Postmodern Marketing', *Ad News*, September 26, 1997, 28.
89 David Keig, 'Brands Face a Timely Private Crisis', *B&T*, July 15, 1994, 20.
90 Chris Pearson, 'Brands Rebound', *B&T*, July 15, 1994, 2.
91 'Standing by their Brands—Some of Them', *B&T*, March 3, 1995, 20.
92 David Keig, 'Brands Face a Timely Private Crisis', *B&T*, July 15, 1994, 20.
93 Stephen Byrne, 'Brand Indifference', *Ad News*, May 9, 2003, 20.

94 'Bryson: Brands Aren't Working', *B&T Weekly*, November 27, 1998, 1.
95 'Brands are Back', *B&T*, May 19, 1995, 30.
96 Tim Heberden, 'Brands: What's in It for Agencies', *Ad News*, May 7, 2004, 32.
97 Martin Lindstrom, 'Brands Brace for Tough Time with Solid Signals', *Ad News*, October 24, 2001, 38.
98 'Aussies Crave More Trustworthy Brands', *Ad News*, May 6, 2005, 3.
99 Rex Briggs & Nigel Hollis, 'Advertising on the Web: Is there Response before Click-through?', *Journal of Advertising Research* 37, no. 2 (March/April, 1997): 44.
100 Ibid.
101 Victoria Lea, 'Living, Talking the Brand', *AdNews*, May 19, 2006, L4.
102 Victoria Lea, 'Brands Play Catch-up', *AdNews*, July 28, 2006, 1.
103 Michael Abdel, interview by author, July 19, 2019.
104 Sean Cummins, interview by author, May 29, 2019.
105 Ibid.
106 Ibid.
107 Catherine Benson, 'The State of Client/Agency Relations', *ANA Magazine*, February 2005, WARC Database.
108 Martin Mayer, *Whatever Happened to Madison Avenue? Advertising in the '90s* (Boston: Little, Brown & Co., 1991), 4.
109 Bob Isherwood and Kevin Roberts, 'How an Agency Evaluated a Client', *ANA Magazine*, February 2005, WARC Database.
110 Bob Miller, interview by author, May 7, 2020.
111 Kate Henley, interview by author, May 15, 2020.
112 Ibid.
113 Max Sutherland, 'Marketing's Mid-Life Crisis', *AdNews*, June 20, 2003, 20.

3   The media coup

As the clock ticked down to the new millennium, media agencies looked forward with great anticipation. The coming decade, they predicted, would be theirs. Looking at the decade that lay ahead, Gary Hardwick, managing partner of media agency Ikon Communications, explained that 'Australia will experience more change in the next ten years than in the past 30 years as the range of media channels of all kinds expands, new digital formats proliferate and audiences fragment or segment as a result'.[1] Anne Parsons, CEO of Zenith Media, was even more optimistic, declaring that '[t]he arrival of the new century will mark the millennium of media'.[2] 'This media-led millennium', she continued, 'will push the prominence of media planning and strategy further to the fore'. As principals of leading media agencies, it is hardly surprising that they would make such bold predictions. However, time would prove them right. Speaking in 2013, Alan Robertson, whose career in media business spanned almost four decades, observed that a fundamental shift had indeed occurred: 'In the last ten or fifteen years, media has … grabbed more of the ground in the decision-making process of communications than the creative agencies. Creative agencies have fallen behind'.[3]

For many in the advertising agencies, the rise of the media agency from the 1990s had been something of a surprise. 'I remember in the small agency I worked for, Harold Mitchell was the guy who did the buying, because he used to buy for little agencies', recalls creative director Peter Murphy, 'I didn't even notice, and suddenly Harold became a billionaire. I said, "How did that happen?", because the last time I saw him, he was floating around buying ten by twos in the newspaper'.[4] Of course, a closer examination of this apparent rags to riches story reveals that it was neither sudden nor unexpected.

The perception of the media industry contained in Murphy's anecdote was not limited to those working in the agencies' creative departments. Academic accounts have followed a similar path, prompting Joseph Turow to note that 'the influence of media buying' on current media practices and their future has largely been overlooked by scholars.[5] Less overt and glamorous than the creative side, the media side of the advertising industry has attracted scant attention from critical scholars. Noting that 'the center of gravity in the industry has moved so that the media-buying and planning function has taken outsized importance', Turow offers an accurate summary of the media industry.[6] Significantly, he contends that the rise of the media agency cannot be solely attributed to the emergence of digital media.

Turow thus underscores the importance of longer-term forces that revolved around 'a growing desire to measure and label consumer responses'.[7] In his study of British agencies in the mid-1990s, Sean Nixon attributes the rise of the media agency to the 'process of media proliferation that began in the early 1980s' along with the 'policy-driven opening up of media markets—especially television markets—and the emergence of new media technologies and delivery systems'.[8]

In her account of the rise of the media buyers and planners in Australia, Liz Ferrier presents a more detailed explanation, identifying four interconnected factors at play: the increasing sophistication of media research and market research, client demands for accountability in relation to advertising expenditure, the fragmentation of media audiences, and, the trend towards media convergence, which has called for a whole-of-media strategic approach to advertising.[9] While both accounts are accurate, these factors need to be teased out in greater detail and, indeed, contextualised. As we saw in Chapter 2, marketing as both a practice and a management process underpinned the client's relationship with the advertising agencies. Marketing would exert a similar impact on the media side of the advertising business, underpinning the marketers' successful campaign to dismantle the accreditation process. However, this incursion did not necessarily strengthen the client's dominance—far from it. Coinciding with the emergence of a more complex media ecosystem that demanded more sophisticated analysis and strategic thinking, this intervention would in fact play a key role in giving rise to a powerful and confident media industry that would be perfectly positioned to capitalise on the digital revolution that lay just around the corner.

In the shadows

The title 'advertising agent' can be traced back to the eighteenth and nineteenth centuries, when individuals first began to selling press space to clients.[10] They derived their income not from the client (who, upon purchasing the space from the agent was left to fill it themselves) but rather the commissions paid by the press outlets. With little to no formal auditing of press circulations, this first generation of advertising agents developed a shady reputation for exaggerating or simply inventing circulation figures to snare clients.[11] Over the second half of the nineteenth century, the next generation of advertising agents sought to build up advertising as a profession by distancing themselves from these nefarious practices. J. Walter Thompson's enormous success in selling space in America's 'best magazines' in the late nineteenth century led it to create the position of 'account executive' to ensure that clients' needs were being met.[12] The advent of full-service agency was the next step in the process. In addition to offering space and account service, the full-service agency would produce the creative work.

As the full-service advertising agencies began to attract more clients, they progressively established separate departments for account service, creative, and media. Within this hierarchy, the media department stood at the bottom. Viewed as a clerical department, it was deemed a 'backwater' by creatives and account executives. The mundane tasks performed by the media department meant that it was often left to women and junior staff.[13] Alan Robertson, who had worked at J. Walter Thompson in the 1960s and 1970s, vividly outlines the lowly status of the media department:

The media department guys were regarded as blokes with green shades and a light bulb hanging down, the next best thing to an accountant, sitting there in a boring, dusty room while all the creative Johnnies were upstairs cracking champagne bottles and having fun with all the girls kind of thing, and we were the boring farts putting numbers and x's in squares. That's how we were regarded, and a lot of guys resented the fact that they weren't the heroes of the piece. And that kind of hung on for many years.[14]

John Steedman recalls that little had changed at J. Walter Thompson in the 1980s. Outlining a standard J. Walter Thompson pitch to clients, Steedman recounts the account service would open proceedings with discussion of strategy before giving the floor to the creative team to discuss their big idea: 'And if there was enough time, they'd get to media. Generally speaking … media would probably get 5 to 10 minutes. By the time the presentation was coming to a conclusion you probably had about 2 minutes'.[15] Of course, not everyone in the creative department viewed their media colleagues in the same light. Sean Cummins recalls how he would 'always go to the media department because the media department knew their shit. They knew the audience. They knew where it would they go best. … They could tell me who this person was, and then I could write to that person'.[16] Similarly, progressive media people sought to reach out to their creative counterparts. Tony Hale, who had started his career in the media department in the 1970s before moving across to management, explains his attempts to develop a more cohesive strategy: 'I always figured developing media plans in isolation of understanding the content and the media was absolute folly. And I equally thought that creative might have some thoughts that could impact on the choice of media channels that I selected'.[17]

The media department's presumed lowly status was not unique to Australia. Andy Pratt cites a similar pitching experience from the UK, where the media department is given a few minutes at the end—even though its work accounts for 90 per cent of the client's advertising expenditure.[18] The inferior status of the media department in Japan in the early 1990s reflected a different media environment. Dealing with a homogeneous market where a small number of vertically integrated media groups produced a relatively small number of publications, the Japanese agency's media department had a relatively simple job. More importantly, the media department's inferior status in Japan was further compounded by the fact that it struggled to earn money (and were viewed as a cost centre rather than a profit centre).[19]

Although the rise of the full-service advertising agency signalled a commitment to legitimacy and professionalism, advertising did not completely shake its somewhat shady reputation. Concerned by the inflated, incorrect, and often invisible press circulation figures for publications in the USA and Canada, the Association of National Advertisers succeeded in establishing the Audit Bureau of Circulations in 1914 (renamed Alliance for Audited Media in 2012). Similar bodies were established during the interwar period (Japan, 1918; France, 1922; the UK, 1931; Australia, 1932) and in the aftermath of the Second World War (India 1948; Germany 1949; Malaysia, 1975). For their part, press proprietors were similarly concerned by advertising agents' shady practices—defaulting on client payments, apportioning space to multiple advertisers, underquoting rates, and pressuring publications for free publicity. Accreditation provided a means by which the press could keep rogue agents at bay. As the Great Depression hit in 1929, Australian newspaper proprietors implemented an accreditation system for advertising agencies to ensure that they received full and timely payment.[20] By the end of the decade, a standard 10 per cent commission was set as the nationwide standard. These actions would have long-term consequences.

When the Media Council of Australia (MCA) was established by peak publishing and broadcasting bodies in 1968, it would adopt both the processes for accrediting advertising agencies and 10 per cent commission rate set in the interwar period.[21] All advertising agencies in Australia were paid using the same formula: 10 per cent media commission and 7.5 per cent service fee. While the agencies' income streams were highly lucrative, the process of accreditation was an onerous one, as agencies needed to demonstrate that they were in a financial position to guarantee full payment to the media outlet within 40 days, irrespective of the client's capacity to pay.[22] The process worked to the advantage of the larger, well-established agencies. However, two enterprising media men saw an opportunity to offer a more bespoke media service, particularly for the new generation of 'creative boutiques' that were in no position to secure accreditation from the MCA.[23] In Sydney, Dennis Merchant established Merchant & Pettett in 1974, while in Melbourne, Harold Mitchell formed Mitchell & Partners in 1976. While they were not the first independent media agencies to open in Australia (Media Buying Services had unsuccessfully entered the market in the early 1970s),[24] their impact was felt both immediately and in the longer term. The new independent media agencies not only threatened to cut into the advertising agencies' stranglehold over the 10 per cent media commission, they also provided smaller agencies an opportunity to compete on a more equal footing. George Patterson, which boasted that it was responsible for placing one in five commercials on Australian television, argued that the new media agencies were 'unaccredited' and were therefore operating illegally.[25] The challenge ultimately failed, and the two media agencies quickly found their place in the local advertising landscape.

The emergence of independent media agencies was hardly unique to Australia. Independent media agencies were also appearing in other markets across the globe. In North America, the first independent media buying services emerged in the late 1960s with the establishment of U.S. Media International (1968) and Media Buying Services (1969) in Canada. The size and nature of the US market meant that neither these nor any other independent media agency was regarded as a serious threat to the status quo until the late 1980s.[26] The impact of newly formed media agencies was more noticeable in Europe. In France, Gilbert Gross spent the 1960s developing a lucrative business in buying and selling media space for large and small clients, which would be subsequently go on to become Carat (Central d'Achat, Radio, Affichage, Television).[27] The first media agencies in Britain appeared in the early to mid-1970s. Media Buying Services established its British office around 1970 and its spin-off, Time Buying Service appeared shortly afterwards.[28] Chris Ingram was responsible for the formation of The Media Department (TMD) in 1972, which brought together the media departments of six agencies. Concerned about the flawed structure and problematic operations of TMD, Ingram would leave before going on to create his eponymous media agency in 1976.[29] As in Australia, British advertising agencies sought to protect their media commission from the interlopers. However, unlike the Australian experience, the British media independents struggled. While they were renowned for their capacity to buy media cheaply (leading their agency competitors to christen them 'bucket shops'), the services of these media agencies were still of 'limited interest to mainstream, blue-chip advertisers', which wanted 'beautifully crafted TV commercials, conveying a complex array of brand values … [and] strategic thinking as well'.[30] Embracing the latter would be the key to the media agencies' future.

Accreditation—'The Moment in Time'

In 1976, the Australian Commonwealth Government's Trade Practices Commission granted conditional authorisation for the MCA's accreditation process for advertising agencies. While accreditation was deemed to be an anti-competitive process, it was deemed that it operated to the public's benefit and therefore was permissible. This exemption would be reviewed and upheld by the Trade Practices Tribunal in 1978, which found that the accreditation system offered efficiencies in terms of resources, lowered costs, and afforded protection to smaller advertising agencies and media agencies, which would also serve to enhance locally owned firms.[31] Reviews of the accreditation system's codes of advertising conduct would also be conducted in 1986, 1987, and 1989, resulting in minor alterations to the ways that advertising standards were upheld.[32]

By the early 1990s, further questions about the accreditation system were beginning to emerge. The Recession saw Australian Media Placements going into receivership in 1991 with $3.74 million owing to media outlets, prompting the MCA to implement more stringent financial requirements for accrediting agencies. Declaring that '[h]istorically the media accreditation system has addressed the moment in time and no doubt it will continue to do that', MCA executive director Garvin Rutherford went on to claim that the accreditation process 'boosts confidence in the system'.[33] In response to the MCA's move, Dennis Merchant observed that 'I don't think we have to change the entire system because of one incident'.[34] A few days later, *Ad News* reported that many agencies were opting out of the accreditation system altogether with the number of accredited agencies dropping by 12 per cent over 1991–92.[35] While the Recession played a role in this downturn, it was not the sole cause. Mark de Teliga, managing director of Omon, explained to *Ad News* that accreditation simply offered little to his agency: 'It provides us with nothing and costs too much … I don't think it has ever been significant to an agency's performance, either financially or creatively'. The costs of engaging media agencies were significantly less than operating an internal media department. Significantly, de Teliga noted that 'clients don't require it [accreditation]'.[36] This point was confirmed by the AANA, which noted that some members were splitting their creative and media accounts between advertising and media agencies.[37]

In early 1995, it was announced that the Trade Practices Commission would be reviewing its 1978 decision and that it would be inviting submissions from the advertising industry. Noting that the Commonwealth was paying greater attention to enhancing competition to improve the economy, *Ad News* predicted that 'the TPC is unlikely to simply make a few minor changes to the advertising agency accreditation system ... It is up to the industry to convince the TPC that public benefits ... outweigh its anti-competitive nature'.[38]

The campaign against accreditation was spearheaded by the AANA. Bob Miller, president of the AANA, recounts that as a big advertiser spending $90 million on advertising per year, he 'objected to being told that if our ad agency wanted to nego-tiate with us on commissions and so on they were forbidden from doing so. ... It's my money'.[39] Speaking to the trade press, he put it another way: 'The system is not in the best interests of consumers and in advertising terms we are the consumers'.[40] As part of their campaign to gain greater accountability from their advertising expenditure (see Chapter 2), many marketers like Miller were now beginning to ask questions about transparency and the nature of the media commission, which lay at the heart of the accreditation process. AANA executive director Kate Henley played an active role in having accreditation reviewed, recalling:

> I put numerous papers and things to the Trade Practices Commission. That was very contentious. Obviously, what the agencies had got for many, many years was 10 per cent commission for little or no work in some places. If you talk about this media charter and media accountability and media transparency, it was very clear that this was just money for jam, really. If I, as an advertiser, paid a million dollars, they got 10 per cent of that. If I had a big media buy ... and I wanted to bump it to $5 million, then you got five times that. A media buy is a media buy. You hadn't necessarily done ... much extra work for extra money. So, this cosy relationship was coming unstuck, and they were not happy...[41]

Speaking to the trade press at the time, Henley also underscored the degree to which the commission process was muddying the waters in terms of the agencies' obligations: 'a shift in the perception of who the agency is working for would remove the current conflict of interest that sits between media buyers and the media'.[42]

On the other side of the fence, the agencies mounted their arguments. Bev Dyke, the federal director of the agencies' Advertising Federation of Australia (AFA), sought to counter the AANA's claims by stating that 'Agencies act for the advertiser clients in dealing with the media and they are not agents for the media'. In terms of the proposal to dismantle accreditation, Dyke argued that 'there would be upward pressure on price in both agency and media costs structures and a less efficient market' with rates increasing as media proprietors sought to safeguard themselves from the risk of non-payment.[43] Alex Hamill of George Patterson similarly focused on the economic argument: 'Clients who believe that by doing this they will reduce the cost of advertising are commercially naïve ... That 10 per cent commission represents a lot of costs covered by agencies. If advertisers deal directly with the media, someone will have to carry those costs'.[44] Such arguments in the trade press sought to win over clients. However, the reality, as Colin Wilson-Brown, the vice-chairman of the AFA, subsequently conceded, was that the advertising agencies would be losing a major source of income:

> The agency business was certainly keen to retain it. It was our structure. We were not keen to let it go. It was incredibly simple and I suppose the restrictive part of it was all agencies—if they were accredited—got 10 per cent. All agencies added a certain 7.5 per cent service fee.[45]

Michael Godwin, who had progressed through the account service ranks of major agencies in the 1990s, notes that the full-service agencies tended to view both income streams in singular terms: 'you made a little bit more on media, your margins were higher in media. They were less in creative but it didn't matter because it all went into the same pot'.[46] However, John Sintras reveals that the media department was well aware of this division. As media director and general manager of Leo Burnett over the 1990s, Sintras relays the media department's frustrations:

> [T]he commissions from media paid for everything in the agency. And that's what used to really piss the media people off that we were earning the money … very little was invested into the media product way back then. The money went to … creatives and sort of the sexy lights, bells and whistles part of the industry. Not the numbers people, as they were back then. And that was really stupid and demotivating for all of those people that were actually contributing a lot of value that weren't able to articulate what that was back then.[47]

As clients paid greater attention to their expenditure, they inevitably focused on the aspect involving the largest outlay on their behalf. The lack of transparency was an abiding concern for many marketers. As Wilson-Brown reveals, such concerns were not entirely unfounded:

> And then, you know, we added a few creative and production fees and there's the 20 per cent margin on the business and everybody did the same thing. So, in that sense it [10 per cent commission] was … the only mandated part. The rest of it was just a practice built up in the industry. And obviously with a 20 per cent margin, you had a healthy business.[48]

Alongside the long lunches enjoyed by agencies and clients alike, this healthy income stream also provided sufficient wherewithal for the advertising agencies to produce high-quality work.

In October 1995, the Trade Practices Commission revoked its authorisation of the accreditation system, stating that public benefit no longer outweighed its anti-competitive detriment.[49] While the decision was expected, it nevertheless spurred the AFA to mount a legal challenge. In his editorial for *Ad News*, Tony Burrett expressed dismay at the AFA move. 'In New Zealand where a deregulated system has been in place for years, the sky has yet to fall in on adland', he noted.[50] However, he was more concerned about the broader statement that was being made. For Burrett, 'the simple act of appealing has allowed clients to accuse the AFA and its member agencies of "showing their true colours" by siding with the media when they had a clear choice to show where their allegiances lay'. The appeal undermined the agencies' relationship with their clients at a time when clients were exerting their strength. Henley recalls 'it was very, very acrimonious. Very acrimonious' with one key media proprietor telling her "'You'll get rid of the accreditation over my dead body." Reflecting on the encounter, she mused '[y]eah, it was almost threatening'.[51]

As the AFA was joining forces with the MCA to take up the fight, agency heads were expressing a level of ambivalence alongside resignation about the inevitability of deregulation. Claims that accreditation had 'forced agencies to be more professional during times like the recession when it was tempting to take financial short-cuts' were lukewarm at best. Despite the loss of income, the larger agencies gave the impression that they were unfazed. Greg Daniel, managing director of Clemenger BBDO Sydney, thus declared that '[a]s an agency we have nothing to fear from deregulation', while Alex Hamill, CEO of George Patterson Bates, mused: 'When the smoke finally settles, I think we'll find it's exactly the same as it is in the rest of the world and not an awful lot will change'.[52] Media buyers expressed a similar stance to their advertising agency counterparts. Merchant reiterated the view that it was 'the high cost of setting up a media department' not accreditation costs that was in fact hampering smaller agencies (an argument that conveniently supported the media buying agencies). Looking more broadly, David Baker, the chief of AIS Media and managing director of Dentsu Pacific saw little need for accreditation: 'Throughout the world, advertisers have become accustomed to purchasing advertising service from the appropriate recognised providers and fees are usually negotiated'.[53]

On 26 July 1996, the Australian Competition and Consumer Commission (formerly the Trade Practices Commission) announced its decision: the authorisation for the MCA's accreditation process would be revoked. In his ruling, Justice Lockhart considered the degree to which there been a material change of circumstances since 1978. The media agencies were cited in the final decision as one of the seven material changes that had swept through the industry. It was found that in 1978 'there were two unaccredited media buying consultancies in Australia, not long formed, and it appears that they held about 3 per cent of the market'. The number and the billings now handled by the media agencies 'to an extent that the Tribunal has been unable to estimate confidently' but it was clear 'that the media buying houses are highly influential in the operation of the market'.[54] Reference was made to overseas trends, where it was noted that some 47 per cent of American advertisers were dividing budgets between creative and media work, while in the UK, media agencies accounted for seven of the nation's top ten billings.[55] The decision also noted the importance of 'parallel changes in technology'. Technology was deemed to be reinforcing 'the trend to specialisation' in small advertising agencies, where 'the talents of imaginative individuals are combined with techniques of computer graphics to prepare finished advertising copy for an advertiser client'. Technology was equally having an impact on media agencies, as:

> computer software for the interpretation and optimum use of the data now
> appears to favour the media buying house that operates on a substantial scale,

over the limited media capabilities that can be mounted in-house by an accredited agency of moderate size.[56]

The decision was hardly a surprise. In the lead up to the final decision, the AFA's announcement that it would not oppose the deletion of the anti-rebating clause (focusing instead on other aspects of the system that it hoped to maintain) revealed that it understood the accreditation process was doomed.[57] Speaking to the trade press immediately following the announcement, agency chiefs accepted the decision before claiming that it would not hurt their operations.[58] Media agency heads were noticeably more optimistic in their outlook. In his comments, Daryl Paterson, managing director of Media Decisions, provided a revealing insight into the cause of such optimism:

> Privately and quietly our company has been making plans for such a thing to happen for some time. We have always supported accreditation in its past form. However media buying companies will benefit somewhat in the new environment as it will probably encourage advertisers to think how they handle media, making it the focus of a little more attention. The change places independents very competitively with full service agencies.[59]

As such comments reveal, it did not really matter to the media agencies whether accreditation was maintained or dismantled—their 'moment in time' had well and truly arrived.

The new order

In the lead up to the Tribunal's decision, advertising agencies, media agencies, and clients were all making preparations for the likely event that the accreditation system would be scrapped. Their plans all centred around 'unbundling'—a term that was being used in the UK in the early 1990s to denote the clients' separation of media expenditure from their creative spend.[60]

While the AFA was fighting to keep the MCA system, various agencies pragmatically looked to pivot to meet the new post-accreditation age. Eager not to lose any business to the media agencies, the larger advertising agencies were aiming to build up their media credentials, investing heavily in computer technology. Mojo media director John Preston thus explained that 'More and more media departments are opening the way for new business with a media platform. Clients are primarily concerned with cost-efficiency but there are other services we can offer'.[61] Expanding on this point, Steve Allen of AIS media agency observed that the 'big agencies are worried about unbundling and accounts moving away from them. They are forever thinking about creating totally new relationships for creative, media, and below the line because clients can select four different suppliers instead of having one doing everything'.[62]

Clients were also readying themselves for the post-accreditation age. Large multinationals looked to import the strategies they were using in other non-regulated markets across the globe. Some seven months before the decision on accreditation was made, *Ad News* reported on the growing trend among advertisers to pay closer attention to the ways they bought media: 'The past 12 months has seen a resurgence of the master media account with clients seeing better prices, better systems, more efficient services and a higher calibre of people'.[63] By buying their media space in bulk, clients were hoping to secure cheaper rates. Coca-Cola's South Pacific operations exemplified this shift, trialling a split between its main advertising account with McCann Erickson and its media planning and buying with Mojo (where Mojo bought off McCann's rate but took responsibility for individual campaign strategy, planning, and buying).[64] Another strategy was to pool resources with other marketers that shared the same holding company. As the amounts being invested in media increased, it was clear that the system was working to the advantage of the largest media agencies. Overseas experiences also indicated that tough times lay ahead for advertising agency. *Ad News* thus observed: 'Australia is expected to follow in the footsteps of the UK, where the full service agency is becoming less common'.[65]

The rise of the media agency in Australia and in markets across the globe did not go unnoticed by the giant global advertising networks, Interpublic, Omnicom, Publicis, and WPP. Having built up their networks on the back of full-service agencies, the networks understood that the rise of the media agency and the clients' propensity for unbundling demanded a response. Zenith had been established by the Saatchi Communications Group in 1988 as a response to media inflation, media-owner growth and domination, the growing sophistication of media planning and media decision-making, and the globalisation of clients.[66] By drawing on the network members' collective size and strength, Zenith provided a model that not only responded to client needs and challengers in the media space, but also ensured that the network maintained its media commissions. This pattern, which was already evident in the UK and Europe,[67] would be easily applied to the newly deregulated Australian market. Writing shortly before the accreditation decision was announced, David Baker of AIS Media and Dentsu predicted that 'it is only a matter of time before the Cordiant group insists that the media operations of George Patterson Bates and Saatchi & Saatchi merge with Media Decisions to form Zenith in this country'. 'The move', he added, 'will really create a massive media agency powerhouse'.[68]

Such discussions intensified in the weeks following the announcement that regulation had been abandoned. Similar suggestions were also being made about other agencies. WPP's Martin Sorrell had told the British trade press that he was laying plans to consolidate the media buying resources of J. Walter Thompson and Ogilvy & Mather. Asked whether the Australian branches were considering this plan, J. Walter Thompson's media director, Greg Graham, responded that '[i]t is something we are examining but nothing will be happening in the short term'.[69] Both agencies, he added, already had 'clear images and good strong media departments'.

In October 1996 came the announcement that the Cordiant group (comprising George Patterson Bates, Saatchi & Saatchi, Media Decisions, Marketforce, and ABKP & Friends) would be establishing Zenith Australia. A franchise of Zenith Worldwide, it would be owned by the George Patterson Bates holding company, The Communications Group.[70] It was estimated that Zenith Australia would be controlling $1 billion in billings.[71] Far from being a spur of the moment decision, the creation of Zenith was the result of almost two years of discussion among Cordiant's Australian companies; the end of accreditation meant that such media shop was not only necessary, but also viable.[72] The outlook for the new initiative was unclear. David Baker predicted that the media behemoth would experience the challenges that advertising agencies had faced when merging: 'The pitfalls are familiar; the bringing together of different, sometimes incompatible cultures; morale problems; executive and staff defections; client defections; the limits of clout philosophy across the advertising categories'.[73] Revisiting the creation of Zenith a few months later, Baker mused that it may severely weaken its key backer—George Patterson. While it had been 'miles ahead of the competition in billings terms', being 'cut off from its main revenue base by its ambitious parent group' meant that Australia's largest agency had lost its advantage and was now vulnerable to more creative competitors.[74]

Other advertising agencies and networks duly moved to establish their own media agencies and, in the process, revealed that they too had been preparing for a post-accreditation world. In Melbourne, Grey had in fact beaten the Cordiant group to the punch with the establishment of its own media shop MediaCom.[75] Six weeks after the Zenith announcement came the news that the Omnicom-owned Clemenger BBDO and DDB, respectively, Australia's second- and third-largest agencies, would be formalising their loose media affiliation with the creation of Optimum Media Direction (OMD).[76] Commenting on the creation of OMD, Clemenger's Greg Daniel took aim at the established media agencies, arguing that they were primarily interested in the cost of media space and had failed to keep up with technological change: 'We have made a major investment in that area of the past five years and we feel we have a definite edge over the competition'.[77] Martin Sorrell's plans for J. Walter Thompson and Ogilvy & Mather would be realised a little later with the creation of Mindshare Australia in early 1998.[78] When Universal McCann was established in 1999, its point of difference was that it was not 'just another media independent or rebadged media department'. Its managing director, Michael Gower, thus declared: 'Universal McCann will become the dominant brand name and acknowledges that it is not trying to hide the fact it is owned by McCann'.[79] The following year Leo Burnett made a more cautious entry into the media business. John Sintras recounts how the agency opted to conduct tests across several markets before determining its media strategy:

> Australia was one of the four test markets and in this market we tested two solutions. We left media in Leo Burnett (I continued to run that), and we had a breakaway unit with another guy running it, where it went out to chase clients independent of Leo Burnett to do media only. And we ran that model for 12 months, side by side … we reviewed the test markets and made the decision that it's all or nothing, and Starcom was created. … We had to create a new brand and Starcom actually came from Australia, the name which nobody remembers, but the breakaway group that we created here was called Star.Com.[80]

Starcom, he adds, quickly built up its operations in Australia by buying out the hitherto independent media agency AIS Media.

The established media agencies were also entering the fray. Already in early 1997, it was clear that the media agencies were generating enormous business—and that it would only continue to increase. AIS Media, for example, had billings of $365 million and employed 117 staff.[81] (It was also the lead member of the Equmedia buying group, which was billing $1.3 billion.) Australia's lucrative media market was attracting interest from abroad. August 1997 *B&T* reported that the 'Australian media-buying scene is about to get some European sophistication' with the arrival of Europe's largest independently owned media agency, Carat. Noting that the new arrival illustrated 'just how global business media buying is these days', the report on Carat's arrival also noted that the firm's capacity to negotiate and buy media space was supported by its technological wherewithal.[82] For smaller local media agencies, the prospect of joining forces with a giant like Carat was highly appealing. Bray Media, for example, had initially affiliated itself with Zenith, but was persuaded to move across to Carat in order 'to gain access to its research and technology capacities, against which small players could not compete'.[83] For a multinational like Carat, bringing in smaller local media agencies meant that it was in a position to handle conflicting accounts.

Not surprisingly, marketers in the post-accreditation age were paying greater attention to costs.[84] However, some were frustrated that the promises of cheaper media had not yet arrived. A survey of marketers in early 1997 revealed that while 25 per cent had unbundled over the last year, almost a third were less than satisfied with the result. The issues appeared to stem 'from the hype generated by agencies about the value of new media specialists … and their inability to completely deliver the goods'.[85] During the accreditation years, media-buying had companies kept 5–10 per cent of direct client billings and 4–5 per cent of ad agency billings. Post-accreditation, these figures had declined to 3–5 per cent on direct billings and 2.5–4.5 per cent on agency billings.[86] While some clients opted to 're-bundle' in order to manage their costs, an overall pattern was emerging. George Patterson's Daryl Paterson thus described the current state of play as 'an evolutionary process' where the 'clients not media buyers were setting the goal posts'. Costs were not the only factor driving marketers to engage media agencies. The importance of the media agencies was further underscored by the fact that changes in media landscape demanded greater expertise: 'As the existing media continues to fragment and new advertising media … come on line over the next two years, advertisers will need people with unique skills to help them through the dizzying maze of media options'.[87] Marketers would also discover that there were other costs. 'The problem with unbundling', commented *AdNews*, 'is that it makes more work for the client, who now has to manage more suppliers and spend more unwelcome hours in meetings every month for little cost or other benefit'.[88]

For the advertising agency, the rise of the media giants in the immediate aftermath of deregulation was not necessarily the unmitigated disaster that many made it out to be. While they watched on as the media commissions flowed away to the self-proclaimed 'independent' media agencies, the reality was that they were not entirely excluded from the process. As *AdNews* pointed out, these new media agencies were not always independent: 'The reality is that some media companies have merged, even moved offices, and some independents have been bought by multinational networks. But little has changed apart from the colour on their front doors'.[89] The advertising agencies' interests did not end there. For many, the carving off of the media department was a profitable move in itself, as it enabled them to reduce their costs. Using a media agency thus presented 'a good way for big agencies to do the same or more work with fewer staff'.[90] Industry scuttlebutt also suggested that some advertising agencies were using their media department as a loss leader, where the discounted costs of the media department were offset by over-charging in other departments.[91]

After a year of deregulation, the new lie of the land was becoming clearer. Various advertising agencies were seeking new approaches. Whybin Lawrence TBWA, for example, sought to 'rebundle' by creating brand teams covering multiple areas of expertise, to develop creative ideas and determine the best way to execute them.[92] DDB sought to foster similarly interdisciplinary solutions by embracing the open office concept. However, it was clear many agencies were feeling the financial pinch. Clemenger's Greg Daniel, who had previously proclaimed that his agency had 'nothing to fear from deregulation', now conceded it had had a significant impact on the advertising agencies: 'It's undeniable that deregulation has had a more compelling impact on revenues than most agencies, including Clemenger, had anticipated'.[93] As advertising agencies embarked on a price war, their media competitors looked to supplement their media buying power by improving their strategic services. Their cause would also be aided the growing number of media channels.

And the old order changeth

In 1990, television was the undisputed dominant advertising medium—'television was king' recalls media research luminary John Grono.[94] Clients loved seeing their products when watching television at home. Advertising agencies were deeply vested in the medium; 'And so every media plan had a 30-second TV ad, whether it was required or not, because they'd committed to that money, and that's how they made money'.[95] However, there were already signs that television's golden age was drawing to an end.

Television's power lay in its capacity to reach a mass audience. However, when it became clear that the mass audience was fragmenting, advertisers, advertising agencies, and media agencies revisited their views of the medium. Under the headline 'TV needs to try harder', the AANA argued in 1991 that Australia's commercial television networks needed to pay closer attention to advertisers' needs:

> One thing is clear, and that is if television wants to maintain its traditional share of ad revenue, then the networks need to provide advertiser with more advance notice on important or interesting programs which will suit their marketing mix.[96]

Harold Mitchell echoed the AANA's concerns about specific markets at a conference on cost-effective advertising in 1992. Claiming that 'mass media will be less relevant to advertisers and marketers' and that the 'age of the target audience media is well and truly upon us', Mitchell predicted 'a steady growth in what we might call niche media and niche media use, and it won't always be the media that we expect'.[97] He wasn't alone in such predictions. Stan May, chairman of Leo Burnett Connaghan & May, thus explained that audiences had become fragmented to the point that 'we're running out of "ordinary people" to shoot for. No longer can we target the "traditional" Ossie and Harriet family with Mum at home, Dad at work and the two kids at school'.[98] Significantly, this was part of a global phenomenon. When visiting Australia in 1993, Jerry Reitman, vice-president of Leo Burnett USA, offered a similar perspective:

> in the US the traditional mass media has become so fragmented … a multi-million dollar campaign has no guarantee of success. This doesn't mean, for example, that television is not an effective medium. It means our way of using television needs to change.[99]

The calls for greater accountability that had been targeted at the advertising agencies also spread to television. Henley recalls that the AANA was increasingly concerned about audience measurement processes. Noting that in the early 1990s 'everything was diary-based', Henley was frustrated that viewers 'just lied about whatever they … wanted to be, not what they actually watched. So we were buying media based on diaries which could've been anything'.[100] The advent of Nielsen's Peoplemeters in 1991 caused a significant change. Although this technology arrived in Australia much later than elsewhere, its timing nevertheless reflected the zeitgeist.[101] As Grono notes, the new technology had an immediate effect, providing detailed data almost instantaneously: 'The TV industry went from 10 "books" per annum—i.e. the 10 four-week survey periods—to overnight ratings available at 9am 365 days a year … Virtually nothing could be hidden'.[102] Despite the advantages, questions about the accuracy of the Peoplemeters, as well as their inability to identify whether people were in fact watching the screen was raised by clients and agencies alike.[103] The technology would also be useful for measuring another media platform that had similarly been long-available in other countries—pay TV

In 1991, the Minister for Communications, Kim Beazley, announced that pay TV would be arriving in Australia. However, he also added that the new platform 'will not be allowed to carry advertising for five years from the start date of 1 October 1992'.[104] 'If that strikes you as blatant self-interest tactics, you're right', mused one media commentator, 'The [free to air] networks didn't want the new kid on the television block stealing their sole source of revenue'.[105] Despite this victory, a spokesperson for the Federation of Australian Commercial Television Stations remained on the offensive: 'They're not likely to be a full scale competitor because as a pay service there will be a limit on how much advertising they can run and, as a national service, they won't be competing for local business'.[106]

Although many advertisers and their agencies were disappointed that they would have to wait several years before they could advertise through the new medium, various parts of the industry saw an opportunity. This was not necessarily an easy task. At Young & Rubicam Mattingly, Matt Donovan worked on the Galaxy Pay TV account. The account executive recalls that the concept of pay TV 'was something that Australians were pretty suspicious of [they would say] "You mean I've got to pay for television?" … It seemed very expensive to people'. However, Donovan recalls that selling the new platform was still a relatively straightforward task:

> You didn't really need to know too much about technology in order to work on these accounts at that time, because you were really selling movies and you're selling sport … agencies have been doing that for a long time. There was nothing particularly new about that.[107]

It was not just the advertising agencies entering this space. Entrepreneurial direct marketers also moved quickly to secure the business of selling the new medium to potential subscribers.[108] Experiences from other countries indicated that direct involvement led direct marketers progressively to extend their operations into the new medium and, in the process, begin to produce mainstream advertising. Drawing on the experiences of BBDO in the established cable market in the US, Russell Norton-Old, media director of Clemenger BBDO Melbourne, predicted that full-service agencies' capacity to connect media, strategy, and creative in one place, the new medium placed them in a good space to respond to the new medium. However, Norton-Old also advocated a shift in mindset. He called for a '"media-first" way of thinking—of identifying the … audience and what it consumes in media terms—allows the creative message to be crafted to fit he chosen medium and address the target audience in appropriate terms'.[109] However, up until the time that pay TV would actually carry advertisements, the outlook remained subdued. A survey of industry attitudes that same year concluded that 'the impact will be slow in coming and when it does free-to-air will remain the dominant source of television'.[110]

In July 1997, the moratorium on commercial advertising on pay TV came to an end. Preparations for advertising on the new platform were already being made at the beginning of the year. Full-service agencies and media agencies not only had to deal with two providers, Foxtel and Optus Vision, they were also dealing with independent channels, causing some confusion about sales hierarchies in the initial phase of negotiations.[111] Such confusion gave a glimpse into the complexity wrought by media proliferation on the one hand and audience fragmentation on the other.

However, the real issue lay with audience size and how many people would see the advertisements placed on pay TV. In March 1998, *AdNews* reported that the advertising industry was still frustrated by a 'lack of hard data on who is watching what and when' and that pay TV were deliberately withholding data 'perhaps fearing the raw figures would detract from the "integrated marketing packages"' that they sold to advertisers and media buyers'.[112] A few months on the first anniversary of the platform's broadcasting of commercials, the ratings were still not forthcoming. However, there were some discernible trends. Although $15 million spent on advertising on pay TV was a mere drop in the ocean when compared to $2 billion being spent on free-to-air, it was found that free-to-air audiences were falling, particularly where niche audiences were concerned.[113] By the end of 1998, things on this front had not improved. Michael Renehan, media director at Singleton Ogilvy & Mather, observed that this reticence to release viewer numbers was inconsistent with client expectations:'A lot of companies simply won't support an unrated medium, especially with only 11 per cent penetration'.[114]

After two years of inaction, pay TV operators announced that they would be releasing ratings figures in mid-1999.[115] When the ratings were finally released in August, they were incomplete and, as expected, relatively low. Peter Hudson, general manager of advertising sales at one of the two networks, Optus Television, sought to reframe the discussion by arguing that pay TV offered different marketing opportunities: 'Despite all we have said, people are still comparing pay TV with free-to-air [ratings], but they are completely different mediums [sic.]'.[116] Overall, pay TV's gains were still modest—its growth of 1.7 per cent over 1999/2000 was only marginally better than the 1 per cent growth for free-to-air.[117] However, there were positive signs. Pay TV audiences were found to be watching more than free-to-air audiences, and were more loyal to their channels.[118] While these statistics indicated that pay TV would not be replacing free-to-air any time soon in the Australian market, they nevertheless revealed that free-to-air would be facing a tougher battle to maintain its proportion of advertising expenditure.

The message that pay TV was an additional advertising medium was sinking in—particularly in media circles. Media consultant Steve Allen thus urged pay TV to promote its differences to its competitor rather than challenging it on the same ground: 'Advertisers can use ... specialist environment intelligently. Playing with niche and the genre of programming offers advertisers more creative options. Pay TV can be more creative and flexible'. Reflecting on the changes sweeping through the media industry more generally, Allen also observed that 'no medium can offer a unique audience. We're about adding to media schedules, not about replacing any medium. The aim is to find consumers wherever they are in the era of fragmentation'.[119] Establishing strategies for locating and reaching these fragmented audience would become an integral part of the media agency operations.

Rethinking the media agency

Up until the mid-1990s, buying media had been relatively straightforward process. Haydon Bray, founder of Bray Media and *AdNews* columnist, thus outlined a typical media approach:

> Ten years ago, a mass market campaign usually consisted of 200 TARPs across three TV stations, one page in the *Australian Women's Weekly*, one page in the *Sydney Morning Herald* and the *Daily Mirror* and 30 spots in a handful of AM radio stations.[120]

Of his early years as a media buyer/planner, Simon Lawson outlines a similar situation:

> I used to work on a lot of FMCG [fast moving consumer goods] brands, and you'd buy annual plans of magazines across *Superfood Ideas, Australian Good*

Taste, Donna Hay, Delicious, Women's Day. You could have the whole year done in a couple of weeks and go out for a few nice lunches. I mean, I don't think I worked on a Friday.[121]

Of course there was much more to media buying than both accounts suggest. However, Bray and Lawson nevertheless make it clear that the primary goal of the agency media department or the media agency was relatively straightforward—get the media space. There initially seemed to be little need to think beyond the purchase of good space at a good price, but this would change. Over the course of the 1990s and the early 2000s, the questions being asked by the media industry went from 'how much' to 'where', 'when', and 'how'.

In 1994, Martyn Thomas, the media director at The Campaign Palace, lamented the 'worrying' trend of advertisers viewing cheap media as 'most important component of their media strategy', a move described as 'a hangover of the recession'. While Thomas stressed 'that buying media at the best possible rates should always be a key priority', he added that 'getting the best rates is not the beginning and end of a great media strategy'.[122] As noted, buying in space bulk and selling at discount rate had been the *modus operandi* of large advertising agencies like George Patterson as well as media agencies like Mitchell & Partners. The status of media buying was outlined by Dennis Merchant, who angrily pointed out that '[i]t is stupid that millions of ad dollars are trusted to inexperienced juniors' who lacked the ability to think beyond 'reach and frequency'.[123] Over a decade later, media buyers still had the drab reputation of 'operating at the less glamorous end of the market'—in contrast to the planners, who were emerging as the new superstars of the media agency world'.[124]

As with media buying, media planning in the early 1990s was still criticised for being a simplistic process. 'Agencies are too often recommending the same media schedules they were ten years ago', complained creative Siimon Reynolds, 'Many times it's just "Put it into 30-sec TV or DPS mags and let's go to lunch"'.[125] However, evidence of growing client interest in the strategic side of media could already be seen in the Recession. In 1990, media consultant Pat Williams observed that clients were 'looking closely at the way their money is being spent and how agencies are justifying that, not just with bulk deal discounts ... but to the effectiveness of the buy'.[126] By 1993, it was becoming clear that the balance was tipping away from media buyers. 'It is the prowess of media planning that will be the "media differentiator" in the '90s, not media buying', asserted Martyn Thomas in his *Ad News* column, 'You need to target the right people in the right place at the right time. Just getting a cheap rate is not enough'.[127] Technology also provided further data on audiences and media consumption, which, in turn, enabled planners to develop more sophisticated strategies.[128] The creation of the Australian Advertising Media Awards in 1996 was deemed a major milestone, signalling the industry's recognition of the ways that creativity in the media space was actively contributing to the success of an advertising campaigns.[129] While there were still questions about the degree to which media planning was being embraced by the advertising industry as a whole, the proliferation of media platforms meant that the importance of planning would only increase.[130]

Aside from being the 'first' of the new mega-independent media agencies, Zenith Australia also broke new ground in the field by splitting its planning and buying operations. At the time, observers predicted that this division 'may result in an upgrading of the planning function in Australia'.[131] This resulted in a shift within the industry whereby 'media people have had to decide where their skills really lie. Are they great thinkers and strategists or solid implementers and negotiators?'[132] Of course, many buyers would have railed at this description, arguing that their role was inherently strategic.[133] However, the emergence of new media outlet coupled with development of better tools to measure audiences meant planning was becoming a more sophisticated process. In his *AdNews* column, Thomas offered a clear definition of what media planning actually involved:

> Media planning is not the distribution of Tarps [target audience ratings points] on a media plan, deal-led 'strategies' or the analysing of Nielsen/Morgan/Panorama etc to arrive at a sterile cost per thousand solution. What it should be about is breaking down traditional media demarcation as the media planning blueprint is established. It should be about an intimate understanding of the advertiser's key market dynamics and media priorities of the target audience(s) coupled with an intimate understanding of the opportune cost associated with choosing one media over another.[134]

Despite the need for the new role as well as the promises it made, many media and advertising agencies were still reluctant to embrace it fully, prompting *AdNews* to comment: 'For all of the song and dance among the bigger agency groups, we are seeing very little innovative media placement'.[135]

There were, of course, agencies that embraced this role. In 1999, The Media Palace won a slew of local and international awards for its strategic media work. With the aim of 'capturing the high ground in the media planning business', The Media Palace positioned media strategy as its point of difference.[136] Its success was not lost on its competition. Mindshare Asia Pacific chairman, John Steedman, thus told the trade press that 'We've employed a strategic planning director'.[137] Claiming that Zenith Australia had always been more than a media buying house, its chief executive sought to link the agency to this trend by declaring that 'we want to be more recognised for what we are and for our abilities in strategic planning'.[138] In a move that reflected both the rise of planning on the one hand and the ways in which ownership structures consolidated their networks on the other, Zenith Australia would absorb The Media Palace in 2004. This embrace of strategy also reflected the clients' increased understanding of media buying.[139] By establishing their strategic credentials in addition to their buying credentials, media agencies ensured that they continued to offer a service that clients could not do for themselves. Not surprisingly, the media agencies roundly condemned claims by media sellers that they played an instrumental role in strategy development.[140]

As the media agencies expanded their offerings, some could not help but note that the media agencies were following a well-trodden path. Observing how the media agency of 2005 now boasted account management and strategic planning departments as well as digital operations experts, Clemenger BBDO strategic planning director Mike Daniels mused that 'the only thing [media agencies] don't have are creative departments and studios—yet.They are becoming indistinguishable from the organisation they separated from'.[141] Other commentators pointed to the possibility of a split within media agency, which would see the emergence of media strategy agencies and media planning/buying as distinct entities in their own right.[142] It was not long before this prediction came to pass—thanks in part to the emergence of a new term, 'media neutral'. While the term had been circulating since at least 1996,[143] it would gain growing popularity in Australia and internationally in the early 2000s as the impact of the division between media and creative agencies became more pronounced.[144] In 2003, Joe Hancock, managing director of Gorilla Communications, defined media neutrality as something altogether different to previous efforts to develop integrated marketing campaigns:

> being media-neutral does not simply mean able to execute through the (above and below) line. It is not even about the thinking that goes into the media spaces bought. ... It means a complete restructure of the way in which the skill required to service clients' needs holistically are organised within individual agencies and/or brought together from a variety of sources. Media-neutral planning cannot become a reality without "solution" neutral or "organisational" neutral structures.[145]

While Hancock later explained 'media-neutral solutions, at their most neutral, need not necessarily involve media at all', he nevertheless observed that media neutrality strategies nevertheless still required the experience and expertise of media specialists.[146] There was also another component, which had largely been overlooked in the Australian context. Jane Asscher, CEO and founding partner of 23red, offered a slightly different interpretation. Writing in *Admap*, Asscher claimed that a media-neutral approach to planning needed to prioritise consumers: 'the phrase "media-neutral planning" is actually a misnomer, it implies that the solution lies in media, and it takes the focus away from both the consumer and the brand. A closer definition might be customer or brand communication planning'.[147]

The first agency in Australia to specialise in the delivery of media-neutral planning emerged in 2000, when Phil Hayden and Simon Bellamy announced that they would be leaving The Media Palace to form their own agency. Of his decision to leave the highly decorated Media Palace, Hayden explained that 'the market has changed an awful lot since six years ago ... the majority of ad accounts are unbundled so opportunities for media specialists have broadened'.[148] Bellamyhayden found a ready market for its services. In less than 15 months, it had billings of over $100 million and by 2004, it had become one of the most awarded agencies at the MFA awards.[149] With interest in media neutrality taking hold across the industry, Hayden sounded a warning: 'Beware the media planner who left work on Friday and started as a media neutral communications strategist on Monday by sitting at another desk'.[150]

However, it was the arrival of the British agency Naked in 2004 that compelled the local industry pay real attention to media-neutral planning. John Harlow, Naked's co-founding partner, identified media neutrality as the agency's cornerstone: 'Media agencies still have a vested interest in putting their clients' money into advertising whereas we don't make our money through the media channels we choose. We work much more broadly across the whole communications mix'.[151] It was a bold move. Imogen Hewitt, media manager at The Media Palace, recounts being invited to join the new venture as well as her reticent response:

> And I said no [laughs], and he [Australian co-founder Mike Wilson] said, "But we're pitching Coca Cola", and I said, "But there's only three of you in a garage at Surrey Hills and I'm not going to join because I've got a mortgage [laughs] and some common sense." And he said, "If we win Coca Cola I'm calling you back." And I said "If you win Coca Cola then I'll join".[152]

Shortly after its Sydney office commenced operations, *AdNews* noted that it already making waves: 'Naked is finding enough weak links to convince marketers they should question the diversified ownership model of the big holding companies, and even the mini-diversification among ad agencies.'[153] Its business plan was simple and stood in contrast to that of its larger competitors: 'Where holding groups acquire companies that perform the various disciplines that make up the marcomms industry, Naked just works with them'. To a lesser degree, Naked also posed a challenge to both media and creative agencies; as a 'pure strategy player' it could 'take the place of a strategy planner in creative agency and almost certainly, the place of a media strategist'.[154] However, the holding groups and the big media agencies would remain the 'enemy'. Within months of opening, Naked had in fact secured the major planning portion of Coca-Cola Australia's account. True to her word, Hewitt also joined what she would subsequently describe as a 'really creative, dynamic, slightly scary at times, place to be'.[155] Not surprisingly, Harlow was delighted with the immediate results from his Australian office. Describing the advertising and media agency sector as 'pretty fucked up', Harlow claimed that agencies needed to change with the media changes that had enveloped the industry: 'Networks have built these huge TV-centric powerhouses but the media landscape has changed. In the '70s there was Coke's "I'd like to teach the world to sing" and there were very few channels to market'. Tellingly, Harlow also added that this major change transcended the media and, indeed, the associated marketing-related industries: 'Now the consumers are in control'.[156]

★★★

In 1998, Malcolm Stewart, the head of a small independent media agency, observed that the media industry appeared to be moving upwards in the marketing hierarchy. 'Media buyers, not advertising agencies, are now responsible for the client's money', he wrote, 'Their senior executives … have ascended from the untidy room next to the agency accounts department to become the major communications suppliers to Australia biggest companies'. As if to rub salt into the advertising agencies' wounds, Stewart added: 'In many instances, they are the main client contact and they commission other agency services—such as creative and production— on a project basis'.[157] The rise of the media industry over the 1990s had come at the advertising agencies' expense.

In losing the battle over media accreditation, the advertising agencies incurred several major losses, which would dramatically impact on their operations. First and foremost, they lost a highly lucrative income stream. Media departments were shut as clients moved their advertising expenditure to media agencies. While the global holding companies actively worked to keep the clients aligned to the agencies within their networks, the individual advertising agency—rebranded as creative agencies in this world order—was losing out. As new media outlets and platforms were emerging, the creative agencies had little option but to look on as the media agencies continued to ride these new waves. While some sought to bring media departments back into the agency, it did little to reduce the might of the media agencies.[158] By 2005, commentators observed that the ongoing predictions of the rationalisation of media agencies in Australia had been proven wrong. Not only were there now 'more media-only brands than ever before', their increasing specialisation in relation to emerging media outlets 'and the need for buying agencies to house conflicting accounts are key drivers' meant that they would remain a fixture in the advertising landscape.[159] Growing competition among media agencies would also see them eat into the creative agency's role of strategy. As the creative agencies' income dwindled and remit declined, so too did their status with clients.

The impact of the rise of media was felt in multiple ways. Media buyer/planner Simon Lawson, who recalled not working on Fridays in the early 2000s, found that the industry progressively got busier and

> as the industry got more and more busy, you'd work in the morning on Friday, then you'd go out for lunch, … now I'll find myself at six o'clock on a Friday still working diligently. … You know, it's really changed.[160]

While media agency workloads increased, their contact with the creative agencies seemed to decrease. Sean Cummins thus contends that:

> there's the generation of creative people … who've actually never met and worked side by side at the start of the process with a media person, and vice versa. Very few media people have actually sat and worked and met and created with a creative person.[161]

This growing gulf between creative and media not only undermined the cohesiveness of campaigns, it was, as TBWA Melbourne's Kimberlee Wells observes, also causing confusion all round 'you would sit in meetings and the creative agency would present their strategy with the creative work, and then the media agency would present their strategy with the media plan, and I would be confused, let alone how the clients would feel about that'.[162] Such confusion would become even more pronounced over the late 1990s and early 2000s when technology gave rise to new technologies and media platforms, and, consequently, new advertising practices and strategies.

Notes

1 Gary Hardwick, 'The Media Decade', *B&T Weekly*, October 22, 1999, 30.
2 Anne Parsons, 'The Millennium of the Media', *B&T Weekly*, December 3, 1999, 10.
3 Alan Robertson, interview by author, November 23, 2012, Title No: 1489300, National Film and Sound Archive (NFSA), Canberra, ACT.
4 Peter Murphy, interview by author, August 2, 2019.
5 Joseph Turow, 'Media Buying: The New Power of Advertising' in *The Routledge Companion to Advertising and Promotional Culture*, ed. Matthew McAllister and Emily West (New York and London: Routledge, 2015), 99.
6 Joseph Turow, *The Daily You: How the New Advertising Industry is Defining Your Identity and Your Worth*, (New Haven and London: Yale University Press, 2011), 19.
7 Ibid., 20.
8 Sean Nixon, *Advertising Cultures: Gender, Commerce, Creativity* (London: Sage, 2003), 45.
9 Liz Ferrier, 'Bring out the "Backroom Boys": The Role of Media Planners and Buyers in the New Knowledge Economy', *Media International Australia*, no.105 (November, 2005): 69.
10 T. R. Nevett, *Advertising in Britain* (London: Heineman, 1982), Chapter 4, 61–66.
11 Jackson Lears, *Fables of Abundance: A Cultural History of Advertising in America* (New York: Basic Books, 1993), 89–90.
12 Stephen Fox, *The Mirror Makers: A History of American Advertising and Its Creators*, University of Illinois Press, Urbana and Chicago, 1997, 30–1.
13 Robert Crawford and Jackie Dickenson, *Behind Glass Doors: The World of Australian Advertising Agencies 1959–1989* (Perth, WA: UWA Publishing, 2016), 216–17.
14 Alan Robertson, interview by author, November 23, 2012, Title No: 1489300, NFSA.
15 John Steedman and Greg Graham, interview by author, January 3, 2013, Title No: 1489320, NFSA.
16 Sean Cummins, interview by author, May 29, 2019.
17 Tony Hale, interview by author, May 13, 2020.
18 Andy C. Pratt, 'Advertising and Creativity, a Governance Approach: A Case Study of Creative Agencies in London', *Environment and Planning A: Economy and Space* 38, no.10 (2006): 1886.
19 Brian Moeran, *A Japanese Advertising Agency: An Anthropology of Media and Markets* (Honolulu: University of Hawai'i Press, 1996), 171–72.
20 Robert Crawford, *But Wait, There's More … : A History of Australian Advertising, 1900–2000*, Melbourne University Press, Melbourne, 2008), 68.
21 John Sinclair, 'Media Council of Australia' in *A Companion to the Australian Media,* ed. Bridget Griffen-Foley (Melbourne: Australian Scholarly Press, 2014), 258.
22 Harold Mitchell, *Living Large: The World of Harold Mitchell* (Melbourne: Melbourne University Press, 2009), 39.
23 Crawford and Dickenson, *Behind Glass Doors*, 108–109.
24 Dennis Merchant, *Media Man: The Life and Times of Dennis Merchant OAM* (Sydney: Dennis Merchant, 2013), 247.0.
25 Geoffrey Cousins, interview by author, March 15, 2013, Title No: 1488631, NFSA; Alan Robertson.
26 Research Services, 'Defining Moments in Agency History: Evolution of Media Unbundling', June 1, 2017, https://www.aaaa.org/evolution-media-unbundling/.
27 Mark Tungate, *Ad Land: A Global History of Advertising* (London and Philadelphia: Kogan Page, 2007), 156–57.
28 Chris Ingram, 'In at the Birth of the Media Independents', *Admap*, November 1989, WARC Database.
29 Ibid.
30 Alasdair Reid, 'Thirty Years of Independent Media', *Campaign*, July 21, 2006, https://www.campaignlive.co.uk/article/thirty-years-independent-media/571048.
31 RE Applications for Review of a Determination of the Australian Competition and Consumer Commission Revoking Authorisation No. A3005, ACOMPT 1, Judgement No. AC1/96, Sydney, July 26, 1996, 12.

32 Ibid., 2–3.
33 Peter Dockrill, 'Accreditation under Security', *B&T*, March 28, 1991, 8.
34 Ibid.
35 Penney Warneford, 'Accreditation: Why Some Opt Out', *Ad News*, June 5, 1992, 20.
36 Ibid.
37 Ibid.
38 Lynne Hughes 'How will You Survive Post-Accreditation?', *Ad News*, March 10, 1995, 20.
39 Bob Miller, interview by author, May 7, 2020.
40 Patrick Dye, 'Shockwaves Rock Adland as TPC Reviews', *Ad News*, January 27, 1995, 15.
41 Kate Henley, interview by author, May 15, 2020.
42 Lynne Hughes 'How Will You Survive', 20.
43 Ibid.
44 Dye, 'Shockwaves Rock Adland as TPC Reviews', , 15.
45 Colin Wilson-Brown, interview by author, May 6, 2020.
46 Michael Godwin, interview by author, November 27, 2018.
47 John Sintras, interview by author, May 25, 2020.
48 Colin Wilson-Brown.
49 Paul McIntyre, 'Advertisers to Appeal TPC Decision', *Australian Financial Review*, October 10, 1995, 26.
50 Tony Burrett, 'AFA's Decision is a Shame', *Ad News*, October 20, 1995, 15.
51 Kate Henley, interview.
52 'Accreditation: The Great Debate', *B&T*, October 3, 1995, 6.
53 Angela Jackson, 'Big Agencies: We Won't be Disadvantaged', *Ad News*, October 20, 1995, 35.
54 RE Applications for Review, 127–28.
55 Ibid., 68.
56 Ibid., 125.
57 Paul McIntyre, 'AFA Takes a Soft Line on Rebate Clause', *Australian Financial Review*, March 12, 1996, 46.
58 'Adland's Reaction', 'Accreditation Special Newsletter', *Ad News*, July 31, 1996, 1–4.
59 Ibid., 3.
60 See Brian Jacobs, 'Trends in Media Buying and Selling in Europe and the Effect on the Advertising Agency Business', *International Journal of Advertising* 10, no. 4 (1991): 283–91; Nicholas Staveley, 'Conference Report: Relationship—"Advertising Accountability" and the Double Bind of the Full Service Agency', *Admap Magazine*, April 1992, WARC Database.
61 Heather Jacobs, 'Big Agencies Scramble for Media', *Ad News*, December 1, 1995, 19.
62 Ibid., 20.
63 Ibid., 18.
64 Ibid., 19.
65 Ibid, 20.
66 Ray Morgan, 'A New Order in Media Buying', *Admap Magazine*, July 1989, WARC Database.
67 Jacobs, 'Trends in Media Buying'.
68 David Baker, 'Agencies Forced to Unbundle Post Deregulation', *Ad News*, June 28, 1996, 16.
69 Heather Jacobs, 'Agencies to Create Media Shops', *AdNews*, August 9, 1996, 8.
70 Edward Charles, 'Editor's Apology', *AdNews*, May 8, 1998, 6.
71 Edward Charles, 'Media Splits from Creative', *AdNews*, October 18, 1996, 16.
72 Ibid., 16–17.
73 David Baker, 'The Next Unbundlers', *AdNews*, October 18, 1996, 16–17.
74 Ibid.
75 Charles, 'Media Splits from Creative', 16–17.
76 Angela Jackson, 'Omnicom Agencies Unite', *AdNews*, November 29, 1996, 3.

77 Scott Morton, 'Media Shops Behind the Times—Clems', *B&T Weekly*, January 19, 1996, 3.

78 JWT and O&M Merge Media Departments', *AdNews*, 16 January 1998, p.1.

79 Rochelle Burbury, 'Universal McCann launched', *Australian Financial Review*, November 2, 1999, 41.

80 John Sintras, interview by author, May 25, 2020.

81 Ed Charles, 'Media Buying has Changed Forever', 'Top 150 Agencies Supplement', *AdNews*, February 14, 1997, 18.

82 Tony Burrett, 'Carat Entrance to Shake up our Media Market', *B&T Weekly*, 22 August 1997, p.48.

83 Andrew McKenzie, 'New Future for Bray with Carat', *AdNews*, March 27, 1998, 1.

84 Charles, 'Media Buying has Changed Forever'.

85 Tony Burrett, 'Media: Something's Wrong', *B&T Weekly*, April 4, 1997, 1.

86 Neil Shoebridge, 'Media Buyers feel the Squeeze in the New, Deregulated Order', *BRW*, 9 March 1998, 68.

87 Lara Sinclair, 'Accreditation to Die Quietly', *B&T Weekly*, January 31, 1997, 1.

88 Charles, 'Editor's Apology'.

89 Ibid.

90 Sinclair, 'Accreditation to Die Quietly'.

91 Ibid.

92 Sunita Gloster, 'The Advertising Agency in 2010: Problems and Opportunities of Unbundling', *AdNews*, April 24, 1998, 22.

93 'Agencies feel the Weight of Client Demands', *B&T Weekly*, December 5, 1997, 15.

94 John Grono, interview with author, June 19, 2920.

95 Sean Cummins.

96 Kate Henley, 'TV Needs to Try Harder', *Ad News*, November 2, 1990, 23.

97 'Mass Media on Way Out, Says Mitchell', *Ad News*, May 22, 1992, p.4.

98 Stan May, 'Agencies must adjust to "Mass Market" Loss: May', *Ad News*, April 24, 1993, 18.

99 Ian Kennedy, "The Mass Media is Dying, says US Agency Executive', *Ad News*, July 30, 1993, 21.

100 Kate Henley, interview.

101 Tom O'Regan, et al., 'Ratings in Transition: Industry Implications', *Media International Australia*, no. 105, (November 2002): 16.

102 John Grono, email to author, June 20, 2020.

103 'Meters Can't Give Involvement Factor', *Ad News*, April 10, 1992, 7.

104 'Pay TV Decision—Implications', *Ad News*, October 18, 1991, 24.

105 Fred Brenchley, 'Ads on Pay TV: What to expect', *Ad News*, October 8, 1992, 25.

106 Deborah Soden, 'FACTS welcomes Pay TV Restrictions', *B&T*, October 25, 1991, 8.

107 Matt Donovan, interview by author, May 29, 2020.

108 Penny Warneford, 'Pay Television Set to be Bonanza for Adland and Direct Marketers', *Ad News*, September 24, 1993, 18.

109 Russell Norton-Old, 'Pay TV—It's No Couch Potato', *B&T*, June 23, 1995, 14.

110 Heather Jacobs, 'Pay TV Will Have "Minimal Impact"', *Ad News*, March 10, 1995, 19.

111 Heather Jacobs, 'Channel Surfing—You've Got to Pay to Play', *Ad News*, January 31, 1997, 21.

112 Andrew Mckenzie, 'Hard Numbers Still Wanted for Pay TV', *AdNews*, March 27, 1998, 16.

113 Andrew Mckenzie, 'Is Pay TV Impacting on Free-to-Air Audience?', *AdNews*, 3 July 1998, 18.

114 Andrew Mckenzie, 'Nervous wait for Pay TV Ratings', *AdNews*, November 20, 1998, 15.

115 'Pay TV and Networks Band Together for Ratings', *AdNews*, February 7, 1999, http://www.adnews.com.au/yafNews/2720015E-3776-4815-AB679621A04E2C06.

116 'At Last, Who's Watching, When', *AdNews*, August 27, 1999, http://www.adnews.com.au/yafNews/6569550B-2BF6-4F13-A5D17A4029C87E0C.

117 Jeni Goodsall, 'Faithful Viewers Create Niche Advertising Opportunities', *AdNews*, June 2, 2000, 37.

118 Barbara Messer, 'Pay TV Numbers Grow', *AdNews*, January 31, 2003, 13.

119 Jeni Goodsall, 'Faithful Viewers'.

120 Haydon Bray, 'Media Set for Some Explosive Changes', *Ad News*, October 20, 1995, 15.

121 Simon Lawson, interview by author, June 14, 2019.

122 Martyn Thomas, 'In Media, Clout is just the Start', *Ad News*, October 7, 1994, 13.

123 Heather Jacobs, 'Get Rid of Brain Dead Media Buyers', *Ad News*, February 24, 1995, 10.

124 'Media Buyers', *AdNews*, July 4, 2003, 26.

125 Siimon Reynolds, 'Why We Need Creative Media', *Ad News*, August 28, 1992, 6.

126 Tony Burrett, 'Media Planning gets Creative', *Ad News*, November 2, 1990, 18.

127 Martyn Thomas, 'Planning not Buying is Key to Efficiency', *Ad News*, May 7, 1993, 7.

128 Anne Parsons, 'The Millennium of the Media, *B&T Weekly*, December 3, 1999, 10.

129 Heather Jacobs, 'The Rise and Rise of the Media Department', *Ad News*, June 14, 1996, 21.

130 Ed Charles, 'Editor's Letter', *AdNews*, June 6, 1997, 7.

131 Ed Charles, 'Media Splits from Creative', *AdNews*, October 18, 1996, 16.

132 Pauline McCredie, 'New Rules for a Changing Game', *AdNews*, 6 June 1997, 17.

133 Dennis Merchant, *Media Man: The Life and Times of Dennis Merchant* (Sydney: Dennis Merchant, 2013), 103–110.

134 Martyn Thomas, 'The Rise of Creative Media Planning', *AdNews*, 11 September 1998, 12.

135 Ed Charles, 'Editor's Apology'.

136 'The Media Palace', *AdNews*, January 28, 2000, L15.

137 Paul McIntyre, 'Sellers' Strategy a Time Waste', *AdNews*, April 12, 2002, 14.

138 Paula Bombara, 'Zenith Rejigs for Strategy', *B&T Weekly*, February 19, 1999, 4.

139 Paul McIntyre, 'Slim Margins and Strategic Thinking Drive Change to Bulk TV Buying Deals', *AdNews*, September 14, 2001, 13.

140 Paul McIntyre, 'Creativity vs Commodity', *AdNews*, 29 March 2002, p.14. Paul McIntyre, 'Sellers' Strategy a Time Waste', *AdNews*, 12 April 2002, 14.

141 Mike Daniels, 'Is History Repeating Itself?', *AdNews*, August 12, 2005, 24–25.

142 Haydon Bray, 'Media's Move up the Pecking Order', *AdNews*, December 3, 1999, 10.

143 Ander Gronstedt and Esther Thorson, 'Five Approaches to Organizing an Integrated Marketing Communications Agency', *Journal of Advertising Research* 36, no. 2 (March/April 1996): 55.

144 Alastair Ray, 'How to adopt a Neutral Stance', *Marketing*, June 27, 2002, 27.

145 Joe Hancock, 'Media Neutral Planning, Fad or Fundamental?', *AdNews*, April 11, 2003, 10.

146 Joe Hancock, 'Start Neutral, think Creative!', *AdNews*, April 22, 2005, 26.

147 Jane Asscher 'Is Media Neutral Planning Viable', *Admap Magazine*, no. 438, April 2003, WARC Database.

148 'Hayden and Bellamy quit The Media Palace', *AdNews*, July 28, 2000, http://www.adnews.com.au/yafNews/84928D5D-6C74-4805-A6E78C8DA97C99DD.

149 'GSK takes Bellamy to \$100m', *AdNews*, January 3, 2002, http://www.adnews.com.au/yafNews/6F8476C9-C4E9-475C-8805294B524B1991. 'bellamyhayden defends Awards Dominance, *AdNews*, October 22, 2004, http://www.adnews.com.au/yaf-News/CBCB3085-4282-49E5-A8530558860992DC.

150 Phil Hayden, 'Media Neutral Myth', *B&T Weekly*, September 17, 2004, 17.

151 Barbara Messer, 'Naked Lays its Plans Bare', *AdNews*, May 7, 2004, 23.

152 Imogen Hewitt, interview by author, June 1, 2020.

153 Paul McIntyre, 'Naked Exposes Weak Link', *AdNews* September 10, 2004, 14.

154 Dave Clutterbuck, 'Agencies Face up to Naked Truth', *AdNews*, September 24, 2004, 10.

155 Imogen Hewitt.

156 Dave Clutterbuck, 'Coke Fuels Global Naked Growth', *AdNews*, January 14, 2005, 6.
157 Malcolm Stewart, 'The Rise of the Media Specialist', *AdNews*, February 27, 1998, 16.
158 Maria Ligerakis, 'Media in the House as Agencies Seek Control', *B&T Weekly*, March 5, 2004, 5.
159 Lara Sinclair, 'Harold Mitchell Under Attack', *Australian*, October 20, 2005, 19.
160 Simon Lawson, interview by author, June 14, 2019.
161 Sean Cummins.
162 Kimberlee Wells, interview by author, June 3, 2019.

4 The rise of the machine

Since its broadcast in the *Super Bowl*, Apple's '1984' commercial launching of its Macintosh personal computer has assumed an iconic status within advertising circles. Created by Chiat/Day and directed by Ridley Scott, the campaign sought to introduce Macintosh by dramatically contrasting it against the dull and dreary machines produced by its competitors. As marketing academic Linda Scott observes, the commercial appeared to break all the rules of advertising; it contained 'no product shots, no on-camera demonstrations, no litanies of product specs, and only minimal corporate identification'.[1] It not only set industry tongues wagging, but audiences watching the *Super Bowl* were also discussing it. Within days, the product had completely sold out. Subsequent critical accounts of the success of '1984' have sought to locate its message within the broader context of the rise of information technology. Communication scholar Sarah Stein thus notes that in retrospect, it was a 'defining moment' that heralded the computer revolution.[2] Christina Spurgeon, another communication scholar, echoes this point, adding: 'This execution famously anticipated the demolition by digital media of the one-to-many architecture of transmission media, and the associated social relations of Orwellian thought control'.[3] Like the rest of the world, advertising would also be caught up in the revolution wrought by the very product it helped introduce.

In *Computer: A History of the Information Machine*, Martin Campbell-Kelly *et al.* identify the mid-1980s as the key turning point in the development of the personal computer market. The standardisation of the personal computer market around the IBM-compatible personal computer produced a more accessible product—from both user experience and financial viewpoints. Such shifts would also give rise to a handful of information technology firms to emerge as major global corporations and, indeed, advertisers.[4] While Campbell-Kelly *et al.* observe that the history of the personal computer is still waiting to be written,[5] broader studies of the impact of technology on office work practices nevertheless offer useful approaches to understanding the computer's impact on the advertising industry. Historical and more contemporary examinations of the relationship between gender and technology offer particularly insightful accounts into its social and cultural impact on everyday work practices.[6] Arguing that 'the gender/technology relationship is one in which a mutual process of shaping takes place', Juliet Webster's *Shaping Women's Work: Gender, Employment and Information Technology* seeks to identify 'the ways in which gender relations contribute to the shaping of technology and then the role of technology in affecting women's jobs and relations at work'.[7] Applying this lens to the advertising industry's relationship with information technology up until the mid-1990s, this chapter reveals a similar dynamic relationship at play, whereby industry identities and practices inform the use of technology, which, in turn, influences industry identities and practices.

The computer arrives

Set in 1970, the final series of the AMC drama *Mad Men* depicts Sterling Cooper & Partners entering the computer age. Having mispresented its technological capabilities to clients, the agency was forced to invest in a state-of-the-art IBM 360 computer. The computer's arrival generates particular tension among the agency's creatives, whose breakroom was given over to the beaming new machine. Such concerns would be reiterated in a scene featuring the conversation between Don Draper, the agency's mercurial creative director, and Lloyd Hawley, whose firm was installing the computer in the agency's office:

> LLOYD: 'Well, I go into businesses every day, and it's been my experience these machines can be a metaphor for whatever's on people's minds'.
> DON: 'Because they're afraid of computers'?
> LLOYD: 'Yes. This machine is frightening to people, but it's made by people'.
> DON: 'People aren't frightening'?
> LLOYD: 'It's not that. It's more of a cosmic disturbance. This machine is intimidating because it contains infinite quantities of information, and that's threatening, because human existence is finite. But isn't it godlike that we've mastered the infinite? The IBM 360 can count more stars in a day than we can in a lifetime'.
> DON: 'But what man laid on his back, counting stars and thought about a number'?[8]

In pitting technology's infinite possibility against its inability to understand the human soul, this conversation seeks to position the arrival of technology in a people-focused industry like advertising as a paradox. The reality, however, was more prosaic.

Sterling Cooper & Partners would have in fact been a latecomer to the computer age. Already in 1968, some 25 agencies in the United States were operating their own IBM 360.[9] By this time, it was also clear that these machines had little to do with the work of the creative department. A 1966 article in *B&T* thus explained that it was the media department that would be the key beneficiary: 'The computer is a purely mechanical innovation designed to sift information at high speed and produce a desired pattern of operation based on given facts. It reduces labor required for media selection, and frees staff for more essential tasks'.[10] Given the media department's lowly status (see Chapter 3), few creatives would have seen their agency's first computer as anything more than a very large and expensive calculator.

Australia's entry into the computer age would begin in 1963, when George Patterson announced that it would be installing an IBM 1440 computer, 'the first contract for a computer by an advertising agency outside the US'.[11] Describing this investment 'as one of the most progressive steps in the advertising field in Australia for many years', the trade press indicated an awareness of the growing importance of information technology in advertising and across the marketing sector more generally. Two years later, George Patterson's IBM 1440 was finally in operation. Observing the agency's computer in action, the *Newspaper News'* correspondent was impressed:

> In its air conditioned "no smoking" room is the first computer to be owned by an Australian advertising agency—an IBM 1440. The computer, which is still building up its store of knowledge, has been in operation only a few months, but it is learning fast. Under the care of Mr E. S. Hall, and served by three male programmers and five female punch card operators, it is already doing a number of jobs for the agency in a time which, by labour saving, and man hour standards is staggering. When I saw it operating it was digesting the results of a survey on milk drinking habits in Malaysia, breaking down figures into area, race, and socio-economic groups, then cross tabulating them. It is also used for invoicing and accounting and for the preparation of various schedules. Later the company plans to use the computer for media selection, but in order to do so a considerable amount of information has yet to be fed into its memory system or "brain".[12]

While the correspondent felt that he had indeed been given a glimpse into the future, his account also addressed some of the current anxieties around automation and displaced that *Mad Men* had dramatised. His report thus noted a recent advertising conference in Chicago, where delegates concluded 'the machine won't replace humans who still must make subjective judgements both as to what they put into the system and as to what significance they attach to the answers'.[13]

When speaking to the trade press and clients, George Patterson sought to present its computer as a tool to assist with media and research. However, the agency's chief financial officer, Russell McLay, recalls that it was 'essentially ... just an accounting machine' and that the computer was as much a 'public relations' initiative as it was an attempt to streamline the agency's operations.[14] Its public relations function was noted by others. It was said that the lifts at George Patterson were always programmed to stop at the floor where the IBM 1440 stood so that clients could physically see and, indeed, marvel at the agency's technological prowess.[15] An article in *Advertising in Australia* also noted that the 'current general opinion is that there is not sufficient information available with which to feed computers'.[16]

Over the 1960s, American and British agencies progressively invested more heavily in information technology systems and hardware. Australians visiting the USA and the UK regularly contrasted such developments against the Australian experience, which seemed slow and backwards in comparison.[17] The relatively slow adoption of computers in Australia was twofold. Firstly, only the largest agencies like George Patterson could afford to make the significant investment of money, time, and space. Secondly, Australia's media market was both smaller and less complicated than either the USA or the UK—a computer was therefore desirable but hardly essential for media planning at this time.[18]

Although Australia's media landscape had changed little over the course of the 1960s, the fear of losing their competitive edge led many agencies to invest in a computer. Local branches of international agencies led the way. In 1966, Lintas' Sydney office proudly announced that it had installed a 'Friden Flexowriter data processing machine in its media department to prepare television media schedules for its clients' which would work 'in conjunction with an NCR 315 computer'.[19] When Thomas F. Sutton, executive vice-president of J. Walter Thompson international, visited Australia in 1969, the trade press noted that it 'coincides with the introduction by JWT in Australia of the use of computers for internal administration, such as billing, cost accounting and payroll, and media evaluation'. Such computers, Sutton explained, were already 'being used by the company in New York, Detroit, London and Frankfurt'.[20] With the large agencies embracing technology, smaller local agencies had little option but to join in or risk falling behind.[21]

Over the 1970s and into the 1980s, the uptake of information technology among advertising agencies would continue to accelerate. The tasks being undertaken by the computer were also expanding. In 1978, Young & Rubicam announced that in addition to the standard coordination and centralisation of 'routine agency financial procedures like booking, billing and paying for all offices', its new computer would 'also link up with computer systems being used by Y&R internationally'.[22] At J. Walter Thompson's Melbourne office, the activities of the traffic department were computerised in 1981.[23] Those who had already made the investment now faced that perennial task of upgrading and expanding their computer systems. Already in 1969, George Patterson was announcing that it was 'conducting a study of our computer needs for the next 10 years. Our present computer … is now five years old'.[24] In 1971, Hansen Rubensohn-McCann Erickson proudly announced that its upgrade to a Honeywell H115 would see 'significant changes made, mainly to media processing, resulting in improved media booking, presentation instructions and client invoicing'.[25] By 1976, George Patterson's CEO, Keith Cousins, was telling the trade press that 'The computer used to be a luxury … now it's a necessity'.[26] While some continued to complain that Australia still lagged behind overseas developments,[27] it was clear that the computer had become an essential tool in modern advertising agencies across the globe.

And then things got personal …

Looking back on his first days at Leo Burnett's Sydney office in 1982, John Sintras reveals that the image of the tech-savvy advertising agency did not necessarily match realities of agency life:

> [W]hen I started, we had telex machines, photocopiers, there were no computers. There were typewriters, not even a word processor. Like it was another world. Everything was manual. Telephones, someone called and left a message and you were called on a landline. You could not be contacted at lunch. You

could not do an email to the office. It was mail boys delivering memos. Like it was another time in every way you can possibly imagine.[28]

It would be the launch of Apple's Macintosh two years later that truly sparked a revolution in the advertising industry.

While the '1984' campaign generated significant industry discussion about its aesthetics and appeal, it was the Macintosh itself that would have the greatest impact on the advertising industry. And it was felt quickly. At the 1985 Caxton Awards' weekend celebration of creativity in print, guest speaker Joe Lowe told attendees: 'Word processors make great anchors for dinghies. Go out and buy yourself an Apple IIc'.[29] John Bevins, whose eponymous creative agency was just a couple of years old, recalls acting on the advice: 'I dutifully went out the next day and bought myself an Apple IIc and started working on that'.[30] He was not the only one. Graham Nunn, the principal of another small creative agency, was similarly moved to invest in an Apple IIc following Lowe's talk. However, Nunn recounts that not everyone was as enthused: 'I remember at the Caxtons … a lot of people were really sceptical and saying "oh, bullshit, we don't need any computers". But it didn't take long really … for them to come in and revolutionise [things]'.[31] The momentum was already evident in other agencies. George Patterson also spent 1984 acquiring new personal computers, but not Macs. Where its previous 'visual display units' had been linked to the mainframe, its newly installed personal computers would provide access to the mainframe while also functioning as 'an intelligent workstation within the media department itself'.[32]

The uptake of personal computers in agencies may have been gaining momentum over the late 1980s, but they were still far from being commonplace. '[E]ven in the early 90s, the idea of having a computer on the desk was completely foreign', notes Tony Hale. Phil Hayden, who had arrived at The Campaign Palace from Britain in 1989, was pleasantly surprised that his new agency had computers—his last agency in the UK had none.[33] But by the mid-90s, Hale could see a discernible shift:

> The Campaign Palace was the first place that I'd ever been to that had a computer on every desk. And I thought at the time—and they were those big clunky Macs—I thought at the time—wow, how sophisticated is this![34]

The laptop took even longer to take root. Victor Maree thus recalls that costs continued to exert an impact on the uptake of technology:

> [I]f you wanted a laptop in the early '90s, you bought your own laptop, because it just wasn't supported by anything … I bought my first Acer laptop, because I think … you could buy a car for the cost of a Toshiba.[35]

Although computers were finding their way into more agencies, Hale observes that having computers did not necessarily mean that the agency had entered the computer age: 'Half of us couldn't type at all. And the idea of having them on the desk was a bit of a folly because nobody knew how to use them'. The lack of computer

literacy skills was also an issue in other agencies. In 1990, Hertz Walpole's production manager explained to *Ad News* that 'We chose the Macintosh software system
because it could be easily adapted to suit our specific needs and is very easy for
people with no computer experience to understand and use'.[36] Advertisements for
Macs inserted into the trade press provide an insight into the skillset and concerns
of the target audience, along with illustration of the product's capacity to revolutionise the advertising world:

> The people who develop graphics software just naturally start with Mac. If
> MS-DOS versions do appear, they usually don't show up until about 18
> months later. By then, you're most likely already looking at new, improved
> versions for Mac. One reason why the Apple Mac has become the industry
> standard. Another is ease of use. Because all Mac software works in a consistent
> way, once people have learnt the basics of one program, they can move right
> along to another. … [W]e've put this entire ad together on an Apple Mac. And
> while it only took us a few days, this is just a modest effort.[37]

Nevertheless, the costs and ease of using a Mac meant that by 1993, observers felt
sufficiently confident to proclaim that 'very few [agencies] do not currently have
some type of [computer] system installed'.[38]

The impact of the computer affected different parts of the advertising agencies
in different ways. Secretarial staff were the first to be displaced by the desktop
computer. As a junior dispatch boy at George Patterson in 1994, Paul McMillan
encountered:

> the older kind of creative guys and the older sort of account people' who still
> had secretaries and they would stand behind them and talk to them and say,
> can you write this. And they were just clacking away on their typewriters.[39]

Around the same time, Matt Donovan, who had joined Foote, Cone & Belding
(FCB) as a 22-year-old account director also had a secretary during his first time
at the agency. However, this would be a short-lived experience: 'within about a
year, the secretaries all disappeared. Only the CEO and the managing director had
one and the rest of them were all cut out of the business and we all had computers
on our desk'.[40] As Sintras recalls, there were efforts by secretaries and other staff to
stave off the inevitable:

> And there were some people who had secretaries typing their emails for them
> because they refused, seriously, they refused or didn't know how to use a key-
> board, or they were still doing everything handwritten, and passing it to other
> people to email. I remember secretaries that refused to use a word processor that
> insisted that they all type and that's all they will do and they refused to change.[41]

For smaller creative agencies, the desktop computer meant that they could dispense
with secretaries altogether. Graham Nunn, who cofounded Foster Nunn Loveder

in 1983, thus muses: 'I've never had a PA or secretary of my own. Computers were the reason you didn't need one'.[42]

The impact of the first generation of computers had been largely restricted to the finance and media departments. While they would also be affected by the new generation of personal computers, it was not as disruptive as that experienced by the production department and, to a lesser degree, the creative department. In 1990, Clemenger BBDO's Sydney office decided that it was time to update its production and art department. The move would not only bring the agency into the computer age, it would also send the right signals to one of its key clients — Apple. Over four days, it dismantled its old art studios and replaced them with six Mac workstations. Roger Rigby, who led and oversaw the upgrade, recalls the staff were offered training for the new equipment. Younger staff were excited by the move as 'they were starting to think in computers', but a few of the older staff were less enthused. Rigby remembers the ultimatum he was forced to give them: 'either you learn it or you go. And I had to fire two people'.[43] The state of the technology, however, meant that production jobs across the agencies did not disappear over-night. Peter Caley, the managing director of a production house and avid Macintosh user, told the trade press 'the role of typographers ad typesetters would not be effected [sic]'.[44] Within twelve months, these jobs were already in the firing line with the production manager of Harvie Advertising explaining: 'Now we can change an illustration or typeface in about 15 minutes and produce something that can be shown to clients'.[45] And clients were impressed, particularly those who had not encountered computer technology in their own workplaces.[46] Looking back on the demise of the production departments across the industry, production staffer Greg McIntyre glumly observes: 'Technology has taken away so many jobs from so many people, and so much craft'.[47]

Concerns about job losses and lost skills echoed a common fear that computers were not only putting skilled workers out of work, they were replacing them with unskilled staff. Visiting Australia in 1991, American designer Joe Duffy articulated this view stating that 'Companies that don't have a good attitude towards design … think they can hire a Mac and have a secretary or someone do a job that a trained professional should do'.[48] Lance Ross, principal of his own small agency, similarly complained that 'clients are putting their own ads in newspapers and magazines … All because their computers are capable of performing neat typesetting'.[49] At a glance, such concerns echo Harry Braverman's deskilling thesis, whereby management's interests in accumulating profits see a progressive simplification in worker skillsets.[50] However, others saw a different pattern emerge, whereby the computer was in fact requiring staff to upskill and to expand their repertoire: 'Operators need to be allrounders, skilled in a range of areas because technology has blurred the divisions among designer, typesetter and finished artist'.[51]

The ripple effect of the changes to the production department meant that the work of creatives was slowly but surely beginning to be affected by the computer. Keith Aldrich, who worked as an art director for multiple large agencies, explains that up until the 1990s, his briefcase contained 100 magic markers, pentels, pens, and a type rule for measuring the space between letters:

> And everybody used to say "oh, you're not going to use those anymore—computers are coming", and I'm thinking "I don't want to use a computer, why would I want to use a computer, I just want to draw things out" ... and it went on for years.[52]

The computer revolution soon caught up with him, and Aldrich found himself learning to use QuarkXPress:

> So, we were all desperately getting ourselves Mac computers and trying to learn this technology, but not really wanting to because it was far quicker to just scribble it out and present it. But, inevitably, it got more, and more, and more popular.[53]

By late 1992, it was noted that the issue facing creative and production departments was 'no longer in the technology, but rather the amount of talent available to operate it'.[54]

With each passing year, the financial case for agencies to invest in personal computers grew stronger. As noted in Chapter 1, the Recession of the early 1990s had compelled the agencies to pay closer attention to their bottom lines. Such concerns would remain in place even after the economy improved, and as agency profitability began to be measured in terms of the billings to staff ratio, keeping staff numbers at a minimum remained a priority for agency management. The computer's impact on the agency's finances was vividly revealed by Roger Rigby. Clemenger BBDO's decision to computerise its production department saw its turnover grow from $384,000 annually to $1.2 million with the first twelve months. In this climate, there was little chance that agency staff numbers would return to their previous size. The financial case for the computer was further bolstered by the fact that more could be done for less. John Bevins thus claims that the computer made his agency: 'intuitively more productive'.[55] Reports confirmed this to be true with early adapters explaining how their output grew exponentially following the purchase of personal computers.[56] By 1993, it had become an accepted truth. 'Our guys are doing three times or four times the amount of work the same number of people could do two years ago', asserted Robin Chiew, George Patterson's creative director of electronic art (formerly production manager).[57] The computer had not only made things easier and quicker, it was also enabling agencies to do more things in-house. This not only provided confidentiality for the client, it also established an additional income stream for the agency through the design and production of labels, packaging, and other print-based materials.

Beyond the immediate financial and time-saving returns, the personal computer also offered other benefits that would only become apparent later. Many recalled how the personal computer enhanced their agency's professional image. John Bevins explains that his Apple IIc enabled the agency to produce 'documents that looked so much more professional than Lintas were producing with their daisy wheel typewriters'.[58] Such appearances gave the impression that the agency was a large business. Bevins thus tells the story of one client being slightly disappointed to learn that the agency only employed six people. Similar experiences led Tony

Hale to invest even more into information technology systems by leasing an Apple laser printer:

> Now, from memory, those things were about $12,000 or $15,000. So, it was a big investment. But it was an investment that we needed because the look and sophistication that your documents gave—and your work gave—was so much better, because we were used to doing hand-drawn boards and things like that.[59]

Of course, many of the older agency staff continued to express a degree of reservation over the new technology. A 1991 special on technology and presentations in *B&T* thus noted how many agencies were 'not eagerly embracing the new technologies, choosing to stick with the tried and true slides and overheads'.[60] Saatchi & Saatchi was one of the agencies looking to change its practices by investing in Apple Macs for presentation purposes. The agency's business development manager thus explained that '[w]e are moving towards hi-tech, very flexible presentations as opposed to the standardised ones ... agencies who do not use these techniques will be the losers'.[61] Such claims, however, should not overshadow the realities at the ground level. In the late 1990s, Matt Donovan decided to use a laptop in a pitch for a new account: 'but my senior leadership made me print the presentation out on acetate [sheets] just in case'.[62] Although the use of analogue backup may have been a sound precautionary measure, the process of producing the transparent sheets coupled with the task of finding an overhead projector negated any time savings to be had, while the task of lugging such a projector around presumably undermined the image of the professional, tech-savvy agency.

Discovering the computer market

The success of Apple's '1984' campaign revealed that advertising and those responsible for creating it were to play an important role in the expansion of the personal computer market. During the late 1980s and early 1990s, the Apple account in Australia was handled by the highly creative Campaign Palace. In the lead up to securing the account, The Campaign Palace's research revealed that the 'market was widely spread with computer high-flyers at one end and the potential personal computer users still untapped at the other end ... this was the market we had to address'.[63] Martin Williams recalls that his direct marketing agency Cartwright Williams was also engaged by Apple in Australia as the information technology firm 'recognised that they needed to talk to people that were IT people in order to sell their machines'.[64] Such research revealed that the advertising industry itself was one of Apple's key markets. As we have seen, their need for the production and administrative efficiencies that the computer offered made them early adapters. More importantly, they also possessed the finances to make such an investment.

The increasing popularity of the personal computer saw information technology brands evolve into household names. Competition among advertising agencies for information technology accounts duly intensified. Dell, for example, commenced operations in Australia in January 1993, using a direct marketing agency.

While the agency had succeeded in growing sales by 30 per cent per month, it was dropped in June. Speaking to the trade press, Dell's marketing manager explained that 'being such a high-profile account, I've been approached by almost every advertising agency in Australia'.[65] He also sounded a caution to the new agency, adding that it would also be reviewed after six months. Those that managed to keep their information technology clients happy discovered that they had somehow metamorphosised into 'IT' experts in their own right. Cartwright Williams, for example, was able to leverage its work for Apple to reach other businesses in the same field, including Toshiba and Hewlett Packard.[66]

The market for computers and information technology grew steadily in the 1980s before rapidly expanding in the early 1990s. Data collected by the Australian Bureau of Statistics estimated that 29 per cent of Australian households had a computer in 1994.[67] The popularity of computers, software, and other information technology systems meant that this was an important and, indeed, lucrative market for the advertising industry. An estimated $45 million was thus being spent on advertising computers in 1994.[68] The popularity of computers was evident in the magazine market where no less than 25 titles like *Computerworld*, *PC Week*, *PC World*, *PC Review*, *Australian Personal Computer*, *Australian Macworld*, and *MacNews* were all desperately vying for the attention of this market.[69] Noting that '[t]raditional demographics are irrelevant in computer magazines with job titles being a more accurate indication of spending power' underscores the newness; a report on the burgeoning computer market indicates that this was not only an evolving market but also one—as we shall see in the following chapters—that was in many ways unfamiliar to the advertising industry.[70]

★★★

Surveying the state of computers and information technology within Australia's advertising agencies in 1994, *B&T* reported that the industry had undergone a significant change:

> The agency of the 1990s is a very different proposition to that of even five years ago. Most are now fully equipped with sophisticated equipment and a new generation of enthusiastic, computer literate staff. The desktop phenomenon revolutionised agencies, producing creatives with print-based tools boasting greater scope and control.[71]

However, the report also noted that this embrace of information technology had been neither a simple nor an inevitable development. It claimed that aside from the production department segment, the agencies had been 'slow to embrace the developments which are affecting communications industries worldwide' and that 'despite the industry's well-cultivated image of youthful vigour, it is fundamentally conservative' with an innate 'fear of change'.[72] While this interpretation accurately captures the ambiguities that underpinned the industry's approach to information technology, its suggestion that the industry was both a late and reluctant entrant into the computer age ignores the fact that agencies had been actively engaging with it for over three decades.

The nature of the advertising agencies' relationship with computers and information technology was, in the first instance, informed by their needs on the one hand and the technology's capabilities on the other. During the 1960s and 1970s, the growing size and scale of the work being conducted by agencies led them to make significant investments in computers in order to assist their media and accounting departments. Being advertising professionals, they also seized the opportunity to use their investment for publicity purposes.

Over the late 1980s and the early 1990s, the new generation of computers lent themselves to supporting the work being undertaken in the administrative sphere as well as the production and creative departments. In contrast to the earlier period, this second wave had a more profound and visible impact on agency practices. Secretaries almost disappeared from the agency while processes in the production and creative departments were revolutionised as a result of the personal computer. The speed of such changes was also hastened by the broader shifts. As clients were reducing their advertising budgets but demanding the same level of service (see Chapters 1 and 2), computers and information technology provided a conveniently cost-effective solution. And as the market's appetite for computers and information technology rapidly expanded, advertising agencies understood that it was in their interests to be actively engaged in the computer revolution—as both consumers and, indeed, promoters. While the advertising agencies had had three decades to integrate and then adapt to computers and information technology, the next phase of the revolution—the arrival of the internet—demanded a much more immediate response.

Notes

1 Linda M. Scott, "'For the Rest of Us': A Reader-Oriented Interpretation of Apple's "1984" Commercial', *Journal of Popular Culture* 25, no.1 (1991): 68.
2 Sarah R. Stein, 'The "1984" Macintosh Ad: Cinematic Icons and Constitutive Rhetoric in the Launch of a New Machine', *Quarterly Journal of Speech* 88, no. 2 (2002): 169.
3 Christina Spurgeon, 'From Mass Communication to Mass Conversation: Why 1984 wasn't like *1984*', *Australian Journal of Communication* 36, no. 2 (2009): 149.
4 Martin Campbell-Kelly, William Aspray, Nathan Ensmenger and Jeffrey R. Yost, *Computer: A History of the Information Machine*, 3rd edition (New York and Abingdon: Routledge, 2018), 254.
5 Ibid., 229.
6 See Sarah Hartman Strom, *Beyond the Typewriter: Gender, Class and the Origins of Modern American Office Work, 1900–1930* (Urbana and Chicago: University of Illinois Press, 1992); Katherine Durack, 'Gender, Technology, and the History of Technical Communication', *Technical Communication Quarterly* 6, no. 3 (1997), 249–60; Delphine Gardey 'Mechanizing Writing and Photographing the Word: Utopias, Office Work, and Histories of Gender and Technology', *History and Technology: An International Journal* 17, no.4 (2001), 319–52; Kate Boyer and Kim England, 'Gender, Work and Technology in the Information Workplace: from Typewriters to ATMs', *Social & Cultural Geography* 9, no. 3 (2008): 241–56.
7 Juliet Webster, *Shaping Women's Work: Gender, Employment and Information Technology* (Abingdon and New York: Routledge, 2013), 8, 10.
8 'The Monolith', Mad Men, Series 7, Episode 4, 2014.
9 Matthew Creamer, '*Mad Men* Recap: Madtech!', *AdAge*, April 28, 2014, https://adage.com/article/special-report-mad-men/mad-men-recap-madtech/292920.
10 'The Computer in Advertising—The Right Perspective', *B&T*, June 30, 1966, 3.

11 'Top Agency's Two Major Statements', *Newspaper News*, August 9, 1963, 1.
12 'Australia's First Advertising Agency Computer Working', *Newspaper News*, April 2, 1965, 6.
13 Ibid.
14 Robert Crawford, '"But Nobody talks to Accountants": The Growing Influence of the Finance Department in the Advertising Agency', *Accounting History Review* 30, no.1 (2020): 102–103.
15 Mike Satterthwaite, interview by author, September 12, 2012, Title No: 1489306, National Film & Sound Archive (NFSA), ACT.
16 'What makes a Top-Class Media Director', *Advertising in Australia*, 20 August 1965, 26.
17 'Agencies moving into Computer Age', *B&T*, September 15, 1966, 15, 27. 'US Media Size is Perplexing', B&T, January 16, 1969, 13.
18 'The Computer in Advertising—The Right Perspective', *B&T*, June 30, 1966, 3.
19 'Unique Media Scheduling', *B&T*, December 8, 1966, 34.
20 'Ads "More Creative"', *B&T*, June 5, 1969, 1.
21 'Agency's Computer Plan', *Advertising & Newspaper News*, June 21, 1968, 20.
22 Pam Mawbey, 'Profile of a Y&R Vice-President', *Advertising News*, July 21, 1978, 8.
23 Neil Shoebridge, 'Coming out of the Gloom', *B&T*, January 20, 1984, 16.
24 'George Patterson Bill $24.5 mill', *B&T*, July 24, 1969, 4.
25 'Computer ordered for Big Agency', *B&T*, May 3, 1971, 4.
26 Deborah Light, 'Keith Cousins 9 to 5', *Advertising News*, June 10, 1976, 7.
27 'The Ken Landell-Jones View of Agencies in the Future', *Ad News*, May 21, 1982, 28.
28 John Sintras, interview by author, May 25, 2020.
29 John Bevins, interview by author, May 10, 2013, Title No: 1488437, NFSA.
30 Ibid.
31 Graham Nunn, interview by author, May 21, 2013, Title No: 1489208, NFSA.
32 Ron Selsby, 'Media Muscle', *B&T*, November 9, 1984, 44.
33 Phil Hayden, interview by author, July 10, 2020.
34 Tony Hale, interview by author, May 13, 2020.
35 Victor Maree, interview by author, July 23, 2019.
36 Michael Coutts-Trotter, 'Computing a Macintosh Solution', *Ad News*, 1 June 1990, 30.
37 'Mac of all Trades', *Ad News*, March 13, 1992, 24–5.
38 Ian Robinson, 'Power to publish set to spread', Desktop Revolution Supplement, *Ad News*, 27 August 1993, 7.
39 Paul McMillan, interview by author, March 18, 2019.
40 Matt Donovan, interview by author, May 29, 2020.
41 John Sintras, interview by author, May 25, 2020.
42 Graham Nunn, interview by author, May 21, 2013, Title No: 1489208, NFSA.
43 Roger Rigby, interview by author, May 2, 2013, Title No: 1489295, NFSA.
44 'Technology cuts into Artwork', *Ad News*, June 1, 1990, 31.
45 Chris de Bono, 'Anything becomes Possible as Technology opens More Doors', *Ad News*, 31 May 1991, 19.
46 Chris Pearson, 'Prepress logs in', *B&T*, October 11, 1991, 22.
47 'McIntyre, Greg, interview by Rosemary Francis, September 9, 2014, Title No: 1489187, NFSA.
48 Mark Miller, 'Designer Doubts over Computers', *B&T*, November 1, 1991, 3.
49 Lance Ross, 'Desktop is giving Adland Bad Name', *Ad News*, November 19, 1991, 14.
50 Harry Braverman, *Labour and Monopoly Capital* (New York, NY: Monthly Review Press, 1974).
51 'Keying up Desktop Staff', *B&T*, November 1, 1991, 27.
52 Keith Aldrich, interview by Rosemary Francis, June 15, 2012, Title No: 1485200, NFSA.
53 Ibid.
54 'Digital Design: A Virtual Reality', *B&T*, November 20, 1992, 18.
55 Bevins, John, interview by author, May 10, 2013, Title No: 1488437, NFSA.
56 Justin Mansfield, 'The Desk top Revolution', *Ad News,* May 31, 1991, 21, 26.

57 Tony Burrett, 'Big Agencies beef up Computer Power', Desktop Revolution Supplement, *Ad News*, August 27, 1993, 2.
58 John Bevins, interview with author, May 10, 2013, Title No: 1488437, NFSA.
59 Tony Hale, interview with author, May 13, 2020.
60 Chris Pearson, 'Finding Targets Face to Face', *B&T*, May 17, 1991, 25.
61 'Saatchi goes Hi Tech', *B&T*, May 17, 1991, 28.
62 Matt Donovan, interview with author, May 29, 2020.
63 Lea Wright, 'All Aboard the Planning Wagon!', *B&T*, January 24, 1986, 14.
64 Martin Williams, interview with author, May 22, 2020.
65 Paul McIntyre, 'Dell Reboots in a Bid to Taste New Blood', *B&T*, June 25, 1993, 3.
66 Martin Williams, interview with author, May 22, 2020.
67 4102.0 Australian Social Trends, 1999, Australian Bureau of Statistics, https://www.abs.gov.au/AUSSTATS/abs@.nsf/2f762f95845417aeca25706c00834efa/37615266badb1dceca2570ec0011493c!OpenDocument.
68 Heather Jacobs, 'Computer Ads spread to Mainstream', *Ad News*, 18 November 1994, p.36.
69 'Top Computer Titles – A Quick Guide', *Ad News*, 18 November 1994, p.34.
70 'Nichers to win in a Crowded Market' *Ad News*, 18 November 1994, p.34.
71 Andy Bizorek, 'Smart Agencies confront Tecnhnofear', *B&T*, June 24, 1994, 38.
72 Ibid.

5 Ambiguity and the information superhighway

In the concluding chapter of *Advertising and the World Wide Web*, one of the first edited collections of academic work on the internet and advertising, David Schuman and Esther Thorson declare that '[t]he advertising industry has definitely found the Web and is there to stay'.[1] The web's 'ability to target, customize, and provide massive volumes of information on the spot', they add, meant that it was 'unparalleled as an advertising medium'.[2] Published four years later in 2003, Joe Cappo's *The Future of Advertising* offers a more subdued account. He observes that 'despite all of its many capabilities, the Internet has yet to provide itself as an effective advertising medium', noting 'This is not as much an inherent failing of the Internet as it is of marketers who have not yet mastered an advertising technique'.[3] Such comments neatly characterise the internet's ambiguous status in advertising circles in the 1990s—they could certainly see the medium's promises, but they were much less certain about how and when such promises would—or even could—be realised.

In many ways, the advertising industry's ambiguous treatment of the internet reflected the reference points that have been used to make sense of it. Cappo's misgivings were in part informed by the relative lack of advertising expenditure in the internet in comparison to television. Comparisons with television, the premier advertising medium, could do more to obscure contemporary understandings of the internet than to clarify them. For example, Richard Lei's claim that the 'World Wide Web … has not developed like other media. Traditional media have been based on an entertainment platform: the Web is almost exclusively an information based medium' correctly identifies a key difference between the internet and broadcast platforms such as television, but its neglect of the press and its origins indicates the need for greater historical nuance in such comparisons.[4]

Rather than comparing the internet with television, it is more appropriate to consider the emergence of the internet as an advertising medium during the 1990s, in relation to the emergence of commercial radio in the 1920s and 1930s. As an aural medium, radio was fundamentally different from print-based media and would require the development of new, bespoke forms of communication. Radio's commercial applications were not immediately evident and its emergence as a medium for advertising, in countries such as the USA and Australia, was neither planned nor inevitable.[5] The advertising industry's entry into radio was therefore gradual if uneven rather than immediate and wholehearted, but its impact on the medium's early development would be profound. In turn, the medium would also have a significant impact on the agencies themselves as well as their understanding of advertisements and advertising in general. The arrival of the internet and its commercial evolution displayed marked similarities: it was an unprecedented medium; it needed and developed new modes of communication; its commercial applications emerged gradually and unevenly; and it required agencies to reconsider their work along with their identity.

In her 2008 study, *Advertising and New Media*, Christina Spurgeon observes that the 'established advertising industry was not a significant stakeholder in the early commercial period of the internet' and that 'creative advertising agencies in particular tended to be comparatively late new media adopters'.[6] Spurgeon only offers a speculative explanation for the industry's sluggish response, noting the degree to which the advertising industry was 'closely tied to mass media and the transmission view of communication'.[7] As we shall see in this chapter (and the next), this interpretation certainly has merit, but it is incomplete. In many ways, Spurgeon's explanation describes the Web 2.0 period of the new millennium rather than the period leading up to the Dot-Com Crash of 2001/2 (see Chapter 7). Although the discourse surrounding the arrival internet in the 1990s identified its participatory capabilities, the actual state of the technology meant that the advertising practitioners were not yet in a position to use or, indeed, to experiment with the medium and its advertising potential in any significant way. Spurgeon also fails to recognise broader changes sweeping through the advertising industry in the 1990s and their impact on the creative advertising agencies. As the previous chapters have shown, the rising power of clients and media agencies had progressively eroded the strength and influence of the creative agencies within the marketing space. While the agencies certainly paid attention to the internet and were willing to consider and explore its advertising potential, their outlook was ultimately an ambivalent one. Desperate to forestall any further losses, creative agencies deemed that it was better to stick to what they really knew rather than to risk too much time, money, and effort on a new medium that did not seem particularly well suited to their immediate needs.

Turning on to the information superhighway

In 1995, the Federal Networking Council, a forum comprising representatives from US government federal agencies whose programs utilised interconnected internet networks, met to provide a clear definition of the internet as a 'global information system' that is 'logically linked together'.[8] The need to define the medium illustrated its novel status as well as the difficulties that many had in comprehending what the information superhighway was and how it worked. Nicholas Negroponte's 1995 account of the impending digital age, *Being Digital*, offers a case in point. 'The information superhighway', he explains, 'is about the global movement of weightless bits at the speed of light'.[9] Such a concept seemed fantastic if somewhat bewildering. The interchangeable use of the terms internet, information superhighway, and World Wide Web similarly added a further layer of complication.

The evocative term information superhighway initially captured the attention of the general public. While variations of the term had already been used prior to the

1990s, it was Al Gore's advocacy of the medium early in his term as vice-president of the United States that brought the term into the general public's attention.[10] The take up of the phrase in the advertising trade press revealed that the industry's interest was in line with that of the broader population. With its allusions to speed, openness and competition, as well as its masculine connotations, the masculine connotations, information superhighway resonated with many of the advertising industry's values.

The first reference to the information superhighway in both *Adweek* and *Advertising Age* occurred in 1993.[11] There would subsequently be marked increase in articles using the term occurring in 1994 following the Superhighway Summit in Los Angeles. This growing interest was also reflected in British journals *Campaign* and *Marketing Week*, which first made reference to the information superhighway in early 1994.[12] In the Australian trade press, the first reference to the information superhighway occurred in 1993 with direct marketer Malcolm Auld noting that new media forms such as 'CD ROMs, interactive disks, pay TV, [and] flopticals … are here to stay. And if you don't try to understand their potential, you'll get run over on the superhighway'.[13] A 1994 article featuring the term in its title offered similar advice, telling Australian readers 'agencies that don't keep up with the whirl-wind of change will get left behind, doing their clients and the industry a disservice. That's the warning from overseas and from key players in the industry in Australia'.[14]

Although the terminology and the explanations surrounding the internet could often be expressed in confusing and complicated terms, the key concepts underpinning the new medium were familiar to readers of the industry press. The notion of an interactive media, for example, was already being raised in the early 1990s. Articles on the prospect of interactive television had been appearing since 1991.[15] Introducing new media platforms and channels, Dave McCaughan, the information and research manager of McCann Erickson's Sydney office, noted the emergence of 'Interactive Home Media' which would offer 'significant two-way communication, through which there is the potential to have "one-on-one" conversations with individually targeted consumer'.[16] McCaughan adds that this proliferation of new media outlets and new ways of connecting with audiences would not only demand 'imagination and courage to make good use of any new medium' but also greater flexibility in the ways that advertisers and their agencies approached and, indeed, selected the right medium.

By 1995, the trade press began to reveal a perceptible shift in the discussions of the internet with the conversation moving on from introductory descriptions and predictions to discussions of how and why it could be used as an advertising medium. Rob Oliver, whose agency, Frontline, handled the Microsoft account, thus observed that '[t]here's a lot of talk about the information superhighway, there's a lot of talk about hot technology … but cut through the bullshit and you soon find there's more hype than realism … it's time to look at what can be done'.[17] Articles with headings such as 'How to advertise on the New Media', 'Surfing the "Net for Profit" and "To Net or not Net?"' thus appeared in the trade press.[18] They were complemented by a raft of books with similarly instructional titles, including *How to Make a Fortune on the Information Superhighway*, *How to Advertise on the Internet*, and *Advertising on the Internet*.[19] While such publications uniformly extolled the commercial opportunities that were available online as well as the need for the advertising agencies and their clients to pay serious attention to them, the reality was that the advertising industry was still wary of what was commonly deemed 'the new media'. John Sintras, who was the media director and general manager of Leo Burnett Sydney in the 1990s, recalls the agencies' response, which combined scepticism with a dollop of hostility: 'So somewhere the internet was invented and nobody went, "Yippee." Nobody went, "This is amazing." Nobody was super keen to adopt it'.[20] Its arrival in the advertising industry, then, did not commence with a bang, but rather the less assuming ping sound announcing the arrival of an email.

You've got mail

The arrival of electronic mail in the advertising industry went largely undocumented in the trade press. However, personal reflections tell a different story. Email, as it would become known, was adopted as a business tool by individual firms with relatively little fanfare. Its humble status could be seen in a 1997 report on the use of personal computers in *Marketing Week*, which expressed surprise at the growth of email and the fact that a third of users 'now use it from home for both business and personal communication'.[21] Over the course of the 1990s, email would incrementally change the ways that everyone across the advertising sector conducted business.

First experiences of email could be exciting if not a little confusing, as the new digital communication tool seemed to operate outside of the normal conventions of analogue mail. Such sentiments were vividly recalled by Tom Moult, the creative director at Euro RSCG in Sydney, when he was first introduced to email in the early 1990s. On a visit to his client Compaq in Houston, Moult remembered that

> we had a little tech presentation, and at the same meeting, we learnt about email addresses and websites. I remember them saying to me, "So, you'll be tom.moult@something dot, dot, dot," and I'm going, "Yeah, how does this work?" They said, "So, I'll send you a message on the computer," [and] I'm going, "But you don't know where I live." And then they said, "And then there'll be websites, there'll be Tom at dot dot dot com and then they can see." We went away going, "This will never happen".[22]

Moult was not the only one to view email as something of a fad. While email was certainly being used by various business and organisations in the early 1990s, most Australian agencies would only set up email accounts for staff in the second half of the 1990s.

Intra-office communication in the early 1990s had scarcely changed for decades. Ed Brice recalls that when he joined George Patterson Bates in the mid-1990s, internal office memos were the primary mode of communication across the agency. The young recruit was perplexed by the process of placing memos in a tray for someone to carry it to another tray just metres away: 'I just thought it was so strange ... Why don't I just go and give it to them, you know. It's like "No, no, you just put it in the out tray. The person will come and pick it up and go and put it in their tray." I'm going "'It's not that far to go!'".[23] It was the replacement of this slow and cumbersome process rather than the actual arrival of email that stood out in the memory of Kimberlee Wells, a young account manager at Samuelson Talbot & Partners in the late 1990s: 'I remember the Teledex notes no longer came on your desk where reception had taken a phone call while you were out, and now all of a sudden it was an email sitting in your inbox. Yes, slips of paper with the clock on it'.[24] For Paul McMillan, it was the speed of the change that stood out. Like Brice, McMillan was a dispatch boy at George Patterson in 1995. He recalls how his job 'was to hand around inter-office memos through the mail cart in my first year', but by the time he left the role, the task was already redundant: 'late '95/'96 was when email was on fire and everybody had a computer on their desk and everybody was emailing each other and sitting in their offices'.[25] Internal memos were not email's only victims. When Michael Abdel launched his own agency Sphere in 1998, he did not have email—'everything was fax'—but by the turn of the century 'we started dabbling in sending digital files off'.[26]

The advantages of email were quickly felt by those agencies that embraced it. Efficiency was the first advantage. Tony Hale, director of client service at The Campaign Palace, thus explains that 'rather than handwriting a note and have somebody type it up and put copies all around the office—you could actually, via email, for the first time send stuff to the office, or even external to clients'.[27] Speed was the second major advantage wrought by email. 'You could be more organic. You could be faster', enthused creative director Sean Cummins, 'And I think just the speed and the ability to communicate faster was a really fantastic thing, and it's always been the case. It's amazing what can be done'.[28] Of course, there were some who were unwilling to embrace. John Sintras tells how the decision to use email for all internal communication at Leo Burnett 'was not a popular decision in its day' and that some staff who would not or could not comply: 'there were some people who had secretaries typing their emails for them because they refused … or didn't know how to use a keyboard or they were still doing everything handwritten and passing it to other people to email'.[29]

Although email's enhancement of speed and efficiency was experienced across agency departments and, indeed, the advertising industry more generally, the nature of this impact varied considerably. Within the creative agencies, it was the account service department that was the first to see the benefits of speedy and efficient communication with clients. Victor Maree, who had arrived at Box Emery's account service department from Johannesburg via London, remembers a computer with email being installed on his desk so that he could be in direct contact with the agency's new account, Medibank: 'So I would get back from meeting or something and I'd get a message from Gary "Can you look at blah, blah, blah?" and it was quite amazing. It was a very expensive setup for us, but I have to say that I thought "Look, this is really good."'[30] Maree notes that the agency's introduction of email did not necessarily mean that established systems were immediately abandoned, musing 'we were still sending memos and nonsense like that'. Of course, the account service department's use of email similarly reflected the growing use of email among clients.

In addition to facilitating speedy communication between the agency and clients, account service staff found that email offered a way of reducing error. Michael

McEwen was an account executive at Young & Rubicam's Melbourne office in 1997. He vividly recalls the instance with a retail client that led the agency to invest in digital technology as a means of eliminating costly errors. With the client being based in Sydney, the primary modes of communication were fax and the newly installed Integrated Services Digital Network (ISDN). The client's 'beautiful cursive handwriting' meant that he would firstly have to decipher what was written. He explains that he would then 'go to the library and find the relevant stock image. The guys would lay it out. And then I would have to courier the artwork or fax it to her'. On this one particular occasion, the ISDN was consistently crashing, and the agency was struggling to send the electronic artwork to the client in time for a newspaper deadline. Images were faxed to the client, which were then signed off after hours on Friday evening. With it being too late to use a courier service, the agency had to organise an alternative way of physically transporting the artwork to Sydney over the weekend. The discovery that negatives rather than positives had in fact been delivered to the client meant that McEwen had to travel on the Monday morning to hand deliver the artwork himself. When the advertisement was finally published, it was discovered that there had been an error in the advertised price. The client, McEwen recalls, was outraged:

> And at that stage there was an enquiry into what happened and why did this happen and why did that thing now work? And at that stage, the business said okay we need to actually work out how we can make this internet thing work. One of the guys at [advertising production house] Show Ads said "Oh we've been testing this high speed thing where we can actually send an artwork electronically. And we've been trailing it with *Sydney Morning Herald*." And that was it that was the catalyst for Show Ads to cease production of bromides and film and actually upgrade the system so they could send material electronically to the newspaper.[31]

As McEwen notes, production houses, as well as agency production departments, would also play a key role in introducing staff across the agency to new technologies.

Email also reduced errors in other client service areas. Prior to the arrival of email, conference reports were produced following face-to-face meetings clients. Such reports functioned as quasi 'minutes of the meeting but it was also there to just safeguard both sides. And also to be something that the rest of the agency who may not have been in that meeting could see what was going on and understand it'.[32] By providing an instant and accessible record of what was said and agreed, email effectively eliminated the need for such reports. In the process, it also reduced the need for face-to-face meetings and telephone calls.

For those working in the direct marketing side of the marketing business, email was not just a form of communicating with colleagues and clients, it was also a way of reaching out to the consumer. By the time that Kimberlee Wells became head of direct marketing at M&C Saatchi in Sydney in 2001, she found that 'email was a conversation that was constantly coming up' as the agency and its clients considered whether or not they should transition from direct mail to email. Bob Miller,

General Manager of Marketing at Toyota Australia, saw email as 'a miracle … just the simple fact of being able to write an email to all your customers, like 100,000 customers without paying a dollar for a stamp, let alone for the packaging, that's a miracle, right? It's a revolutionary miracle'.[33] As email assumed greater importance for direct marketers, it also become a resource within itself. Wells thus recalls how the Qantas Frequent Flyer account was initially tasked with the role of email acquisition: 'The strategy was let's grab as many email addresses as we possibly can, and then at some point we flipped it to be more about how to monetise the data'.[34]

Staff working in the media agencies and dwindling number of media departments in agencies similarly found that email had a significant impact on their work practices. Imogen Hewitt was working as junior media planner/buyer in the media department at FCB in Sydney in the late 1990s when she received her first email address. At that time, television spots were bought by fax, with buyers identifying what spaces they wanted and television stations responding with large reports of what was ordered and what was available. Explaining that some programs had 'hundreds of 30-second bits of air time', Hewitt outlines the onerous task of having 'to sit there and, literally with a pen and a ruler, see how close what you'd asked for was replicated in what you got'.[35] The process would then be repeated after the commercials had been aired, as media buyers worked out 'how many of the spots you paid for went to air in the places that you'd paid for them to go to air'. She recalls that email not only 'made the transportation of large pieces of paper that you needed to cross reference a little bit easier', it also provided immediate access to media sales staff to query any discrepancies or inconsistencies.

While the benefits of increased speed and efficiencies saw email become an entrenched business tool for the advertising industry (and, indeed, the world at large), there were also costs—many of which would only become apparent with the aid of hindsight. Peter Murphy, whose advertising career started in the pre-email 1980s, identifies two major changes. Firstly, email reduced personal contact between the agency and client. 'I think that's a loss for the industry', he observes 'because … when you're talking to someone, the amount of information you get from their body language and all that stuff is enormous. Unless you are an incredibly gifted writer, you will never be able to precisely put that exactly in an email'.[36] To this end, Murphy notes that email also increased the scope for miscommunication as 'people get the wrong meanings, the right meanings but the wrong outtake'—an ironic development given email's accuracy in documenting words. The reduction in personal contact and meetings also opened the scope for more fractured discussions between individuals rather than teams. As Sean Cummins muses, 'that was possibly good and possibly bad, depending on what the outcome was'.[37] The second major change that Murphy witnessed was the fact that agencies and clients no longer needed to physically go to one another's premises. Murphy recounts how in the past visits to the client often led to serendipitous jobs being given to the agency: 'you'd know what was going on in their business, and they'd give you projects that you didn't even know existed, because they'd see you there. Because, you know, advertising is like one 60th of their job, so they weren't thinking about you'.[38] Murphy's accounts of the impact of email on agency–client relations are not only consistent with the broader changes discussed in Chapter 2, they also appear to have played a role in exacerbating them.

The growing accessibility of email created a different type of challenge. Hotmail, the first free, online-based email service, had grown exponentially during the late 1990s. Launched in 1996, it boasted 30 million users across the globe in 1998—with one million in Australia.[39] As Tony Hale discovered, email meant that the distance between advertising agencies and audiences had become much shorter. Hale had worked on a campaign advertising Queensland's Hamilton Island as a tourism destination. Part of the campaign was a single outdoor billboard near Sydney airport which featured a couple lazing in a rowboat with the headline 'Chronic Fatigue Syndrome'. Hale thought little of it until he began to receive emails from the public castigating him, the agency, and the client for mocking the health condition:

> And I'm getting inundated with these emails. I never know how they got it—but they got my email address. And I'm getting something like 30 emails a day—from all around the world—abusing me and threatening me and calling me a disgrace and saying that they're going to attack my family, and calling me the worst part of Madison Avenue set. Stuff like this … it was coming from everywhere.[40]

Hale also discovered that a website had been created featuring his image, his home address, his phone numbers, and his email. By illustrating the ways in which the speed, efficiency, and ubiquity of email (and the internet) could be harnessed by the public to communicate back to the advertising industry, this incident provided an early demonstration that the traditional broadcast model of communication was not applicable to new media. Of the incident, Hale concludes: 'it became clear to me, at that stage, the power of the internet. And the ability to connect the world from very remote parts. … it also gives a voice to the disaffected … and allows them a platform to disseminate messages that they wouldn't have had in the past'.

Living up to the hype

In April 1995, *Ad News* announced that 'the Internet has finally hit Adland, with a clutch of new agencies claiming to help marketers access it'.[41] *B&T* similarly saw this development as the beginnings of 'a new era in advertising'.[42] However, the fact that only 4 per cent (262,000) of Australian households had internet access in 1994 indicated that these agencies' investment in the new medium was still very much an act of faith.[43] As one agency's managing director observed, the advertising industry was struggling to come to grips with the internet: 'as an industry we're either ignoring this new medium, or allowing Web enthusiasts to hype us into premature action'.[44] However, the explosion in the number of Australians going online over the coming years would vindicate the agencies' decision to venture into the digital space. By 1998, the number of Australian households with internet access stood at 19 per cent (1.3 million). Internationally, the figures showed a similarly exponential increase with 170 million people online by 1999 (and it was predicted that this figure would increase to 250 million by 2002).[45]

The impressive number of people going online along with the attendant proliferation of websites and web activity prompted many to look optimistically to the future—particularly those who worked in the digital field. 'Marketers cannot afford to ignore the internet and the provision of online services', asserted Daniel Petre, a former managing director of Microsoft Australia who now worked with PBL media.[46] Predicting that 'an increasing amount of retail and other business would be done online in future', Petre added that this growth would be driven by cheaper computers and more desirable online content. Tony Faure, who launched Yahoo in Australia, similarly extolled the virtues of the new medium and the need for the advertising industry to embrace it: 'How many times have you heard, "Sure, when it gets big, we'll think about it." Well, the time is NOW. and yes, we are absolutely serious. ... There are millions of Australians using the internet, and hundreds of advertisers. The message is simple: the opportunity is now'.[47] Others, however, warned against getting too carried away. A 1995 report by Brisbane agency Knowles Bristow Advertising thus found that the 'Internet has been oversold as a marketing medium ... Marketers have become caught up in all the hype and have unrealistic expectations. Driving the hype is the mainstream media'.[48] Writing in 1999, Simon van Wyk, managing director of an online auction site, similarly offered a more sobering interpretation by situating the internet within the broader media landscape: 'And while the Web is rapidly establishing itself as a significant new medium, it's not at the stage where it can become as universal as TV, radio, newspapers and the cinema'.[49]

By 1998, a shift can be discerned in the ways that the advertising industry was viewing the internet. This was evident in the press reports surrounding two conferences focusing on the online medium. The first was organised by Guy Satterthwaite, print production manager at Euro RSCG. 'Digital will be as big a revolution as Macs were for advertising production', he excitedly told *B&T*, 'Macs changed the business and now digital technology is going to make Macs look like playtime'.[50] Significantly, the conference would be the first to be run by and for advertising and creative services personnel. The topics to be addressed included the significance and impact of digital technology on their roles, the current applications of digital technology in the communication industries, and the likely impact of digital technology on the agencies and agency staff. The second report concerned the response to *B&T*'s sponsored forum on web advertising at the Internet World trade exhibition in Sydney. *B&T* editor, Tony Burrett, observed that the attendees at the forum and the questions they were asking indicated that the internet was no longer the stuff of hype:

> [T]he interesting thing about the attendance at this event was that the usual faces in the audience weren't there. This time there were mostly marketing executives whose bosses had given them the task of building the company's Web site. They wanted to know how to build a site, how to attract people to it, how to advertise on other sites and how to build their online brands. This was a clear indication to me that some marketers, at least, are beginning to take the Web more seriously as an advertising medium and marketing vehicle. [51]

Australia's advertising industry had finally logged on to the internet, and it was now time for action rather than words.

Agencies get webvertising

Under the heading 'Welcome to the Infobahn Marketing On-Ramp', a 1995 report in *Ad News* explained that marketers and advertisers in the United States were embracing the internet: 'Previously the realm of a few computer nerds, the interactive market is growing to the extent that serious, mainstream marketers are rushing to get a piece of the action … *Advertising Age* recently estimated the total amorphous market was worth \$US11 billion'.[52] Australian agencies, it added, had not embraced the new medium with the same level of enthusiasm. However, the agencies' cool response did not stem the flow of advertising revenue moving online. In July 1997, internet advertising revenue in Australia had hit the \$300,000 mark, prompting predictions that over \$2 million will have been spent on online advertising by end the of the year.[53] 'Compared with other media, this is a tiny amount', *B&T* bluntly conceded, before putting the development into a broader perspective: 'Yet all the major agencies and most of the major media are now falling over themselves to get involved in advertising and marketing on the Web. … Only now can media players see some light at the end of the marketing-generated revenue tunnel—even if it's only \$2m now'.[54] *B&T* was right. Within three years, online advertising expenditure had reached \$5 million a month and was still climbing.[55]

Writing in his regular column in *Ad News* in 1995, media agency head Haydon Bray offered an insightful if somewhat crude analogy to describe the status of the internet within business circles: 'Business and the Internet are like teenagers and sex. Everyone's obsessed with it. Everyone thinks everyone else does it. Everyone wants everyone else to think they do it, too. But hardly anyone really does it, and most of them do it badly'.[56] The same could be said for advertising agencies at that time. A report in *B&T* from the same year offered some candid insights into the ways that the Australian agencies were moving into the online space. Libby Doyle, a young marketing information assistant at McCann Erickson Melbourne, was the only person in the office whose computer was connected to the internet. The placement of the agency's only computer with an internet connection in the hands of junior was revealing in itself—senior staff had evidently dismissed it and were happy to leave it to others to decipher its potential. Doyle thus explained that over the past two months, 'staff had been '"having a play" with the Internet … to assess it as a business tool and in terms of its value to clients'.[57] Reflecting on the medium as an information source, she was a little underwhelmed by the internet's American focus and its application for Australian business, although she could see the medium's future potential. Anthony Armstrong, the managing director at J. Walter Thompson's Sydney office, similarly noted that his office had been 'playing' around with the internet and that the medium had a promising future: 'Once they get high quality video images on there, then you'll be able to provide a lot more involvement', he surmised.[58]

For some agencies, outsourcing was a quicker and cheaper of way of enhancing their digital credentials. While George Patterson Bates' use of multimedia CD ROMs to advertise automotive manufacturer Nissan and telecommunications provider Optus was viewed as innovative, *Ad News* questioned the agency's actual commitment to the new format: 'Patts did not create the ads … that task was left to The Frontline Agency, which has Microsoft as its major client. ... Frontline produced the ads, sold the space, and published them in its client's magazine'.[59]

By 1996, it was becoming apparent that more firms were in fact going online and that there were actual improvements in the ways that they were going about doing it. Advertisers involved in the information technology sector would play a pivotal role in pushing agencies online. Tom Moult thus recalls that his agency, Euro RSCG, had the local accounts for both the Compaq and Intel. Intel was particularly keen on partnering with its agency on developing websites as a promotional strategy for its products: 'So, they ... would say, "Look, here's money to build ten company websites. Can you go and find some companies and build them a really fantastic website as a showcase to other companies?"'. The experience would have a fundamental impact on the agency's image as well as its practice: 'We got ahead in the web build business, and I think ... we bought the first banner ad sold in Australia, the first in the world'.[60] With the multinational technology company Apple on its books, direct marketing agency Cartwright Williams similarly found that it was being recognised as a specialist in the information technology area and, in turn, willing to make use of the opportunities afforded by the new technology in its marketing work.[61]

With agencies like Euro RSCG making a splash in the digital space, a growing number of agencies also began to take the medium more seriously. In July 1996, *Ad News* ran an extended feature on the agencies' efforts to drag themselves into the digital age. It identified two key factors that were accelerating the agencies' efforts to embrace the new medium. The first was simple—competition:

> a sprinkling of top agencies now have decided to claim their share of web business by employing their own webmisters [sic] ... The idea is that they will concentrate efforts on getting larger clients a web presence before one of the smaller specialist shops steal the work. These ground-breakers ... have a common goal. They want to provide a turnkey new media service for their clients.[62]

In addition to the competition from the newly established internet specialists, the full-service agencies also faced the prospect of losing out (again) to the media agencies. Concerns about the media agencies also contributed to the advertising agencies' second major motivation for increasing its online capabilities—their clients. Advertising agencies understood that clients would be looking to them for advice concerning online communication: 'What these guys are all about is adding value for their existing clients, and if an agency doesn't have someone specifically working on web sites, the client is missing out'.[63] Although it was noted that 'many clients see web work as computing, which is something outside the realm of the traditional agency brief', the report revealed that advertising agencies nevertheless understood that they faced 'the potential to lose the controlling hand in client brands' if they did not implement appropriate measures to improve their online capabilities.[64]

As advertisers and their agencies began to pay more serious attention to the internet, their first question was whether they should set up a website. Explanations in the trade press reveal the level of understanding among readers. 'A website is more than a media face. It can include hundreds of pages worth of information, interactive databases, hyperlinks to the third parties and content-driven sites', explained a 1996 article.[65] Simon van Wyk's observations in his *B&T Weekly* column a year later revealed that many clients still had a rudimentary understanding of websites: 'most people still view the Internet as an extension of the old media they're most comfortable with. Some businesses treat their Web site like their annual report, while others build one which is essentially a paper-based magazine or brochure with a few interactive bits bolted on'.[66] With only a vague understanding of what a website was and how it worked, many advertisers were altogether reluctant to make any significant in developing a website.

The attitude of advertising agencies towards websites was in many ways little different to that of their clients. 'Only a handful of the traditional agencies have taken the plunge in building their own home on the World Wide Web', observed *B&T* in early 1996, 'The vast majority of those … are the newcomers—the internet marketing companies which have sprung up over the last 12 months, offering internet design and consultancy service but usually with little grounding in the disciplines of marketing and adverting'.[67] Explanations varied. Some agencies used their clients to justify their inaction. Richard Arbon, a group account director at Mattingly & Partners, thus explained that his agency did not consider a web presence to be a pressing matter as 'the people who select an advertising agency for their company, are the most time-pressured people in the workplace. Our research shows that surfing the web is not part of their process for selecting a new agency at this time'.[68] Others felt many agencies were simply not interested. 'The reason there aren't many [agency websites] around is that there is either a real reluctance to get involved in new media, or a drive within the agency to learn and explore the new media. Most of the agencies out there are in the first category', stated Homaxi Masalawaha, the IS and Computer Network Manager at Singleton Advertising.[69] Bob Miller, the marketing director at Toyota Australia, offered a different perspective. Miller did not consider engaging Toyota's agency to create its website: 'because they didn't have any interest in it. It was not their line of work … I went to the PR supply and said, "Look, I don't think this is an advertising thing"'.[70]

Those agencies that were willing to venture online and to establish a web presence of their own seemed eager to assure stakeholders that their investment was not a kneejerk response to a passing fad. Justifying the investment was a priority. Sydney agency Foster Nunn Loveder was one of the first to create a website for itself 'as learning process' but made it clear that it would not be establishing a formal online or interactive department any time soon.[71] Singleton Advertising's Masalawaha offered a similar explanation: 'We're getting into it [online] here not because we expect to gain any business from our web site, but so we can use it as a test-bed for our theories and our clients' needs'.[72] The same justification was also used by J. Walter Thompson's Sydney office when it announced the launch of its new website: 'The agency designed its site in-house, as a practical exercise and an effort to familiarise itself with the new medium … The page will essentially be used as a marketing tool and to demonstrate that JWT understand the new technology'.[73] Despite his office's investment of time and energy, managing director Anthony Armstrong nevertheless felt a need to demonstrate his and his agency's credentials by distancing themselves from the internet hype: 'I am not a great proponent that the 'Net will take over the world but it does have applications to some clients ... It isn't going to replace TV but I think it is suitable for clients whose product requires a lot of information'.[74]

Advertising agency attitudes were also informed by the emerging discussions concerning the concepts of integration and convergence. Building on Don Schultz's pioneering work, the iconic text *Integrated Marketing Communications*, Stanley Tannenbaum and Robert F. Lauterborn espoused the need for marketers to understand the interconnectedness of marketing communications approaches along with the abandonment of the division of 'above the line' and 'below the line' marketing activities.[75] While Schultz would later reflect that the concept of integrated marketing communications (IMC) in the early 1990s was still 'fairly simple and often simplistic' insofar as it focused on those responsible for creating and disseminating the marketing communications, it nevertheless resonated with many marketers and advertisers.[76] Coca-Cola's marketing director for the South Pacific region thus revealed the impact of the IMC concept when he declared that '[a]dvertisements are no longer the centre of the universe ... Ads are just one part of the contemporary marketing campaign along with all the other components'.[77] The Recession of the early 1990s also played a key role in enhancing the popularity of IMC with agencies expanding their services to include public relations and strategic marketing advice in order to secure clients and 'to make up the shortfall' caused by declining advertising budgets.[78] Over the second half of the 1990s, the case for IMC was bolstered by the internet. Looking at current and future practices, Patrick Keane, the strategic director of online advertising agency Jupiter, predicted that 'media integration and the erosion of traditional markets will be more important than the effects of growth' and urged advertisers to rethink 'online as being separate from off-line advertising, and focus on better integration'.[79] While many agencies remained steadfast in their view of what constituted advertising (and what didn't), IMC concept nevertheless provided the support for progressive agencies to move into the online medium. Early internet advertisements certainly reflect this thinking and, indeed, reinforced it. Euro RSCG Creative Director, Tom Moult, illustrated this process when reflecting on his agency's early efforts to go online: 'When we built early websites for companies ... they were brochure-ware websites, they just showed what the ... the product was and did, and if you clicked on it then maybe your email went to the company'.[80]

The concept of IMC dovetailed neatly with the emergent concept of convergence. 'The decade opened with the technologies and services associated with broadcasting, telecommunications and computing being relatively independent', explained Mike Windram in a 1992 article *Admap*: 'However, before the year 2000, most aspects of these technologies will have converged into the new common ground referred to as multi-media'.[81] Windram therefore predicted that '[t]he overlap between the power of the broadcasting medium, the scale of the telecommunications infrastructure and the rapid rate of development in computer and information technology will have a dramatic impact on all three sectors'. The internet's burgeoning popularity in the mid-1990s saw the concept gain greater currency. In 1995, the AANA's monthly newsletter introduced Australian advertisers and marketers to the idea of convergence and ruminated on its significance. Claiming that convergence 'is set to dissolve the boundaries between telecommunication, broadcasting and computing', the report then moved its focus on to the impact that convergence would have on the advertising and marketing sector:

> The creative challenge to agencies is enormous. There is every suggestion that creatives in the future will need to be involved in the brief in the early stages of development. Will this bring an end to the sometimes rigid demarcation between the creative and media departments so often apparent in existing agency structures? The next decade should see major changes in advertising agencies as they respond to advertiser requests for the use of new media.[82]

As IMC blurred the line between 'above the line' and 'below the line marketing', convergence appeared to be blurring the line between advertising/creative agencies and media agencies. Explaining that '[t]he reasons media buyers need to peak beyond the traditional boundaries is that consumers are rapidly changing their media diet', media agency proprietor and commentator Haydon Bray revealed that convergence was affecting the practices media agencies as much as it was affecting creative agencies.[83] Bray's comments further illustrate the way that convergence not only necessitated a rethink of the divisions within the advertising industry, but also their relationship with another key stakeholder—the audience. With convergence and IMC both encouraging the advertising industry to move away from the siloed approach to marketing, many in the industry began to see the internet as something more than the information superhighway.

At the bleeding edge

The first firms to enter the digital space were the entrepreneurial consultancies and small agencies. Already in 1995, *Ad News* was excitedly reporting on the first wave of specialist agencies such as Globe Media, Virtu Advertising, Netheads, and InterGalactic Marketing, which all claimed to be 'able to educate marketers about how they can access the Internet or use it and interactive marketing to their advantage'.[84] Rob Belgiovane would later recall that the decision to start up Globe Media shortly after leaving the agency he had created (Belgiovane Atkinson Moses—BAM) was met with derision: 'At the time people said: "What the fuck is he talking about?" We were right at the bleeding edge'.[85]

NetX was another early entrant into the online space. It was established in 1998 by Craig Wilson, an ex-managing director of the Sydney office of Mattingly & Partners, and Miles Joyce, who had previously been the interactive marketing manager for the insurance firm FAI. Funded by FAI's CEO Rodney Adler, NetX sought to differentiate itself from the other digital agencies by offering more than web strategy and web production. NetX's founders wanted it to be a full-service agency. 'To me, if you wanted to make yourself a full service interactive agency, then you needed to have media', Joyce explained to the trade press. However, the problem that NetX faced was simple: '[P]eople weren't really making money on media, but you needed to have it. It took us a while to work out that you're not going to make money from day one on media, but to offer the whole thing you have to have media because you can then deliver properly to clients'.[86] An early success for the agency was the launch of Hewlett-Packard's online store, where NetX was given the media planning and buying and online activity. Significantly, Hewlett-Packard's IT credentials did not mean it had fully embraced the digital medium as an advertising platform. It thus announced that NetX would be working alongside its existing agency, M&C Saatchi, which had the responsibility of producing 'mainstream activity'.[87] It was the media buying side of the new agency's business that took off, and by the turn of the century, its list of clients also included such agencies as Whybin Lawrence TBWA, Euro RSCG, Batey Kazoo, and Jack Watts.[88]

However, it was Euro RSCG Partnership which stood out as the first agency to be truly successful in the digital media space. Launching in 1996, the agency's first client was IT firm Intel. Its rapid growth reflected the growing interest in the internet as a business and communication tool. In 1998, it scooped the pool for the inaugural 'Interactive Agency of the Year' awards for *AdNews* and *B&T* respectively. *B&T* justified its decision on the fact that Euro RSCG Partnership displayed a deeper understanding of the opportunities afforded by the internet and, indeed, was willing to act on them:

> while many others still categorise online marketing as little more than putting creative content online, Euro has laid much of the groundwork for the introduction of phenomena such as "rich media"—or taking online advertising beyond the banner without side interference. Euro was also at the forefront of tapping direct marketing opportunities through Web sites with the integration of database systems into all online sites.[89]

While it was noted that 'interactive' (digital) accounts constituted 16 per cent of the agency's income, this figure accounted for approximately 40 per cent of all online advertising in Australia. *AdNews* was similarly impressed by the figures, noting that its increase of almost 92 per cent on the previous year indicated that 'it could even overtake income from traditional advertising and marketing'.[90] Like NetX, Euro RSCG Partnership seized on the opportunity to undertake media planning and buying in the unknown digital space—earning its owners over $1 million for 1997/1998. In addition, its creative work was earning international recognition and winning awards at the One Show in New York and at the Asian Direct Marketing Awards. The Sydney office thus became a creative leader within the Euro network, exporting advertisements and campaigns for client such as Intel, Mercedes Benz, and Proton.[91]

Euro RSCG's successful run would continue and in 2000 *AdNews* named it 'National Agency of the Year & Interactive Agency of the Year'—a significant achievement that truly marked the internet's coming of age for creative agencies. In its justification of its decision, *AdNews* echoed some of the earlier explanations: 'What overwhelmed me was that Euro was the only mainstream agency to be able to claim any in-depth understanding of the new media landscape ... Euro is the agency of the Noughties'.[92] Interactive accounts, including Intel and Ninemesn, now constituted 21 per cent of the agency's income, bringing in $4.9 million in the last year alone. Significantly, the agency was not exclusively digital—it also placed a strong emphasis on being integrated. Creative director Matt Cumming proudly lauded the depth of his agency's integration:

> We believe we are the first agency that is capable of creating brand advertising delivered through media such as TV, print, out of home and the coupling those campaigns with the customisable power of the internet which will deliver direct marketing and sales promotions more accurately and effectively than ever before.[93]

While it was important to emphasise the agency's broader credentials, Cumming nevertheless reveals the strength of the agency's emerging brand lay firmly in the new media realm: 'If you are not growing rapidly in interactive, you are doing something wrong'.

Over before it even started?

In 1998, *WIRED* magazine declared that '[t]he honeymoon's over' for online marketers. The internet's promises of providing marketers with a 'more intimate knowledge of customers than has ever existed before … so much more than those dinosaurs in print and broadcast can give' had not arrived.[94] Discussing this article in his *B&T* column, Simon van Wyk similarly noted that '[t]he Brave New World has not arrived. The promise of the ultimate one-to-one marketing has simply not materialised'.[95] While *WIRED* blamed the lagging state of the technology for these undelivered promises, others felt that the agencies—both creative and media—as well as their clients were collectively hindering and even obstructing the realisation of this brave new media world.

The promises of having the most interactive medium at their disposal counted for little if there was no real audience with which the creative and media agencies could communicate. While the number of internet users was growing rapidly in Australia and, indeed, internationally, the medium was still in its infancy in terms of the number of actual users. A 1999 survey of internet users found that '[n]ot all Australians want to get on to the Internet, with research results indicating only 50%–60% of the population will be online in two years' time, rather than the commonly forecast 80%–90%'.[96] Non-users were primarily identified as 'seniors, the unemployed and females', while 'men and those of working age will continue to comprise the majority of Australia's Internet users'. The reasons for not going online included 'the Internet was not a priority to them, they had no personal computer, [and] they had no need of the Internet or they couldn't afford it'. Writing a couple of years earlier, David Rollins, principal of creative agency Sargant Rollins Vranken, was already concerned about the rate of take up and what it actually meant for the advertising industry: 'The bad news is that the Net is a hopeless advertising medium for the simple reasons that it does not present a mass audience we can advertise to, even though there are supposedly 50 million people using it, and despite the attempts of many software companies to make it so'.[97] 'The Net', he cautioned, 'doesn't deliver on the very high levels of expectation generated by the hype'. Others expressed concerns about those who were using the internet. 'Most diehard Net users have tiny attention span and scant respect for the ad culture', commented *AdNews*' Jason Walker, 'Your carefully considered banner might still go unnoticed by the majority of users unless browsers are actually looking to purchase'.[98]

The creators of websites were another target. While the development of a website revealed a very real commitment to the new medium on the advertiser's behalf, many felt that they were too niche or, worse, just hollow attempts to give the impression that they (and their agency) were digital—even if they were not. Rollins, thus claimed that 'web sites are, in the main, being created by surfers for surfers ... Anyone who's actually tried to use the Net—as opposed to being entertained by it—can't help but be frustrated by marketers' and their agencies' understanding of the way it's used'.[99] Rod Bryan, the managing director of online advertising agency Doubleclick Australia & New Zealand, similarly raised questions about the actual audience of marketers' websites and the degree to which marketers and their agencies were engaging with them. He thus urged advertisers to take a closer look at their decision to go online and to ask themselves whether they had created a website for the right reasons: 'Is it a fantastic experience [for the consumer] or is it done for the marketer's own gratification?'.[100]

The traditional full-service advertising agencies' inability to fully embrace the internet stemmed from its own established structures and operations. Such issues were already evident in 1995. Jeff Reeves, a former managing director at Young & Rubicam and The Campaign Palace, who had started up the digital agency InterGalactic Marketing, claimed that the internet was of little interest to advertising agencies because it was (still) not a 'commissionable medium'.[101] While Reeves had a vested reason in criticising the agencies' level of online literacy, others highlighted structural problems

A 1997 article by J. Geoffrey De Weaver, the managing director of Ammirati Puris Lintas Interactive, identified four key reasons why Australian agencies were struggling with the online medium.[102] Firstly, he argued that 'New media is not in their "comfort zone"'. Agencies that had been built around the 30-second television commercial that could reach 90 per cent of the population were struggling with the fragmentation of audiences and the proliferation of media platforms. De Weaver secondly points to the absence of any 'successful Australian case studies to learn from'. This lack of relevant examples left creative agencies with little inspiration to embrace the new medium, let alone excite their clients about it. Building on the previous two points, De Weaver's third point held that '[a]gencies do not understand how to integrate "online creative executions" into a meaningful brand experience'. This was exacerbated by the fact that 'most agencies have very limited technical prowess at best' and, as a result, 'it is almost impossible for them to communicate a consistent, integrated brand image through all the environments which their clients' customers will come into contact with their brand'. His final reason similarly underpinned his previous points: 'There is a drought of qualified, professional and creative Internet advertising sales companies and representatives'. To underscore this state of affairs, De Weaver recounted an anecdote: 'It was only about three months ago, I even had a sales representative (who was trying to get one of my clients to advertise on his site) ask me who or what Yahoo! was'.

Writing three years later, Andrew Antinou, online media manager at WSA Online, offered similar explanations for why advertising agencies were still 'following, not leading, the interactive revolution'. Like De Weaver, Antinou argued that the advertising agencies were fundamentally ill equipped for the digital age: 'Traditional agencies have a lot to worry about. Advertising is about mass marketing, whereas new media is about liberating and empowering consumers'. This effectively left agencies in a bind. 'They cannot afford to tell a client they do not understand new media', he observed, adding 'The reality is that most agencies preach integration but aren't equipped to deliver'. Antinou noted that the agencies also faced an uphill struggle to bring themselves up to speed. In addition to coming to grips with the fact that experiences with other media outlets were obsolete ('you cannot book an ad in the front half of a site like you can in a newspaper or magazine and expect it to work'), agencies needed to invest real money into upgrading their software and digital equipment.[103] Costs were also an abiding issue—not only was the amount being spent on digital small (albeit growing quickly), the scale and nature of online advertising meant that the established systems of costing were inappropriate.[104]

The creative department seemed particularly reluctant to embrace the internet. Reporting on his visit to the 2000 Cannes Lions awards, *AdNews* reporter Paul McIntyre observed that '[l]eaders from some of the biggest international networks were trying hard to convince a somewhat apathetic creative fraternity that this technology thing was for real. The agency business brains have realised they have to stop allowing others to take the digital high ground in marketing communications'. 'The creative brains', he added, 'don't yet care'. Their apathy stemmed from their own background. As Nick Brien, CEO of Leo Burnett London, pointed out: 'A lot of creative people quite rightly have been trained in a business that was built before the Internet or digital domains. … They don't want interactive yet … They really want to make short sexy films under the guide of TVCs'.[105] For them, digital advertising was not interesting because it was not the main game. Moreover, the type of advertisement being created for the internet simply seemed bland and unappealing. Describing the work done by his agency, Craig Wilson, chairman of NetX, explained that '[o]nline work is retail to the extreme. Fast turn around and lots of work. You're doing six or 12 banners a day instead of one press ad a week'.[106] While the energy and pace may have been appealing, the likening of online to the less glamorous retail advertising would have won few creatives over. Similarly, online advertising's principal tool, the banner ad, was equally unglamorous. As Dale McCarthy, strategic director at Harrow Group Sydney observed: 'The banner ad is a largely unsatisfying piece of marketing real estate. Usually a thin rectangle that take s up less than 20% of a screen, it offers a highly restrictive creative space—the equivalent opportunity of a drink coaster or matchbox top for delivering a brand message'.[107] Websites, as Tony Hale recalls, were also a mystery. Creative agencies not only lacked 'the expertise to be able to build websites', they also struggled with content: '[Y]ou didn't really know what you wanted on the website. You didn't really know what they were for. But boy you knew you had to build one. And in many cases that was just like a glorified Yellow Pages thing'.[108] Early client attitudes also did little to stimulate the agency's creativity. Of the arrival of the internet at George Patterson, Group Account Director Michael Godwin recalls:

> we used to talk about it [the internet] because clients wanted their web address on every piece of communication. And again from … a traditional creative agency point of view that was really our level of involvement. We didn't build websites we didn't do any of that. … [Y]eah, we used to just make sure that as part of the call to action it was go to www dot whatever.[109]

Media agencies and agency media departments were also cautious of the internet. As Dominic Pearman, founder and managing director of Pearman Media, recalls, the new medium seemed somewhat unassuming, if underwhelming: 'I didn't really look at it and go, wow, this is going to upset the advertising industry or where money gets spent'.[110]

Their outlook was similarly informed by structural and operational issues—most notably media commissions, their primary source of income. While many media agencies seemed reluctant to dismiss the internet altogether, they nevertheless displayed a marked desire to stand up for the established media platforms. 'Much is discussed about how unique, immediate and targeted Internet advertising is—about how it is different from other media', commented Liam Walsh, a senior planner/buyer at IM Netmedia, before explaining that 'the same principles apply to Internet advertising as far as media planning and buying are concerned as apply to television, radio magazines etc. All media are compared on similar criteria, that is cost efficiency, environment, reach, campaign objectives, etc.'[111] Examinations of current trends revealed both changes and consistencies. A 1998 survey by the Newspaper Advertising Bureau, for example, revealed that unlike magazines and weeklies, daily newspapers were not facing a serious decline in circulations.[112] The finding that '[n]ewspapers—which tend to be used early in the day—were not affected by the increased use of the Internet' revealed that the mode of consumption, in this case, the desktop computer, played a key role in the popularity of the medium. Of course, there were problematic signs. Commenting on the topic of classifieds moving from newspapers to online, Roger Parkinson, president of World Association of Newspapers, put on a brave face: '[N]ewspapers very creative and will find a way to overcome it'.[113] Geoffrey Smith, strategic director of multimedia development at Roy Morgan Research, similarly contextualised the internet alongside other media outlets. Stating that 'there is little evidence to suggest that new media will result in old media disappearing' and that 'the launches of the Internet and pay TV have not resulted in the disappearance of any mainstream media and are unlikely to in the foreseeable future'.[114] In surveying media consumption patterns, Smith found that 'the portion of the population that watches commercial television in any given week has been almost constant' but significantly 'the number of hours spent with the medium has declined' with audiences moving across to the Internet and pay TV. Such trends prompted him to predict that '[i]t is inevitable that while television remains a mass medium, its future will be more niche orientated as digital TV and datacasting segment the market even further'.

Media agencies' cautious entry into the online space also reflected their concerns about audience measurement—a point that was shared by their clients, and, to a lesser degree, creative agencies. The issue of audience measurement was first discussed in the trade press in 1996 with observers expressing reservations about the fact that the advertising industry was entirely dependent on the data supplied by 'the owner of the vehicle … whether it be an online publication or an Internet Service provider'.[115] For an industry that placed a growing emphasis on accountability (see Chapter 2), this was a worrying situation. 'The advertising community is obsessed with accountability. There is accountability everywhere you go', observed Tim Trumper, general manager of Murdoch Magazines, before seeking to assuage the sceptics: 'We believe this medium is the most accountable medium of all time. By a long way'.[116] Despite such assurances, questions about the accuracy of audience measurement would continue to dog the medium over the following years.

While the number of visits or click-throughs to a website could easily quantified, many felt that this was a crude measurement that said little and ignored even more. It firstly overlooked the question of who was online and, in turn, how they were behaving. A 1996 *B&T* report thus noted that '[s]urveys which paint a picture of a "typical" Internet user are largely irrelevant for advertisers trying to decide whether to buy space on the Net … the results of such surveys, while important often do not give the full picture of Internet use' as they failed to distinguish 'aimless surfers' from 'dedicated users'.[117] Two years later, little had changed. George Patterson Bates national media director Peter Gallucci thus explained that '[w]e are still working out the differences in how people use the Web compared to other media'.[118] Gallucci also called for a more comprehensive way of measuring audiences and their activities when considering a campaign's overall effectiveness and patterns of consumption, as 'traditional measurements don't apply'.

The advertising industry's second major problem with the existing internet audience measurement approaches concerned their lack of consistency. In February 1997, Marc Phillips, marketing manager of Nielsen Interactive Services, complained that 'the massively inflated balloon of Internet hype is still adrift with advertising and media companies unable to make informed decisions about which sites to use … without reliable comparative data being measured'.[119] A few months later, *AdNews* editor, Ed Charles, extrapolated these concerns, stating that media planners and buyers were being confronted by a vast range of surveys 'which measure completely different things. This means it is difficult to identify which web sites should be advertised on'.[120] *AdNews* reiterated these concerns in 1999, noting that 'web site measurement is still wobbly' and that the continuing lack of a standardised approach for measuring web usage and site performance resulted 'in conflicting reports … [which] in turn leaves advertisers and media byers confused as to where to direct advertising dollars'.[121]

As the internet's popularity continued to increase, calls for greater consistency in measurement increased in volume and frequency.[122] 'The lack of consensus over Web measurement can make offline media buying look like a walk in the park', observed *B&T* in 1999.[123] The problem was not necessarily realised with the advertisers, media agencies, or creatives, which collectively shared the common desire for a standardised unit of measurement, but rather the firms undertaking the research and the intense competition to establish themselves and their approach as the industry standard. Andrew Barlow, the managing director of Sinewave Interactive, thus observed: 'Our competitors seem too focused on defending their own reputations and the public knocking of other products'.[124] With so much at stake, such conflict was inevitable. Efforts to establish a standard approach nevertheless continued. In April 1997, the Audit Bureau of Circulations, which had primarily been involved in the measurement of newspaper and magazine circulations, was making moves so that its 'Internet audits could gain currency by December'.[125] The result was the establishment of the Internet Advertising Association of Australia, whose membership include major publishers alongside key web media companies. By mid-1998, its goal of establishing a standard measure was still unrealised and, as one member noted, it remained 'some way off'.[126] In February 1999, the Audit Bureau of Circulations resumed its campaign, this time looking to collaborate with a private auditing company, Sofres IMR.[127]

By the turn of the century, the issue of measurement remained unresolved—a point that did not go unnoticed by Yahoo!, one of the new major players in the online space. But rather than wallowing in the unknowns, Yahoo! sought to take on the advertising industry's cynics by inserting a simple text-based advertisement in the trade press. Its headline declared: 'Online is still an inexact science' and was followed with the wry observation: 'Unlike outdoor, radio and TV, which are all perfect'. The copy then went on to outline the new medium's growth and accuracy: 'You wanna put your brand in front of over 2½ million Australians? Yeah, we can do that. You wanna know exactly how many people click on your ads? We do that too. You wanna know the psychology behind it all? Hire a shrink'.[128] While the need to be accountable remained in place, the growing number of Australians heading online certainly helped to ameliorate some of the advertising industry's scepticism and doubts.

★★★

By the turn of the century, it was clear the internet had become an integral part of the advertising and marketing communications environment. 'This new world, driven by media fragmentation, the Net, WAP and eventually digital TV, has huge implications for anybody with an interest in marketing', mused Simon White, managing partner of media agency Ikon Communications. 'The only certainty', he added, 'is that traditional creative and media people are going to have to adapt quickly'.[129] However, Paul McMillan's subsequent recollections of this new world were little different. Of his experience of the 1990s, the former group account director at George Patterson Bates recalls that the industry 'didn't really change … there was a slow turn. People were still, like, "the most effective, most powerful channels to market are still radio and TV and outdoor. So there's nothing new here. All we've got at the moment is an electronic communication space"'.[130] Creative director Peter Murphy similarly noted how little things had changed: 'So we were doing exactly the same thing. Rather than walking down a floor, or looking at a book, we were then getting it online … So, the behaviour didn't change, just the frequency and ease of getting information changed'.[131]

Over the course of the 1990s, the advertising industry's response to the digital revolution had been characterised by its ambivalence. On the one hand, the advertising industry actively bought into the hype surrounding the information superhighway. Many were excited by the advertising opportunities afforded by the new medium and could see its synergies with concepts such as IMC. Unlike many of the ideas surrounding the new medium which were still abstract, email illustrated the strengths of the digital world—speedy, efficient, and relatively easy to use—as well as its capacity to change advertising practices. The success of agencies such as Euro RSCG and NetX similarly demonstrated the opportunities afforded by the internet. However, on the other hand, many in the industry were disappointed by their experiences of going online or simply struggled to accommodate the new medium within their operations. Despite the promises of offering a uniquely interactive and engaging experience to audiences, the state-of-the-art technology meant that the reality was banner advertisements—a much more prosaic form of advertising that did little to excite audiences or agency creative departments. The difficulties in measuring audiences meant that advertisers were unwilling to spend large amounts on online campaigns. And with traditional agency structures built around television and press campaigns, there was still little real impetus to fully embrace the online medium at this point.

Hindsight would reveal such ambivalence to be costly. With only a minority of agencies willing to embrace the new medium, the advertising industry—notably the creative agencies—effectively lost an opportunity to reinvent itself and to reassert the importance of advertising within the marketing hierarchy. And, as the next chapter will show, subsequent efforts to re-establish the creative agencies' flagging fortunes would be further complicated by the audience's transformation from passive onlookers to active stakeholders.

Notes

1 David W. Schuman and Esther Thorson, 'Thoughts Regarding the Present and Future of Web Advertising', in *Advertising and the World Wide Web*, ed. David W. Schuman and Esther Thorson (Mawah, NJ: Lawrence Erlbaum Associates, 1999), 303.

2 Ibid., 307.

3 Joe Cappo, *The Future of Advertising: New, Media, New Clients, New Consumers in the Post-Television Age* (Chicago, Ill.: McGraw Hill, 2003), 192–93.

4 Richard M. Lei, 'An Assessment of the World Wide Web as an Advertising Medium', *The Social Science Journal* 37, no. 3 (2000): 465.

5 Susan Smulyan, *Selling Radio: The Commercialization of American Broadcasting, 1920–1934* (Washington, Smithsonian Institution Press, 1994); Cynthia Meyers, *A Word from Our Sponsor: Admen, Advertising, and the Golden Age of Radio* (New York: Fordham University Press, 2014); Bridget Griffen-Foley, *Changing Stations: The Story of Australian Commercial Radio* (Sydney: UNSW Press, 2009); Robert Crawford, '"And Now, a Word from Our Sponsors": Radio and Its Early Impact on Australia's Advertising Industry' in *Radio in the World: Papers from the 2005 Melbourne Radio Conference*, ed. Sianan Healy, Bruce Berryman and David Goodman (Melbourne, Vic., RMIT Publishing, 2005), 311–19.

6 Christina Spurgeon, *Advertising and New Media* (Abingdon and New York: Routledge, 2008), 13.

7 Ibid.

8 Federal Networking Council Charter, 20 September 1995, available at: https://www.nitrd.gov/fnc/FNC_Charter.pdf. Federal Networking Council Resolution: Definition of "Internet", 24 October 1995, available at: https://www.nitrd.gov/fnc/internet_res.pdf.

9 Nicholas Negroponte, *Being Digital* (New York: Vantage Books, 1995), 12.

10 William J. Broad, 'Clinton to promote High Technology with Gore in Charge', *New York Times*, November 10, 1992, Section c, 1.

11 See Rance Crain, '"Superhighway" or Dialogue Dead-End', *Advertising Age*, October 18, 1993, 28; Michael Schrage, 'Survival Test', *Adweek*, Eastern edition, November 1, 1993, 27.

12 See Mike Elms, 'The New World: Advertising in Suspense–Part 4', *Campaign*, March 18, 1994, 22; Nick Higham, 'Ted's Starship Enterprise', *Marketing Week*, February 25, 1994, 19.

13 Malcolm Auld, 'Don't get run over on Info Highway', *Ad News*, October 22, 1993, 9.

14 Rosemary Ryan, 'Keep in the Fast Lane or prepare to be burnt off on the Information Highway', *Ad News*, August 26, 1994, 17.

15 'Interactive Television: Prospects for Advertisers', *Ad News*, 22 February 1991, 56; Richard Luke, 'Interactive TV is on its Way', *Ad News*, April 10, 1992, 18.

16 Dave McCaughan, 'New Media means New Opportunities', *Ad News*, January 31, 1992, 30.

17 Rob Oliver, 'Fear and Confusion in the Info Age', *Ad News*, June 16, 1995, 18.

18 Dave McCaughan, 'How to Advertise on the New Media', *Ad News*, 16 June 1995, 19; Pauline Hayes, 'Surfing the 'Net for Profit', *B&T*, September 22, 1995, 23; Allan Bonsall, 'To Net or not to Net?', *Ad News*, May 3, 1996, 29.

19 Laurence A. Canter, *How to Make a Fortune on the Information Superhighway: Everyone's Guerrilla Guide to Marketing on the Internet and Other On-line Services* (New York: Harper Collins, 1994); Michael Strangelove, *How to Advertise on the Internet: An Introduction to Internet-facilitated Marketing and Advertising* (Ottawa: Strangelove Internet Enterprises, 1994); Neil Barret, *Advertising on the Internet: How to get Your Message across on the Worldwide Web* (London: Kogan Page/LPC, 1997).

20 John Sintras, interview by author, May 25, 2020.

21 John Cleen, 'PC Makers need "Common Touch" to boost Their Sales', *Marketing Week*, November 13, 1997, 32.

22 Tom Moult, interview by author, May 11, 2020.

23 Ed Brice and Peter Murphy, interview by author, August 2, 2019.

24 Kimberlee Wells, interview by author, June 3, 2019.

25 Paul McMillan, interview by author, March 18, 2019.

26 Michael Abdel, interview by author, July 19, 2019.

27 Tony Hale, interview by author, May 13, 2020.

28 Sean Cummins, interview by author, May 29, 2019.

29 John Sintras.

30 Victor Maree, interview by author, July 23, 2019.

31 Michael McEwen, interview by author, November 28, 2018.

32 Sean Cummins.

33 Bob Miller, interview by author, May 7, 2020.

34 Kimberlee Wells.

35 Imogen Hewitt, interview by author, June 1, 2020.

36 Ed Brice and Peter Murphy.

37 Sean Cummins.

38 Ed Brice and Peter Murphy.

39 'MSN Hotmail, World's Largest E-Mail Provider, Surpasses 30 Million Member Milestone', PR Newswire, 1 December 1998; 'Hotmail hits a Million with free E-mail Service', *B&T Weekly*, October 2, 1998, 19.

40 Tony Hale.

41 Tony Burrett, 'Adland meets the Internet', *Ad News*, April 21, 1995, 1.

42 Ross Gow, 'Agencies bet on Internet', *B&T*, April 28, 1995, 8.

43 Lifestyle: Information technology in the home, 4102.0 - Australian Social Trends, 1999, available at: https://www.abs.gov.au/ausstats/abs@.nsf/2f762f95845417aeca25706c008 34efa/37615266badb1dceca2570ec0011493c!OpenDocument.

44 Allan Bonsall, 'To Net or Not to Net?', *Ad News*, May 3, 1996, 29.

45 'Web Population to top 250 million', *B&T Weekly*, March 19, 1999, 18.
46 'Ignore the Net at your Peril', *B&T Weekly*, October 24, 1997, 5.
47 Tony Faure, 'The 21st Century Medium', *B&T Weekly*, August 28, 1998, 17.
48 Mara Lee, 'Internet: Don't believe the Hype', *B&T*, November 3, 1995, 2.
49 Simon van Wyk, 'www: A Medium Unlike Any Other', *B&T Weekly*, July 9, 1999, 15.
50 Tony Kelly, 'Conference Prepares for the Digital Ad Age', *B&T Weekly*, July 3, 1998, 5.
51 Tony Burrett, 'Conference shows Strong Web Interest', *B&T Weekly*, August 14, 1998, 44.
52 Tony Burrett, 'Welcome to the Infobahn Marketing On-Ramp', *Ad News*, June 16, 1995, 15.
53 Kate Lyons, 'Internet Ad Sales to top $2m Mark', *B&T Weekly*, September 5, 1997, 16.
54 Tony Burrett, 'Webvertising is now a Serious Business', *B&T Weekly*, September 26, 1997, 32.
55 'Online Ads top $5m a Month', *AdNews*, January 14, 2000, 21.
56 Haydon Bray, 'Sex and the Internet: Who's doing It', *AdNews*, November 17, 1995, 14.
57 Ross Gow, Agencies bet on the Internet', *B&T*, April 28, 1995, 8.
58 Ibid.
59 Tony Burrett, 'Interactive Marketing set to explode', *Ad News*, 19 May 1995, 8.
60 Tom Moult.
61 Martin Williams, interview by author, May 22, 2020.
62 Charlotte Harper, 'Agencies wake up to the Big Wired World', *Ad News*, July 26, 1996, 24.
63 Ibid., 28.
64 Ibid., 24.
65 Ibid., 24, 25, 28.
66 Simon van Wyk, 'Spinning Synergy into your Website', *B&T Weekly*, August 1, 1997, 18, 19.
67 Mike Hanlon, 'Agency Web Sites: The Cobbler's Children's Shoes', *B&T*, Intercreative Supplement, March 1996, 18.
68 Ibid.
69 Ibid.
70 Bob Miller.
71 Charlotte Harper, 'Agencies wake up to the Big Wired World', *Ad News*, July 26, 1996, 24, 25, 28.
72 Hanlon, 'Agency Web Sites'.
73 'JWT's Site for Sore Eyes', *B&T*, 22 March 1996, 18.
74 Ibid.
75 Don Schultz, Stanley Tannenbaum and Robert Lauterborn, *Integrated Marketing Communications*, (Lincolnwood, Ill.: NTC Business Books, 1993).
76 Don Schultz, Charles Patti & Philip Kitchen, 'The Evolution of IMC: IMC in a Customer-driven Marketplace' in *The Evolution of IMC: IMC in a Customer-driven Marketplace*, ed. Don Schultz, Charles Patti & Philip Kitchen (London and New York: Routledge, 2011), 1.
77 Ivor Thomas, 'Integration is Wildly over-used and underdone', *Ad News*, May 7, 1993, 21.
78 Lara Sinclair, '"Integrated" Agencies shoring up Income', *B&T Weekly*, January 17, 1997, 7.
79 'Web Ad Growth leads to more Integration', *B&T Weekly*, August 27, 1999, 23.
80 Tom Moult.
81 Mike Windram, 'Developments in Communications Technology', *Admap Magazine*, December 1992, WARC Database.
82 'Convergence: What does it mean for Advertisers?', National Advertisers Supplement, *Ad News*, March 10, 1995, 23.
83 Haydon Bray, 'Escape the Clutter with Integration', *AdNews*, February 13, 1998, 15.
84 Tony Burrett, 'Interactive Marketing set to Explode', *Ad News*, May 19, 1995, 8.
85 'Power of Two', *AdNews*, 8 September 2006, http://www.adnews.com.au/yafNews/7EAC510E-5CC1-4AE0-83466C80002F0BE5.
86 Tony Burrett, 'Internet Shop this the Big Time', *B&T Weekly*, June 18, 1999, 8.

87   'NetX helps HP', *AdNews*, June 18, 1999, http://www.adnews.com.au/yafNews/ 36628E46-2B44-428B-A4A955872E1AE731.
88   Tony Burrett, 'Internet Shop'.
89   'Euro RSCG–Interactive Agency of the Year', *B&T Weekly*, December 11, 1998, 46.
90   'Interactive Agency of the Year–Euro RSCG', *AdNews*, December 10, 1998, L12.
91   Ibid.
92   Ed Charles, 'Why Euro RSCG?', *AdNews*, January 28, 2000, L3.
93   'Euro RSCG', *AdNews*, January 28, 2000, L5/.
94   Chip Bayers, 'The Promise of One to One (A Love Story), WIRED, 1 May 1998, available at: https://www.wired.com/1998/05/one-to-one/.
95   Simon van Wyk, 'Marketing: Reality Bytes', *B&T Weekly*, June 19, 1998, 18.
96   Byron Smith, 'All Australians won't go Online', *B&T Weekly*, October 8, 1999, 3.
97   David Rollins, 'The Internet ... Saviour or Saveloy', *AdNews*, February 28, 1997, 38.
98   Jason Walker, 'Hit and Run on the Superhighway', *AdNews*, July 4, 1997, 12.
99   David Rollins, 'The Internet ... Saviour or Saveloy'.
100   'Are You Really being Honest about E-marketing?', *B&T Weekly*, August 6, 1999, 26.
101   Tony Burrett, 'Adland meets the Internet', *Ad News*, April 21, 1995, 25.
102   Geoffrey De Weaver, 'Can You Afford Not to be Online', *AdNews*, September 12, 1997, 18.
103   Andrew Antoniou, 'Traditional Agencies still playing Catch Up', *AdNews*, December 1, 2000, L8.
104   Paul McIntyre, 'Splitting the Business', *AdNews*, May 5, 2000, 37.
105   Paul McIntyre, 'Rewiring Creatives for Interactive Media', *AdNews*, July 14, 2000, 34.
106   Paul McIntyre, 'Splitting the Business'.
107   Dale McCarthy, 'Why Banner Ads are Failing', *B&T Weekly*, July 4, 1997, 22.
108   Tony Hale.
109   Michael Godwin, interview with author, November 27, 2018.
110   Dominic Pearman, interview by author, May 18, 2020.
111   Liam Walsh, 'Debunking the Internet Myth', *B&T Weekly*, February 9, 1999, 17.
112   'Net Users haven't dumped Newspapers', *AdNews*, May 22, 1998, 17.
113   Charlotte Rivers, 'Online Classies still a Threat', *AdNews*, July 28, 2000, 13.
114   Geoffrey Smith, 'The Truth about New media's Impact', *AdNews*, August 13, 1999, 15.
115   Adam Gosling, 'Measuring Online Ad Effectiveness', *Ad News*, May 3, 1996, 28.
116   Ibid.
117   Susanah Petty, 'Net Surveys are "Irrelevant"', *B&T*, November 15, 1996, 4.
118   Kate Lyons, 'Measuring the Web', *B&T Weekly*, April 17, 1998, 24.
119   Marc Phillips, 'How is the Web stacking up?', *AdNews*, February 28, 1997, 29.
120   Ed Charles, 'Editor's Letter', *AdNews*, August 15, 1997, 11.
121   Andrea Sophocleous, 'Measuring Web Sites is an Inexact Science', *AdNews*, July 16, 1999, 16.
122   See Liam Walsh, 'Debunking the Internet Myth', *B&T Weekly*, February 9, 1999, 17; Jason Walker, 'Evaluating the Net', *AdNews*, November 21, 1997, 20; Kate Lyons, 'Measuring the Web'; Andrew McKenzie, 'Ad Agencies still fear the Net', *AdNews*, July 31, 1998, 15; Richard Wilson, 'Buyergraphics: The Future of Advertising on the Internet', *B&T Weekly*, June 20, 1997, 25.
123   Kate Lyons, 'Measurement makes for a Tangled Web', *B&T Weekly*, July 30, 1999, 23.
124   Ibid.
125   Susanah Petty, 'ABC pushes Ahead with New Internet Advertising Audits', *B&T*, April 24, 1997, 13.
126   Kate Lyons, 'Measuring the Web'.
127   'Web Auditors Unite', *B&T Weekly*, February 26, 1999, 25.
128   Yahoo! Australia & New Zealand, 'Online is still an Inexact Science', *AdNews*, April 13, 2000, 5.
129   Simon White, 'The Age of Fast Marketing is upon Us', *AdNews*, March 10, 2000, 13.
130   Paul McMillan, interview by author, March 18, 2019.
131   Ed Brice and Peter Murphy.

6 Following the eyeballs

Reflecting on the major developments that swept through the advertising industry as the internet began to gain traction at the turn of the century, media executive John Sintras points to the rise of the consumer and the realisation of the degree to which the new medium was challenging established practices and outlooks. The advertising industry, he argues, needed to 'create a consumer-centric approach versus the old creative director's approach of, "This is a great idea and you're going to do it. You're going to create iconic advertising even if people don't really want it"'.[1] While the creative agencies' autocratic tendencies and excesses had in fact been curtailed by increasingly vigilant clients and ambitious media agencies, their relationship with consumers had scarcely changed. However, the internet's capacity to empower the consumer would fundamentally and irrevocably disrupt this relationship and, along with it, the operations and outlook of the advertising industry more generally.

Of course, consumers had always featured prominently in the advertising industry's thinking —converting audiences into consumers was, after all, advertising's *raison d'etre*. Over time, gut feelings about audiences and consumers were replaced by more definitive insights gleaned from scientific approaches While such data driven understandings of audiences and consumers provided more accurate insights, they were not infallible. In *Audience Evolution*, Philip Napoli contends that 'the concept of the audience is constructed and defined to reflect the economic and strategic imperatives of media organizations', including the advertising industry.[2] Moreover, Napoli observes that these 'conceptualizations of the audience employed by media organizations evolve in response to environmental changes'.[3] To this end, ideas about audiences over the 1990s and early 2000s were being fundamentally reshaped by media and audience fragmentation, audience autonomy, new audience information systems, and the blurring of the division between content providers and audiences. Such developments were also set against a neoliberal backdrop that venerated individual choice as the key driver of consumption. As this chapter will demonstrate, the advertising industry's discussions about audiences and consumers were equally informed by these technology-related factors as well as their own needs, challenges, and anxieties. They would also be informed by the broader ideas of neoliberalism and its veneration of the individual as the central economic agent.

Significantly, the advertising industry's efforts to identify and conceptualise the consumer in the digital age also prompted it to reflect on its own activities and status. Asked what he thought was the most significant changes in the digital space up until 2006, interactive agency executive Mike Zeederberg answered: 'I think it was the evolution and the understanding of what people were doing. So, as consumer behaviour evolved, so did marketing behaviour and response'.[4] While this chapter reveals the relationship between the advertising industry and the consumer during this period was symbiotic, it also shows that this was neither an even relationship nor a static one.

Fear and control

When the Recession hit Australia in the early 1990s, worried advertisers and their agencies commissioned market researchers to gauge the consumer's thoughts, feelings, and sentiments. The key findings from such reports were regularly published in the trade press. In addition to providing important snapshots of who the consumer was and how they were seeing the world, these reports also established narratives about the consumer which, in turn, informed the way that the industry viewed itself and its future.

The Recession challenged the advertising industry's certainty. After decades of unfettered growth, consumption levels were falling, prompting the advertising industry to look to market research for explanations and, indeed, new insights. Market researchers responded by comparing and contrasting contemporary developments and outlooks with those of the recent past. In her 1991 study of consumer attitudes, Chris Adams looked to the previous decade to account for current trends: 'The invitation for people to spend up in the '80s is now seen as distasteful. Ostentation and avarice have been replaced by decorum ... Consumers these days are a changed people, no longer keen to be seen as materialistic or even glamourous'.[5] Vicki Arbes' 1991 study of consumer attitudes similarly compared the two decades:

> The consumer of the 1990s is shaping up to be a very different person from the one we've grown to know over the past decade. The theme for the 1980s was anxiety. As marketers, our opportunity was to soothe, to placate, to reassure. The consumer felt powerless and alone, so we surrounded our brands with friends and big families, promising the consumer a sense of belonging ... But things have changed. ... The anxiety is changing into anger and the consumer is beginning to take back control. From the Anxious '80s we've moved into the Sceptical '90s. What we are witnessing is the birth of the Sensible Consumer.[6]

Arbes' observations additionally provide an insight into the ways that these insights were also used by the advertising industry to hone their appeals and, indeed, to recalibrate them if necessary.

Other surveys and studies extrapolated on the trends and developments identified by Adams and Arbes. Speaking at the Market Research Society's annual conference, Jacqueline Huie, a former creative director and deputy chair of the Monahan Dayman Adams agency, who had moved into market research in the 1980s, warned of the rise of the 'anti-consumer' society. Consumers, she declared, were now spurning 'packaged goods, status labels, rich cars, ... financial security, bankers, technology, over-commercialism, mass market entertaining, department stores and jobs' in favour of 'culture, barter, simple living, nutritious foods, crafts, creativity, soft values, social disorders, the arts, poverty, self sustenance ... books, nature, movies, self improvement and knowledge'.[7] Hugh Mackay identified similar patterns. Speaking at a conference on cost-effective advertising, the market researcher foresaw 'a resurgence in interest in values and responsibility' and 'a surge of interest in religion and family values' which was 'good news for old brands and heritage brands'.[8] David Mattingly, whose eponymous advertising agency was synonymous with retail advertising, sought to connect this shift in attitude to broader demographic trends:

> It is clear from our own market research that the shopper of the '90s will be a much harder creature to attract and satisfy than its predecessors. Firstly, they will be older; for example, by 2000 over a third of the population will be middle aged and they will control well over half of the disposable income. They will be smarter, more cynical and more discerning in their pursuit of value. They are the "strategic shoppers". That is, their shopping patterns will change from occasion to occasion and purchase to purchase. ... Conventional notions of store loyalty are no longer relevant. ... Rather than middle age bringing about uniformity and conformity, the shoppers of the '90s will be even more individualistic in their states and interests. This will lead to even greater fragmentation of markets and a desire for greater diversity and self expression.[9]

The consumers' declining loyalty was similarly identified by other studies—although some would later raise questions about the studies' lack of nuance.[10] While this shift meant that there would be a greater need for advertising to make sales, it also raised questions about the advertising's capacity to build and maintain loyalty. Understanding the significance of this paradox, Clemenger BBDO went on the front foot to produce *Brands. Ignore Them and They'll Go Away*.[11] Based on Arbes' research, this report used consumer insights to alert advertisers to the need to pay closer attention to their brand and, of course, their marketing more generally.

The finding that consumers harboured negative attitudes towards advertising was hardly ground-breaking. While consumers had long enjoyed individual advertisements and commercials, their overall view of advertising was more negative, drawing on the sense that advertising was becoming all-pervasive along with the fears that the advertising industry was using devious strategies to dupe audiences.[12] However, market researchers' accounts of the growing negativity towards advertising and consumption in the early 1990s revealed a more profound change in the consumer outlook. Writing on consumer attitudes for *B&T*, Chris Adams identified this shift:

> In a world which is already deemed to be running off the rails, the power of advertising threatens consumers' sense of control. That is why their criticism

of the industry is more strident than ever. ... Today's critical consumer is no longer a passive recipient but an active participant in the development of products and communication. Increasingly literate on the subject of advertising and articulate on consumer right, the public is learning to question, challenge and place demands on a system which not so long ago was accepted as the voice of authority.[13]

Hugh Mackay similarly identified growing concerns about control and its impact on both consumer attitudes and the advertising industry more generally. Such sentiment, he argued, had seen a growing interest in 'discipline and regulation and this is a potential hazard for the marketing community, which could be facing much tougher demands for advertising and labelling standards'.[14] Significantly, the issue of control would continue to appear in subsequent market research reports over the course of the decade—long after the economic effects of the Recession had subsided. AMR: Quantum's *Monitor* study of Australian social values and trends for 1994/1995 found that 80 per cent of its surveyed respondents agreed with the statement 'lately I feel more in control of my life'. Such confidence, however, did not mean that consumers were reverting to past practices. Consumers, it was noted, 'are in a mood of saying we are going to build again but because we have got control we are going to do to it in our own way. Not the way any politician says we should or how a brand says we should, but our way'.[15] Two years later, Clemenger BBDO's *Silent Majority* report found that the lack of control remained a continuing issue. Consumers were thus 'much more worried, insecure, suspicious and angry than 20 years ago' and they felt 'increasingly out of control over its prospects and negative about the future'.[16] Grey Advertising's 1998 *Eye on Australia* report observed the impact of such attitudes on advertising. It claimed that 'the adversarial consumer', which had defined shopping trends for much of the early 1990s, had given way to the 'jaded consumer'—willing to spend but weary of the struggle to dig out great value from advertising messages.[17] Finding and connecting with this consumer would require the advertising industry to pay closer attention to consumer demographics.

Rethinking the key demographics

In his address to the 1993 AANA conference Rick Wilson, the managing director of Wilson Market Research, urged advertisers to adopt a more nuanced understanding of their consumers. Demographics, he argued, no longer offered any real insights or strategic advantages: 'A lot of the thinking is that if you buy the highest-rating programs you can't help but reach your target. But I ask, at what cost? ... It is the easy way out of the media problem ... Demographics are not customers they are statistics'.[18] Over the 1990s and the early 2000s, this desire to move beyond crude instruments of the mass market age evolved into a necessity, as advertisers and their clients looked to develop a deeper understanding of consumers that would enable them to make better use of new media and technologies. Of course, this did not necessarily stop the industry from segmenting and homogenising the market.

Women had long been one of the advertising industry's key markets. Yet despite the fundamental importance of this demographic, the industry had notoriously struggled to understand it, resulting in appeals and images that were all too-often sexist, demeaning, and patronising. Although this had been an issue for advertising industries across the globe, the staffing and culture of Australian advertising agencies over the post-war decades were particularly masculine.[19] In an effort to change the advertising industry's perspective, the National Working Party on the Portrayal of Women in the Media produced the educational package *Women and Advertising* in 1991.[20] As part of its efforts to combat the stereotyping of women in advertisements, the package underscored the diversity of women and their experiences. The package thus made use of research conducted by The Campaign Palace for its work on the Australian Meat and Livestock Corporation, which noted 'that diverse attitudes among women made it difficult to achieve a single brand positioning appealing to all segments of the women's' market'.[21] This point had been made by agency strategist Phil Ruthven at an advertising industry workshop 'Communicating to Women'. Ruthven argued the '"standard" family structure has disintegrated, changing the whole culture of "the family at home". The collage of family life has changed women's roles within the family unit'. [22] He foresaw a corresponding shift in women's working lives, as 'opportunities such as franchising, services subcontracting and flexible working hours create greater flexibility for women to mould work to their individual family needs'. Southdown Research Service's 1993 report, *A Woman's Perspective*, reiterated the diversity of readers of Australian women's magazines. Although it found that readers of *New Idea* were 'relatively unaffected by the women's movement', the report noted their growing concerns about the 'unrealistic and idealistic' images of women in television commercials. Based on the report's findings, Southdown Press marketing director, Warren Gillmer, took aim at blunt measurement tools that reinforced stereotypical depictions of women and urged advertisers to adopt a more holistic approach: 'women are not just another advertiser demographic ... there is a texture to the woman of Australia'.[23]

The status of women in the Australian advertising industry certainly contributed to its rather one-dimensional perception of the female market. In 1990 *Ad News* reported that although women outnumbered men in Australian advertising agencies, there still existed 'a huge disparity between the number of women in the industry and the number who reach top management'.[24] There was also a particularly notable gap in the creative department. The increasing number of women entering the account service department appeared to contravene the historical convention which held that clients (who were male) were uncomfortable with women. However, Kate Henley, executive director of the AANA, recalls that many advertisers in the early 1990s continued to view female consumers and their concerns with contempt. Henley recalls the response that she received when raising the topic of sexist advertising at a board meeting: 'they were like, "Why is that important? Why are you going down this track?" And I'm like, "I think it's important. It's going to come up" and they're like, "Really? Do we want to be spending our time on this?"'[25] Such attitudes, she adds, were beginning to change. Advertisers' growing interest in accountability meant that they were becoming more cautious of any risks that might adversely affect their bottom line:

> And then when people started talking about women holding the household budget and women making decisions, and people were going, "Oh my god, women do have more purchasing power. I really don't want to be offending 50 percent of the community". So yeah, I would call it an awakening about the role of women in society in general; not only how you represent them, but their buying power, how persuasive they were in household purchases, all those sorts of things. [26]

Such concerns are evident in Bob Miller's recollections of Toyota Australia's 'discovery' of the female market. Miller recalled that Toyota's research had revealed that 'no-one in the car industry ... advertised for women. And if they did it was some condescending bullshit or a pretty picture of a car with some flowers on the back seat in *Women's Weekly*'. Understanding the size and influence of this market, Miller and his team 'seriously invested in female magazines, first in the Packer Groups [Australian Consolidated Press] and then later on into other areas [such as] *Vogue* magazine and that sort of thing. And so we allocated 6 million bucks a year to female magazine advertising, and that separated us from everybody because no-one would do that'.[27] Toyota's marketing efforts here not only stand out for recognising the importance of women as car consumers, they also reveal an awareness of the diversity within this market and sought to tailor appeals to them through the different publications.

These trends and developments would continue into the second half of the decade. The empowerment of women as consumers was noted in Grey's 1997 *Eye on Australia* report, which observed that 'women today are now more demanding, more assertive, more cynical and more open to new alternatives than ever before ... six in 10 women are much smarter about how they spend their money than before'.[28] Advertising appeals revealed that the advertising industry was listening and, indeed, responding. In 1997, Julie Money, chair of the Advertising Federation of Australia Women in Advertising Awards, observed that entries had displayed 'a move away from stereotyping ... towards a more realistic portrayal of women in their relationships' and that the 'we're seeing a lot of commercials with subtle direction and performances and sensitive scripts'.[29] Such depictions also reflected changes taking place within the advertising industry's own ranks. Imogen Hewitt recalled that advertising 'was not a particularly flexible industry' for women, particularly those that had children.[30] However, by the turn of the century, she could see changes in the agencies' outlook: 'I think it became socially unacceptable [laughs] to be on the back foot there, particularly when you're in an industry that is meant to be a reflection of popular culture'. The changes, she adds, did not end there: 'we went through a period of there being more and more and more senior clients who were women, and simultaneously, one of the advantages of technology was just around the accessibility and the fact that you didn't need to be sitting at your desk 24 hours a day'.

Changes to the media landscape also had an impact on the way that the industry saw women as consumers and audiences. Under the headline 'The Typical Female no longer exists', *B&T* concluded that 'the female consumer presents vast opportunities' but cautioned readers that their 'attitudes will have to evolve if they are to be successful at reaching them. With the increasing numbers of mediums … being on offer, the consumer will be harder to reach'.[31] While familiarity with many of the media outlets meant that the advertising industry was in a position to tailor its strategies and appeal to reach the desired section of the fragmented women's market, the internet was different. Internet users were initially identified as being male. A 1996 survey by CompuServe in the US revealed that this was not necessarily the case. Its finding that women using the internet in the US had increased by 150 per cent since 1993 prompted CompuServe's Pacific manager Allen Sibley to concede that 'in the past, we didn't know how many women were using the service or what they wanted'. [32] However, the survey meant that '[w]e now have a much better understanding of what women are looking for'. By 1999, a survey by AOL found that the number of women going online had continued to grow and that they 'now make up more than half of AOL members'.[33] The internet's appeal was in part attributed to the fact that it 'brings ease and convenience to women's lives—whether at work or at home'. However, a survey conducted that same year on behalf of *Australian Women's Weekly* reveals a slightly different experience with respondents expressing reservations about shopping online.[34] Two years later, things had changed. A study by the online measurement and research company Red Sheriff found that in 1998 'only 11% of women using the Internet made purchases, compared with 24% in 2001'.[35] It also noted that they were more likely to be of a higher socio-economic status and aged between 30 and 49. This was certainly good news for advertisers looking to reach affluent families.

By 2000, it was clear that women not only formed the largest audience online, but that they were also the most active consumers, prompting *B&T Weekly* to observe: 'As women move to dominate Internet usage, e-marketers need to reassess their activity to cater to women's very different online behaviour if they hope to capitalise on this expanding market'.[36] To this end, it was reported that relationships were central to the way that women engaged online. Liz Mandile, marketing manager of TheLounge.com, underscored the significance of such relationships in the digital age: 'Building relationships between consumers and the brand is really important and the internet lets you really link product values with the Web site and with the women.'[37]

A 2003 report by Euro RSCG on women and technology made similar observations. Noting that '[w]omen have a strong relationship with the technology they use, making SMS and the Internet highly effective communications tools for marketers to reach them', Matt Donovan, one of the report's authors, urged marketers to 'think about how women are using technology' and, somewhat curiously, 'to think with a woman's eyes' when designing products and communication.[38] While a 2005 article on 'What women really want' declared that the 'new woman is a complex combination of smart, focused and radical, traditional, committed and feminine. She is rewriting the rulebook on how brands can to talk to her', Donovan's advice to marketers suggests that many in the advertising industry continued to hold on to the outdated images and attitudes of the past.[39] Despite the industry's claims, as well as the irrefutable data demonstrating the impact of women on consumption levels, it seems that the task of overcoming such entrenched sexism and misogyny was easier said than done—and the advertising industry would be the poorer for it.

After gender, demographic breakdowns of audiences and consumers focused on age. Since the 1960s, the Baby Boomers had been the largest and most lucrative market for major advertisers, but by the early 1990s it was clear that their time in the advertising spotlight was beginning to fade. 'Face it. Boomers are getting old', declared Karen Richie of McCann Erikson Worldwide. Urging colleagues to move on from the past, she argued that they needed pay more attention to the next generation of consumers who would soon be 'the primary market for nearly every product category'.[40] Generation X was the new target market for major advertisers, but the focus on the Baby Boomers meant that they were 'the least understood consumers and the most difficult sector to target'.[41] Of course, this would not prevent the marketing industry from categorising this new generation of consumers into a convenient and homogenous market.

A survey commissioned by Young & Rubicam in 1993 sought to introduce marketers and the advertising industry to this new generation. Entitled *Generation X*, the survey claimed that these consumers actively spurned the Baby Boomers' alleged embrace of conformity and 'yuppie values', embracing neoliberal values of individuality and freedom of choice instead. While Generation Xers were not anti-consumption per se, according to the survey's findings, they were expressing greater discretion about the brands that they were consuming. Significantly, their preferences were not unanimously shared by others across their cohort. As with the female market, this market was fragmenting—a process that had appeared to be absent among the Baby Boomers. The realisation 'that there is no way a single campaign can pick up the entire market. All its constituent segment needs to be understood' posed a very serious challenge for an industry that had grown wealthy on appealing to a single mass market (that had largely been a fallacy given the social divisions in terms of class, gender, and ethnicity).[42] Struggling to recalibrate its approach, the advertising industry's difficulties with Generation X would continue through the 1990s and into the early 2000s. In 1997, market researcher Rosemary Herceg observed that '[t]hey are not repelled due to the media's incorrect assessment of them, but more (by the media's) complete lack of effort towards understanding this generation, and the patronising messages they market to them'.[43] Two years later, social researcher and 'Generation X consultant' Mark McCrindle claimed that the industry still had 'a weak grasp of the market' and its sub-groups, and, indeed Generation X's 'scepticism'.[44]

The fragmentation and elusiveness of Generation X along with Generation Y (early Millennials) would also be exacerbated through internet usage. In 2004, it was reported that those aged between 18 and 34 were 'incredibly tech-savvy' and were 'more likely to be online than any other age group', making up 58 per cent of online users.[45] Commenting that '[y]oung consumers are a fickle bunch at the best of times, but the onset of new technologies is making them harder to pin down', *AdNews* noted broadcasters' deepening concerns about this market and its abandonment of television for online platforms.[46] Paul McBeth, media channel director at George Patterson Partners, thus outlined the new approaches to the 18–39 market adopted by progressive marketers: 'Hitting them over the head doesn't work. Some brands have even avoided mass media so that the youth audience might discover them as opposed to being intruded upon. Context—finding the right time and space—is critical with this group'.[47]

As the individualistic values of Generation X intersected with the individualised experiences and opportunities afforded by the internet, the use of demographics began to be questioned. A 2006 article in *AdNews* thus reported:

> Media consumption habits, social behaviour and the living conditions of people aged between 18 and 34 are now so diverse, researchers and the media are employing richer psychographic indicators—such as attitudinal statements, emotional patterns, social awareness and status—to understand what is now an increasingly fractured audience. Many researchers believe that while age demographics still serve a function, information about life stages and attitudinal statements helps to form a wider picture of today's younger consumer.[48]

While the same reports also featured a defence of demographics (based on common experiences, values, and economic sway), Generation X's attitudes and outlooks, along with its unique media consumption patterns, nevertheless illustrated the shortcomings of conventional units of measurement and the need for marketers to adopt a more holistic view of the consumer.

As advertisers and their agencies began to look beyond demographics, they began to see new 'niche' markets. Such markets were not only profitable in their own right, they also offered a more cost-effective way of marketing, as advertisers did not necessarily need to advertise in expensive mainstream outlets in order to reach them. Over the late 1980s and early 1990s, Australia's gay and lesbian community's campaign for social justice was gaining traction.[49] By 1994, the Sydney Gay and Lesbian Mardi Gras had become one of the largest events in Australia that was also broadcast on national television. The increased visibility of the gay community prompted the advertising industry to pay closer attention to this niche market's latent economic power—the so-called 'the pink dollar'. Marketing to gay consumers had initially been conducted by local gay-friendly businesses. However, the liberalisation of social attitudes towards homosexuality coupled with the realisation that the gay market was both affluent and willing to spend meant that many advertisers and marketers were now paying serious attention to the market that was estimated to be worth somewhere between $21 billion to $42 billion annually.[50] It was a 1990 print advertisement for Toyota that signalled a marked shift in the way that major, mainstream advertisers viewed the gay market. The advertisement depicted a Toyota Corolla with two men and a dog standing in front of a terrace house. Its caption read simply: 'The family car'. While this advertisement expressed a progressive viewpoint, Toyota's marketing manager Bob Miller recalls that its impetus stemmed from a more traditional motivation, generating profits during an economic downturn:

> [W]e want to evolve new markets ... Where is our biggest dealership in Sydney? It was on Williams Street, up near Paddington which is where they run the bloody gay Mardi Gras every year [laughs] right past your front door.

You go, "What are we doing about this market?" They go: "Nothing. Well, we don't want to talk to those people." "Really?" "Well, they're all living in poverty. They don't buy new small cars." Oh, so off we go and we discover the gay market. ... Now the gays buy them [small cars] because ... they tended to live in the inner city and so small cars were appropriate to park in the street, in Paddington, right.[51]

Significantly, the campaign was created by staff at the gay magazine *Outrage* as 'nobody at Toyota or its ad agency felt they understood gay tastes well enough'.[52] The campaign's success saw it re-published in the North American gay press, where it generated vigorous protests from the conservative Christian lobby.[53]

Interest in the gay market continued to build momentum. 'More and more advertisers are also succumbing to the temptations of the lucrative gay market', observed *B&T* in 1992, 'In fact, give it another five years, insiders say, and there will be few mainstream advertisers who will completely cross out the idea of targeting this tempting but touchy market'.[54] By 1995, the 'recognition that Australia's gay and lesbian community can mean big business for the corporate world' meant that that '[c]ar makers, airlines, finance brokers, fast food chains and breweries are all ... keen to cash in on the pink dollar. They all agree it is another form of niche marketing, now prevalent in diverse multi-cultural societies such as Australia'.[55] While the Toyota campaign was in part a response to the Recession, subsequent campaigns indicate that a broader shift had occurred. The change was illustrated by David Brooks' frank confession. As the managing director of a suburban hardware store, Brooks made the decision to reach out to the gay market by advertising in *Outrage* magazine:

> Brooks admits he was initially concerned about offending other customers with his advertising, particularly because of the family-oriented Mitre 10 name. "But I spoke with my management team and they said I was being very old fashioned and narrow minded" ... The response to the two-year campaign has been "very good," he says, though he concedes results are difficult to gauge on grounds other than gut feeling. ... "It's just a matter of time before people realise the gay people are there, they have a dollar to spend, and they'll all jump on."[56]

Of course, many did not. Despite being an affluent market, many advertisers remained fearful of a backlash from conservative consumer and preferred to steer clear.[57]

The growing importance of the gay and lesbian market led former lawyer Ian Johnson to create Significant Others, 'Australia's only full-service consultancy specialising in reaching the influential gay and lesbian consumer segment', in 1992.[58] While reports continued to extol the gay and lesbian market's affluence and propensity to consume, Johnson urged marketers, agencies and, indeed, the trade press to avoid stereotypes and simplifications.[59] Responding to an article in *AdNews* that positioned the gay market as early adopters of fashion and new technologies, Johnson reminded readers that the gay market, like any other market, needed to be considered in more nuanced terms: 'we need to be careful to recognise not every gay male is a trendsetter, a point often missed by many marketers ... globalised statements such as "gay people are at the cutting edge" quoted in the article ...

[may be] true for some gay men but certainly not all'.[60] 'The market is strong', he added, 'but expectations must be realistic'.

Blessed are the niche, for they shall inherit the world

In 1995, direct marketer Don Peppers questioned the future of mass marketing. Visiting Australia as part of a world tour, the American direct marketer observed that '[m]ass-marketing seems to be less effective every year … Media efficiency is dropping; there are more products than anyone case assimilate'.[61] Declaring that contemporary marketing was now 'about knowing your customers, knowing how they are different and knowing how to satisfy their individual needs', Peppers asserted that mass marketing would not survive the arrival of 'true interactivity'. At the Pan-Pacific Direct Marketing Conference in Sydney four years later, Don Schultz, the so-called 'father of integrated marketing', observed that Pepper's predictions were coming to pass: 'media fragmentation has dissipated the mass, consumers are less interested in what markets have to say and market companies are talking to individual consumers directly.'[62] As the advertising industry had been built on communicating to mass market, the fragmentation of the market and the media presented an existential crisis.

The softening of the mass market was first felt in the print media. Already in 1995 *Ad News* was reporting that the 'mass-market women's magazines that have for so long led the way have taken a battering over the last 12 months'.[63] Conceding 'to some extent it's easier to launch a niche title than a mass market title', Richard Walsh of Australian Consolidated Press sought to defend magazines by taking aim at their print competitors: 'newspapers are scared shitless by magazines because the relentless growth of magazines has been at the cost of newspapers'.[64] By 2001, the situation was no better with two-thirds of Australian magazines suffering a drop in circulations that year. Mandy Parish, media director at Carat Australia, observed that the difference between the successful and struggling titles was clear. niche titles were faring well, mass titles were suffering. Noting that '[m]ass titles cannot be all things to all people', Parish noted that readers were now 'buying more magazines that offer them exactly what they want. And they want information specifically relation to them and their interests'. Magazines, she continued, were not dead but 'the niche trend will continue in the fragmented media world' and 'those that survive will need to continue offering consumers exactly what they want'.[65]

Speaking at the American Society of Newspaper Editors in 2005, media mogul Rupert Murdoch lamented the newspaper industry's response to the rise of the internet: 'we've been slow to react. We've sat by and watched while our newspapers have gradually lost circulation'.[66] Murdoch not only attributed this decline to consumers who 'want their news on demand' and greater 'control over their media, instead of being controlled by it', he also noted that newspapers had struggled to be 'relevant to our advertisers'. It was a point that advertising agencies had been making for some time. In 1998, Jan Carter, national media director for Ammirati Puris Lintas, took aim at the press' outdated attitudes and approaches: '[T]hey're not at all open to change. They've got to look at releasing readership information, adjust their rate cards and start selling by sections in the same way that television stations sell by program'.[67] Anne Parsons, media director of George Patterson Bates, similarly castigated the newspapers for their arrogance: 'They don't feel that they have to sell themselves because they are always going to be part of media campaigns … because there are going to be clients such as banks and retailers who are always going to use them'.[68] Parsons complained that newspapers had been spectacularly unreceptive to innovations or suggestions made by the advertising industry—in stark contrast to magazines, television, and radio, which all 'try harder'.

Television's amenable relationship with the advertising industry reveals that it was more cognisant of the challenges posed to its advertising revenues than its counterparts in the press. In 2000, Garth Agius, managing director of media and communications agency OMD, noted that aside from the bump in television ratings caused by the Sydney Olympics, 'free-to-air audiences over the past 12 months have diminished somewhat, due in part to a change in lifestyle and a steady migration to pay TV'. The latter, he added, had evolved significantly in the advertising space, working with agencies and advertisers 'to develop marketing programs together, rather than in a supplier relationship'.[69] Although the television stations were more willing to engage advertisers and agencies than the press, they had been willing to play hard ball when it came to increasing advertising rates. However, by 2004, this attitude began to soften. While television rate hikes had long seen advertisers making threats about taking their advertising expenditure elsewhere, media fragmentation meant that they now had alternatives. Gary Hardwick, managing director of media agency Ikon, thus explained that '[t]his time there is a genuine desire to look at costing alternatives'—particularly those that reached the target market in a more cost-effective way.[70]

Wresting control

In 1998, BMCMedia ran a tongue-in-cheek 'Missing Person' style advertisement in the trade press. The missing persons were 'The Consumers', which were '[l]ast seen in 1998 leaving their local shopping centre with a computer and a modem. Extensive television advertising has failed to find them'.[71] The online advertising agency then explained that the advertising and media landscape had fundamentally changed: 'The fact is Australian consumers aren't where they used to be. They're spending less time watching television and more time on the internet. We can help you find them again'. Of course, this was hardly a surprise—the advertising industry had been well aware of this shift for some time. But predictions were now replaced with actual data, providing new insights into the consumer, the medium and, of course, advertising in the digital age.

In 1997, market researchers www.consult released the result of its survey of internet users, which found that the '"second wave" of Internet users' was 'more demographically rounded than previous estimates'.[72] 'They're looking a bit more normal. They watch more TV, and it's hitting the middle income family now', explained the firm's principal, Ramin Marzbani. He also added that while 'the demographics had continued to "normalise" interest in Internet content was totally diverse'. The internet and its audience had gone mainstream. Speaking at the Internet World 1999 conference, Marzbani's colleague Richard Sandlant offered further insights into this second wave: they were accessing the internet from home rather than work; they were accessing the internet for less than one hour per day on account of costs and security; and they tended to use the internet as an entertainment medium.[73] Consequently, other media outlets were showing a decline. A survey by Jupiter Communications in December 1998 revealed '45.2% of active Internet users said the time they spent watching TV had decreased because of internet use' and of these respondents '18% said they now read fewer magazines … 16.8% spend less time reading newspapers, while 10.3% said they listen to radio less'.[74] Moreover, it revealed that this shift was but the tip of the iceberg, as internet usage 'tends to increase over time as they become more familiar with the medium, with Internet users who have been online for more than two years spending three times as many hours online as those who have been using the net for six months'.

The trends documented by market research in the digital space informed the advertising industry that it needed to pay much more attention to the consumer. Declaring that '[w]e have been aggressively ignoring consumers', Don Schultz warned that marketers would 'no longer be able to market products with the same authority as before. The 'future of marketing', he added, 'is interactive, where marketers respond to customers' demands speedily'.[75] Many advertisers had already been moving in this direction. Some five years earlier in 1995, *Advertising Age* reported on a change in the activities and outlooks of Procter & Gamble's brand teams.[76] Where they had previously 'spent most of the time managing sales, line extensions, in-store promotions, allotments of specially marked low-price packages, slush funds', they were now focusing 'on the consumer—on advertising, product development and research'. This shift, noted *Advertising Age*, was a 'big win for the consumers, putting the power back in their shopping cart'. As the consumer moved to centre stage, new perspectives emerged. Richard Sauerman, planning director at McCann Erickson thus urged colleagues to dispense with the word consumer: 'The label "consumer" is institutional marketing jargon, looking at the world from a marketing perspective. This is a mistake, … we should think of our target as people—living beings who are driven by their feelings, emotions, impulses and passions … as opposed to only knowing and understanding them by the things that make them different'.[77] And by 2006, it was clear that the relationship between marketers and consumers had changed—irrevocably so. Philip McDougall, a creative director at experiential agency Jack Morton, had this advice for clients: 'You don't make the rules anymore. Don't try and control it. Don't try and make it hard for consumers. Let them embrace your brand exactly how they want. And if they want to reinterpret your brand, then you need to let them do that'.[78] Imagining the advertising ten years hence in 2015, Saatchi & Saatchi's CEO William Leach predicted that the consumer's power would only increase: 'We'll see consumers actually being the people who will dictate the power of brands'.[79]

The re-conceptualisation of the consumer reflected a broader rethinking of the medium as well as advertising's place in it. Stating that 'it doesn't matter who's using the Internet overall because it's not a blunt medium, it's very specific', Glyn Allanson, media group head of Clemenger BBDO Sydney, identified a fundamental differ-ence between new media and its mass-market predecessors.[80] In an address to del-egates at the 1999 Pan Pacific direct marketing conference, Martin Lindstrom, executive director of internet solutions agency Zivo, similarly separated the internet from mass media platforms, describing it as 'somewhere between the telephone and a personal meeting' which enables advertisers 'to customise their communication'.[81] The concept of the internet as an information superhighway continued to inform the way that marketers and the advertising industry viewed the consumer. Noting that '[o]ne in three visits to the Internet are to seek health-based information', a 1998 report on health advertising suggested building on the medium's strengths as 'direct-to-consumer (DTC) advertising could reap huge benefits'.[82] While it conceded that other media were also important, it nevertheless underscored the latent power in the internet's capacity to connect with individual interest and to communicate at a more personal level.

Others also identified the capacity for marketers to use online tools to develop more sophisticated insights into the consumer. *B&T* editor, Tony Burrett, thus observed how '[i]n the new order, a marketer will have detailed information about her market in a big database. She'll know who her customer is, what the customer wants and when the customer is ready to receive it'.[83] However, Burrett notes that data also serves an important broader function: 'a marketer will know exactly how much each customer is worth in terms of profit contribution'. 'Low-worth customers' are therefore jettisoned in favour of 'customers that deliver the most profit'. Collected and curated through digital and online tools, such granular understandings of customers illustrated the degree to which the new media differed from its mass market predecessors.

While the internet was promising (and delivering) deeper and more meaningful insights into individual consumers, some in the industry feared that its redistribution of power away from marketers towards consumers posed a real challenge to their field. Already in 1996, Toyota Australia's new marketing manager, Matt Callachor, noted that '[i]ncreasingly the consumer is having the chance to get information without advertising. We are looking closely at that'.[84] By the end of the decade, Patricia Duffy, vice-president of online search company LookSmart International, observed that 'there's a body of thought that suggests that marketing as a discipline itself is now irrelevant, and that the figure lies in the hands of "customer relationship managers"'.[85] Duffy, however, dismisses such calls as 'nonsense'. In addition to the claiming that '[g]ood marketers have always been focused on the customer as well as on strategies to take products to market, grow market share, and so on', she also predicted that 'as the amount of information provided by the Internet, and the number of purchasing options, increase, customers will continue to rely on two or three trusted brands for the bulk of their requirements'. Her prediction would prove correct. In 2005, research commissioned by the Australian Direct Marketing Association (ADMA) found that '[r]elevance, trust and control are the keys to successful direct customer contact' with 74 per cent of Australians indicating that they are 'happy to receive direct contact from organisations they know and trust as long as it is relevant and beneficial'.[86] While it seems that advertising was not yet dead, speakers at a panel on advertising and creativity at the 2006 Esquisse Festival for design noted that many senior agency figures harboured deep concerns. Jonathan Kneebone, a writer/director at The Glue Society, thus observed that '[t]here's been a reticence from agencies because they're losing their control over talking at people', adding: 'The extent to which people want to get involved with their advertising has surprised me'.[87] Sam Haysom, managing partner at MP+ was similarly frustrated by the senior management in agencies and their struggle to grasp the new medium and where advertising sat in it: 'The market's miles behind. More than 50% of marketers want to talk about [playing in this space] but don't want to do it. The reality is they can't sell it into the board, they haven't found a way to explain to senior management exactly what they want to do'.[88]

One of the responses to the rising power of the consumer was to hand them the creative reins in terms of devising and creating advertising materials. In 1998, juice manufacturer Berri and shoe firm Clarks each developed campaigns which sought to encourage consumer involvement. Created by 'target demographics rather than ad agencies', Berri's campaign would then be … 'be "finessed" by its agency, J. Walter Thompson Melbourne and formatted into Berri-brand TVCs that will run with the film-makers' credits'.[89] While Ant Shannon, executive creative director of Grey Worldwide Melbourne, observed that this approach was not new and that some industry insiders dismissed it as 'a lazy form of marketing', he felt that 'with the advances in interactive technology it's now an opportunity to do something quite entertaining'.[90] Mat Baxter, Naked's managing partner, similarly viewed this development as an opportunity rather than a setback: 'The democratisation of creativity just means we have to stop creating crap, and there's a fuckload of crap. Around 5% of advertising is good. The rest is crap. This just raises the bar: if agencies don't improve, there's a guy with a Mac in a garage who will show you up'.[91] While there was little real prospect that marketers would actually dismiss creative agencies in favour of garage-based amateurs with Macs, the creative agencies nevertheless understood that they no longer take their proprietorship over the creative process for granted.

Consumers were not necessarily waiting to be invited to engage with advertisers and marketers. Many were actively spurning them. Observing five major trends in the digital space was Rob Ryan, the managing director of the online agency DoubleClick Australia. While Ryan pointed to the growing impact of 'data mining tools [that] will provide advertisers with greater demographic and psychographic inflation, allowing far better targeting of individuals as they browse a Web site', this was counterbalanced by emerging software that 'will filter information from the current clutter of the Web, allowing people to individually establish their own parameters'.[92] Consumers, he added, would be in a position to 'better identify the information and offerings that are of genuine interest and relevance to them'. Marc Phillips, principal of APT Strategies, similarly noted the presence of ad-blocking technology, but urged the advertising industry not to get too carried away as consumers going online had evolved: 'Most of those who initially resented online advertising are less angry, while newer users accept advertising as an integral part of their experience'.[93] The slow but steady growth of online retail similarly revealed that audiences were seeing the internet as something more than an 'information superhighway'. In 2006, ACNielsen's Online Consumer Report found that fewer 6 per cent of Australian shoppers felt uncomfortable about online shopping, a figure that was well down on the 24 per cent that had expressed concern just two years earlier.[94]

The internet and information technology inevitably affected the ways that the industry was beginning to see and understand the consumer. With more consumers going online and engaging with multiple websites, advertisers and researchers not only found themselves dealing with new sources of data, they also had the technology to harvest it and, indeed, analyse it. However, their analysis of this data continued to be informed demographic and socio-economic models. Ross Honeywill's consumer classification sought to move away from using these models as a foundation. Instead, the social economist found that there were two types of consumers: 'Neo consumers' and 'Traditional consumers'. Described as a 'powerful group of spenders who make up one quarter of the population, but represent half of all discretionary spending', NEO consumers were defined as consumers who

> aspire to own things that are better than they have now. They are spenders, not savers, and are comfortable with buying luxury goods. They like to purchase on impulse and, for them, style is more important than price. Cynical of big business, media and governments, Neo-consumers believe in the power of the individual and insist on making connections that are relevant and intensely personal. ... Traditionals and Neo-consumers perceive brands in completely different ways. To a Traditional, a brand is a short-cut to certainty and confidence. A Neo-consumer by contrast delves behind the brand to understand its origins and authenticity. ...[95]

While this description of the consumer shared certain similarities with the upper quartiles in the conventional demographic division of society, its emphasis on values and outlooks meant that it was also connected to contemporary social, cultural, and economic developments. Honeywill thus argues that this bifurcation between Neos and Traditionals 'correlated with the failure of communism in 1989, the replacement of the industrial age by the information age in 1991, the global recession that swept the globe between 1989 and 1993, and the overthrow in 1991 of postmodernity by neo-modernity'.[96] It was, he would later reflect, a confluence of factors, which incorporated technology and knowledge culture but was not exclusively made up of them.[97]

While Honeywill suggests that he was tapping into the zeitgeist concerning technology and knowledge culture, they were nevertheless integral to his thinking. The impact of the digital revolution on the Neo consumer typology was perhaps most evident in the way that it sought to understand consumer actions at an individual level rather than the mass—a perspective that was also imbued with neoliberal ideas. 'In seeking the path less traveled', explained Honeywill, 'NEOs still encounter mainstream culture (such as football), but it is their individual twist on the mainstream that distinguishes them and makes them a challenging audience for mainstream marketing approaches'.[98] Not surprisingly, this typology and the insights it afforded attracted attention from key marketers in the digital space. In 2007, Yahoo! implemented 'a series of initiatives ... which would square the company's service directly against "neo mindsets". The key themes ... were "personalisation and control"'.[99] However, creative and media agencies remained more traditional in their outlook and were therefore more circumspect of this approach as well as its application to their established methods of analysing the consumer.[100]

The digital revolution also prompted questions that went beyond demograph-ics. Market researchers Wendy Gordon and Virginia Valentine took aim at the use of the term 'target market', claiming that the 'marketing model of thinking and the language that underpins it that has prevailed throughout the latter half of the 20th century is one of control. We, the company or brand, believe that we can pinpoint and thus target the customer/consumer in order to own and control them'.[101] In the face of recent rise of the consumer, this assumption seemed untenable. However, Gordon and Valentine warned against dismissing the marketers and their brands altogether. They instead argue that powerful brand–consumer relationships are built on identifying where consumers and brands (marketers) 'collide and join in a moment of identity':

> For successful brands, this will require a revolution in attitude, away from the idea of a fixed market of controllable consumers and towards the idea of a constantly changing cultural space in which people and brands come together for brief moments of empathy.[102]

The consumer, it seems, had not killed the advertising industry—at least not yet.

★★★

At the turn of the century, the claim that the 'consumer is king' had become some-thing of a mantra for the advertising industry. Consumers had not only grown in size and stature, they were also difficult to locate and, indeed, access. In this chang-ing climate, the need to understand the consumer (and audiences) was more important than ever before. Yet many struggled with it. Their difficulties, as well as their interpretations collectively illustrate Philip Napoli's claim that audiences, are 'constructed and defined to reflect the economic and strategic imperatives of media organizations'. Images of the consumer similarly reflect the interests of those defin-ing them. To this end, advertisers, their agencies, and other marketing-related prac titioners and businesses were actively creating and re-creating an image that was consistent with their experiences. Their fears around the economy thus informed their image during the Recession of the early 1990s, while their anxieties around digital media influenced their interpretations in the late 1990s and early 2000s.

Of course, the image and definitions of the consumer and audiences were not entirely self-serving—as a service industry, advertising agencies, media agencies, market researchers, and other allied businesses needed to maintain a level of objec-tivity or risk losing out to competitors. The use of demographics, for example, had been a useful and accessible way of gaining new insights into who the consumer was and how the consumer behaved. Such measures not only provided objective responses to these questions, they also provided an opportunity to identify changes and shifts. Although demographics offered significant insights, the growing realisa-tion that there were other ways of gaining insights into the consumer challenged the advertising industry to rethink its views of the consumer. However, it would be the internet that ultimately compelled the advertising industry to critically examine its views of the consumer and, importantly, its relationship with the con-sumer. The realisation that they were ceding control to the consumer marked a fundamental shift, not only in their efforts to communicate with the consumer, but also in the way that they saw and understood the task of advertising—it could no longer operate as a mass communication strategy for mass marketing. As we will see in the following chapter, the advertising industry's efforts to respond to these changes stimulated a more profound re-think of what advertising was as well as what it would be going into the future.

Notes

1 John Sintras, interview by author, May 25, 2020.
2 Philip Napoli, *Audience Evolution: New Technologies and the Transformation of Media Audiences* (New York, NY: Columbia University Press, 2011), 3.
3 Ibid., 4.
4 Mike Zeederberg, interview by author, May 8, 2020.
5 Andrea Kerekes, 'Do Ads Reflect Consumer Caution', *B&T*, June 7, 1991, 30.
6 Vicki Arbes, 'The Birth of the "Sensible" Consumer', *B&T*, June 7, 1991, 28.
7 'Anti Consumer Rears Its Head', *B&T*, September 20, 1991, p.7.
8 'Consumer Anxiety Epidemic to Impact on Ad Industry', *Ad News*, March 22, 1991, 3.
9 David Mattingly, 'Shoppers Turn Strategic', *B&T*, November 1, 1991, 15.
10 Bronwyn Campbell, 'Cagey Consumers Put Price Tag First', *B&T*, October 2, 1992, 7. Karen Yates, 'Fickle Shoppers Lack in Long-term Loyalty', *B&T*, April 1, 1994, 6; Adrian Dolahenty, 'Most Consumers are Brand Tarts', *B&T*, April 24, 1997, 12.
11 '"Sensible Consumer" Challenging Brands', *B&T*, November 1, 1991, 8.
12 For example, see Vance Packard, *The Hidden Persuaders* (Harmondsworth, Middlesex, Penguin, 1962).
13 Chris Adams, 'Why Consumer Want to Break Free', *B&T*, November 20, 1992, 14.
14 'Consumer Anxiety Epidemic to Impact on Ad Industry', *Ad News*, March 22, 1991, 3.
15 Lynne Hughes, 'Consumers Back in Control', *Ad News*, April 7, 1995, 6.
16 Katy Lyons, 'Consumers Angry and Suspicious', *B&T Weekly*, August 15, 1997, 2.
17 Susannah Petty, 'Consumers: Ads are "Boring"', *B&T Weekly*, June 19, 1998, 6.
18 'Demographics Obsolete', *Ad News*, April 8, 1993, 15.
19 Robert Crawford and Jackie Dickenson, *Behind Glass Doors: The World of Australian Advertising Agencies, 1959–1989* (UWA Publishing: Crawley, 2016), 5.
20 Anne Ross-Smith and Gael Walker, 'Women and Advertising: An Educational Resource Package', *Media Information Australia*, no. 64 (May 1992): 61–6.
21 Deborah Soden, 'Women Act to Improve Ad Image', *B&T*, 7 June 7, 1991, 36.
22 Phil Ruthven, 'Facing the 90s Challenge', *Ad News*, May 18, 1990, 48.
23 'Women Snub Image in Advertising', *B&T*, May 7, 1993, 9.
24 Marise Donolley, 'Bra-burners or Back-breakers? Advertising's Women of the 90s', *Ad News*, June 1, 1990, 10.
25 Kate Henley, interview by Robert Crawford, May 15, 2020.
26 Ibid.
27 Bob Miller, interview by author, May 7, 2020.
28 Adrian Dolahenty, 'Women Demand Value', *B&T*, June 13, 1997, 12.
29 Lara Sinclair, 'Women in Ads get Real', *B&T Weekly*, September 19, 1997, 5.
30 Imogen Hewitt, interview by author, June 1, 2020.
31 Sally Rawlings, 'The Typical Female No Longer Exists', *B&T*, October 8, 1993, 27.
32 'Net Catches Women', *B&T*, January 13, 1996, 12.
33 'The Net Works for Women', *B&T Weekly*, October 22, 1999, 11.
34 Paula Bomarfa 'Women Reject E-commerce', *B&T Weekly*, April 30, 1999, 6.
35 Danielle Veldre, 'Let's Go Shopping: Women Lead Online', *B&T Weekly*, March 9, 2001, 10.
36 Chantal Rumble, 'Relationships Key to Women Online', *B&T Weekly*, June 23, 2000, 17.
37 Ibid.
38 Barbara Messer, 'Women at the Tech Party', *AdNews*, March 28, 2003, 19.

39 Katrina Fox, 'What Women Really Want', *B&T Weekly*, September 23, 2005, http://ezproxy.slv.vic.gov.au/login?url=https://search.proquest.com/docview/195545607?accountid=13905.

40 Scott Donaton, 'The Media Wakes Up to Generation X', *B&T*, February 12, 1993, 24.

41 'Post Baby Boom Market Splinters', *B&T*, February 14, 1992, 5.

42 Ibid.

43 Susannah Petty, 'Research Redefines Gen X', *B&T Weekly*, 14 November 1997, 11.

44 Myron Smith, 'Marketing to Gen X a Failure?', *B&T Weekly*, 7 May 1999, 5.

45 Danielle Long, 'Interactive Motivation', *AdNews*, May 7, 2004, p.L4.

46 Barbara Messer, 'Younger Eyeballs Grow Weary', *AdNews*, May 7, 2004, p.L6.

47 Katie McDonald, 'Looking Outside the Marketing Square', *AdNews*, May 7, 2004, L8.

48 Matthew Eaton, 'Age vs Attitude: The Demographics Debate', *AdNews*, May 6, 2006, L4.

49 Graham Willett, *Living Out Loud: A History of Gay and Lesbian Activism in* Australia (Sydney: Allen and Unwin, 2000).

50 'Gay Marketing', *B&T*, February 11, 1994, 33.

51 Bob Miller, interview by author, May 7, 2020.

52 Ed Charles, 'The Gay Market', *AdNews*,
January 15, 1999, https://www.adnews.com.au/archive/the-gay-market1.

53 Ibid.

54 Sally Rawlings, 'Luring the Big Boys', *B&T*, February 12, 1993, 18.

55 Andrew Hornery, 'Tuned In, Turned On and Cashed Up', *B&T*, February 3, 1995, 13.

56 'Gay Marketing', *B&T*, February 11, 1994, 33.

57 Editorial, 'Power of the Pink Dollar', *AdNews*, January 15, 1999, https://www.adnews.com.au/archive/the-power-of-the-pink-dollar1.

58 'Significant Others' (advertisement), *B&T*, February 3, 1995, 13.

59 Lara Sinclair, 'Lesbians a Lucrative Market', *B&T*, March 1, 1996, 10; Ed Charles, 'The Gay Market', *AdNews*, 15 January 1999, https://www.adnews.com.au/archive/the-gay-market1.

60 Ian Johnson, 'Gay Market "Overstated" in Report, May 19, 2000, https://www.adnews.com.au/archive/gay-market-andquot-overstatedandquot-in-report.

61 Ross Gow, 'Mass Marketing's Grim Reaper', *B&T*, August 4, 1995, 12.

62 Tony Burrett, 'The Age of the Customer Arrives', *B&T Weekly*, July 2, 1999.

63 Rob Johnson, 'Mass Titles Suffer in Circulation Results', *Ad News*, August 11, 1995, 22.

64 Ibid.

65 Mandy Parish, 'Find Your Niche and Pander to It', *AdNews*, August 17, 2001, 27.

66 Rupert Murdoch, 'Murdoch's Speech: Full Text', *Guardian*, April 14, 2005, https://www.theguardian.com/media/2005/apr/14/citynews.newmedia.

67 Jason Walker, 'Newspaper in Crisis', *AdNews*, 13 March 1998, 18.

68 Ibid.

69 'Audiences Migrate to Pay TV's Niche Programming', *AdNews*, November 17, 2000, L5.

70 Paul McIntyre, ' Will Advertisers Really Turn Off TV?', *AdNews*, April 23, 2004, 11.

71 BMCMedia.com, 'Missing', *B&T Weekly*, August 6, 1999, 31.

72 Susannah Petty, 'Internet Users Fragmented: Study', *B&T*, February 14, 1997, 13.

73 'Profiling Web Users for E-marketing', *B&T Weekly*, August 13, 1999, 18.

74 Marc Phillips, 'The Net Ate My Audience', *AdNews*, April 9, 1999, 31.

75 'Time to Consider the Customer', *B&T Weekly*, 25 June 1999, 7.

76 'Time to Perform or Perish', *B&T*, 13 October 1995, 22.

77 Richard Sauerman, 'Forget Consumers. Think People', *AdNews*, May 7, 1999, 20.

78 Victoria Lee, 'Experiential: It's Not All About You', *AdNews*, March 10, 2006, https://www.adnews.com.au/yafNews/32E40749-E40E-4CAC-AD897FFEC738B003.

79 Danielle Long, 'Power to the People', *AdNews*, December 17, 2005, 12.

80 Susannah Petty, 'Net Surveys Are "Irrelevant"', *B&T*, November 15, 1996, 4.

81 Byron Smith, 'Web Marketing, Now It's Getting Personal', *B&T Weekly*, June 25, 1999, 1.

82 Kate Lyons, 'Consumers Take Control', *B&T Weekly*, 19 June 1998, p.30.

83 Tony Burrett, 'The Age of the Customer Arrives', *B&T Weekly*, July 2, 1999.

84 Adrian Dolahenty, 'Callachor: The Customer is King', *B&T*, November 15, 1996, 10.

85 Patricia Darcy, 'Marketing: The Next Millennium', *B&T Weekly*, October 22, 1999, 23.
86 AdNews, 'Consumers Like Relevant DM', *AdNews*, March 25, 2005, https://www.adnews.com.au/yafNews/B2B139D2-743F-43A2-AAABD7BF8B4F159B.
87 AdNews, 'Advertising's Brave New World', *AdNews*, August 25, 2006, https://www.adnews.com.au/yafNews/30C2DD1A-2D56-4A72-9DA540E0B69EBA7C.
88 Ibid.
89 Susannah Petty, 'Consumers Make Ads', *B&T Weekly*, September 18, 1998, 7.
90 'Where is Consumer-generated Content Taking Us?', *AdNews*, May 5, 2006, 9.
91 'Advertising's Brave New World', *AdNews*, August 25, 2006, https://www.adnews.com.au/yafNews/30C2DD1A-2D56-4A72-9DA540E0B69EBA7C.
92 Rob Bryan, 'The Net Must Enhance Consumer Experience', *B&T Weekly*, October 22, 1999, 18.
93 Marc Phillips, 'More Control for Consumers', *AdNews*, January 15, 1999, 15.
94 'Australians Get Comfortable Online', *AdNews*, September 22, 2006, 8.
95 'What is a Neo-consumer?', *AdNews*, July 1, 2004, https://www.adnews.com.au/yafNews/E669954C-D76A-4EC8-A724AD8BAE47CC52.
96 Ross Honeywill, 'NEOs', https://rosshoneywill.com/neos/.
97 Personal correspondence, email, October 19, 2020.
98 Ross Honeywill, 'NEOs', https://rosshoneywill.com/neos/.
99 'Chasing the Big-spending Neos', *The Age*, September 13, 2007, https://www.theage.com.au/business/small-business/chasing-the-bigspending-neos-20090619-cpbt.html.
100 Personal correspondence, email, October 19, 2020.
101 Wendy Gordon and Virginia Valentine, 'The 21st Century Customer: An Endlessly Moving Target', *Market Leader*, no.11 (Winter 2000), WARC Database.
102 Ibid.

7 Reimagining the advertising agency

By the early 2000s, it was clear that advertising and the advertising industry were no longer what they used to be. As its title suggests, Al Ries and Laura Ries's *The Fall of Advertising & the Rise of PR* by Al Ries and Laura Ries argued that advertising and those responsible for it had lost 'their traditional role as marketing partner' and that 'marketing has entered the era of public relations.[1] Their argument is entirely based on the view that advertising 'has no credibility with consumers, who are increasingly sceptical of its claims and whenever possible are inclined to reject its messages'.[2] In *The End of Advertising as We Know It*, Sergio Zyman and Armin Brott argue that advertisers needed to look beyond the 30-second television commercial and reconceptualise advertising as a broader form of communication that ultimately leads to sales.[3] Significantly, neither account made any real effort to consider the impact of the internet. While such gaps seem to stand at odds with the growing attention being paid to the new media platforms in the pages of the trade press as well as academic publications, a closer examination suggests that the two studies were perhaps more in line with contemporary practices at the day-to-day operations level.

The growing number of consumers going online signalled to marketers and their agencies that the future was undoubtedly digital and that they needed to embrace it or risk falling behind. Not surprisingly, advertising agencies were eager to present their digital credentials to clients. A 1999 advertisement for Euro RSCG Partnership opted to discredit its competitors by warning that '[q]uite a number of advertising agencies have leapt on the Internet bandwagon recently, proclaiming themselves to be "Internet experts"'.[4] Most, it added, 'have no real understanding about either the Internet or e-commerce apart that there could be a quick buck to be made somewhere'.[5] While such comments read like typical advertising agency hyperbole, advertising practitioners looking back on the first years of the twenty-first century recall that it was in fact an exercise of truth in advertising. Jhonnie Blampied, the chairman and CEO of DDB Australia deployed a culinary metaphor to explain how the established advertising agencies were engaging with the medium: 'Look, everyone was trying to explore to have an offering, but … it was an offering on the side. So it was a side salad, it wasn't the meal. It was something that would be nice to have to be part of a meal … And it was seen as a bolt on by agencies, much to their detriment'.[6] Michael Godwin, another DDB executive, similarly details the industry's lacklustre response as well as its unintended long-term impact:

> So we sort of kept doing what we did. I guess we put a website at the bottom of the ad and that was us becoming more progressive. But did we build websites? Did we understand digital strategy? Did we understand digital ecosystems? No we didn't. And I would argue that there's still a hangover to this day around that. I think that there are still "traditional agencies" and they aren't as well versed in all things digital and social as other more specialist agencies are.[7]

Such comments contain echoes of the disappointment that Elaine Leong, Michael Ewing, and Leyland Pitt found in their 2003 survey of agency attitudes.[8] However, disappointment about lost opportunities does not really define the broader picture that emerges from the first seven years of the new millennium. While the ambiguity that had characterised the advertising industry's relationship with the internet in the 1990s (as discussed in Chapter 5) was still evident, it would give way to a more pragmatic approach. Such pragmatism was the result of greater exposure to the internet. As the realities concerning the medium's functionality, not to mention its limitations, became more apparent, the advertising industry adopted a more hard-headed perspective of new media and the ways that it affected their advertising work and, indeed, the ways that the entire industry worked.

The Dotcom Boom

At the turn of the century, the Dotcom Boom was in full swing. As the number of people going online grew, so too did the number of entrepreneurial start-up businesses hoping to reach them. This seemingly irrepressible rise was not lost on investors and speculators who were desperate to cash in on the new medium's expanding popularity and its seemingly untrammelled future. Throwing caution to the wind, they were willing to invest increasing amounts in the hope of getting in on the ground floor of the next big thing, prompting further public stock offerings and fuelling higher stock prices.[9] Watching on as their audiences moved online, established media companies increasingly recognised the importance of the internet and sought to join forces with the new kids on the block. 'With the Web's rampant growth and the nascent move to high-speed broadband links that will bring on the vaunted convergence of TV and PCs, the Net is shaking up the media giants' hard-fought oligopoly', observed *Business Week* in 1999, adding 'media companies are in a mad scramble to overtake or at the very least form alliances with Web rivals'.[10] The situation in Australia was no different. In 1997, Publishing and Broadcasting Limited, which owned a major television network along with key print mastheads, joined with Microsoft to form ninemsn, a news and current events website. The advertising industry too would also be swept up into the hype and would profit handsomely from it.

In the US, the advertising industry played an important role in expanding the Dotcom bubble. Matthew Crain outlines how advertising, along with public relations, generated investment capital: 'Dotcoms with a strong market position and positive media profile found it much easier to attract investors … [while] those with investment funding spent heavily on advertising to further build market share and enhance brand image'.[11] One estimate claimed that as much as 80 per cent of venture funding given to internet companies was being spent on advertising.[12] Observers could not help but note the irony of tech companies looking to advertising agencies to market their brands in traditional media outlets. 'Only a year ago, media pundits were predicting that the Internet was going to put newspapers out of business. Yet now dot-com advertisers are clamouring to get into the national press, and the windfall from their new ad revenue is welcome news for traditional media owners', Chris White-Smith wryly observed in *Marketing Week*, 'Accusations have been flying that national media owners have been unfairly cashing in "on the boom and charging dot-com advertisers through the nose" for their space. What's more they want a cheap deal so the national press is being asked to subsidise their attempts to put us out of business'.[13] Crain notes that the dotcom businesses' investment in advertising also had a significant impact on the advertising industry's own efforts to enter the digital realm. Such investment thus provided a 'powerful feedback loop between marketing and finance had the effect of rapidly increasing the scale and scope of online marketing activities during the bubble period' and that 'ad spending in particular drove demand within the emerging online advertising market and contributed to medium's legitimation as a channel for commercial messages'.[14]

Although Australia lacked the same number of dotcom start-ups (and, indeed, cashed up investors) as the US or the UK, their impact on the local advertising was nevertheless discernible. In 2000, *AdNews* reported that 'Above-the-line online advertising revenue is expected to reach $100m this year—compared to $34.6m in 1999' and that this figure was predicted to reach $200 million in 2001 and grow to $400 million in 2002.[15] The estimated figure being invested by local dotcom businesses into advertising and marketing was lower than their American counterparts, with an estimated 50 to 70 per cent of working capital being used for such activities.[16] As the dotcom bubble began to expand, others looked for different ways in. Leo Burnett Connaghan & May, for example, took equity in dotcom start-ups as payment for handling their advertising accounts.[17] However, it was clear that dotcom money was finding its way into the agencies. Looking back on this period, Phil Hayden, founder of media strategy agency Bellamyhayden, recalls the 'bizarre' station whereby the advertising industry 'initially benefitted from … all these dotcom start-ups with local bench capital money for about year or 18 months, [that] wanted to do advertising in the traditional analogue channels'.[18]

Outdoor advertising was one of the key media outlets being used by the dotcom advertisers. In 2000, *AdNews* reported on this upswing with major outdoor advertising firms noting that dotcoms accounted for 7–20 per cent of their business.[19] This investment in out of home advertising was part of a global trend. In the US, dotcoms spent $US13.1 million in 1998, which then skyrocketed to $US101.3 million the following year. British figures were no less impressive, going from £1 million in 1998 to £13 million in 1999. Outdoor advertising conveniently addressed several needs. Noting that 'Outdoor is good for branding, you're seen to be like one of the big boys and it gives your brand credibility, ubiquity and makes it part of the community', Richard Herring, general manager of Cody Outdoor, revealed the ways in which the medium lent legitimacy to start-ups.[20] More importantly, outdoor advertising enabled dotcoms to reach their target audiences. With net users watching less television, outdoor provided a relatively cheap way of reaching them while generating broader awareness. Chris Tyquin of GOA Billboards in Brisbane thus observed, 'The oldest and the newest advertising mediums are coming together because the Internet start-ups realise you can't create a brand in cyberspace because people live and breathe in the real world'.[21]

As dotcom businesses looked to spend more on advertising, entrepreneurial advertising professionals established new agencies to service their particular needs. In 2000, Martyn Thomas relaunched Frank Media with the aim of delivering specialist media planning to dotcom businesses. 'Most of our clients are dot coms, we know what their requirements are and how they're different from conventional clients', he explained, 'We know how to build lifestyle brands through conventional media because we are the audience'.[22] Dotcom businesses, however, were often demanding clients that had no qualms in challenging their agencies' perspectives, approaches, and structures. Their combative attitude stemmed from the assumption that creative agencies possessed little more than a rudimentary understanding of the digital media. Telling *AdNews'* readers that '[i]nternet marketing means more than commissioning an ad and booking it', James Garvie, director of hotjobs.com, claimed that, although agencies did a good job of producing promotion materials, they did not fully understand the internet and the ways that it differed from other media. 'The dot-com client often has a much clearer idea about how to achieve a better return on investment', he declared, noting that dotcoms possessed the ability to 'know immediately which ads are driving traffic' and the agility to change 'the creative or media schedule' accordingly.[23] Such scepticism was not necessarily misplaced. Musing that '[a]t Whybin's we've been doing a lot of Net advertising of late, which involves sitting in meetings with technicians wondering a) what the hell they're talking about, and b) why advertising seems to be the least important part of the equation', Bruce Baldwin, senior art director at Whybin TBWA & Partners in Melbourne, seemed to confirm the dotcoms' view that agencies were out of touch.[24] Dotcoms also castigated agencies for their glacial approach and urged them to embrace the use of digital technology to expedite the approvals process for creative works as well as the dotcoms' capacity to calculate the costs of their own media plans.

On the other side of the fence, agencies discovered that their new clients had some quirks. Euro RSCG's creative director, Tom Moult, recalls that the dotcom clients were often young 'kids' with enormous budgets but little business experience. He thus recounts a popular joke that circulated the agency: '[W]hen kids came in for a meeting, the coffee would be laid out, and they'd say, "How much is the coffee?" and we'd say "It's free," and they'd go, "Wow!"'.[25] Others found that the lucrative new income stream derived from dotcom clients also came at a cost. Many were frustrated by the dotcoms' arrogance—whether it stemmed from their naivete or otherwise. 'Because the clients have created a dot-com media brand ... they think they know how they should be portrayed and may even want to book the media themselves', grumbled Kim Boehm, managing director of Clemenger Harvie.[26] Of course, this was hardly the first time that clients felt that they knew better than their agencies (see Chapter 2). The frustrations with this outlook would be exacerbated by the fast-moving dotcoms' efforts to exploit the hype surrounding their business as well as the agencies' desperation to land dotcom clients. David Jones, CEO and managing director of Euro RSCG, articulated the advertising industry's frustration with the dotcoms' mercenary approach and, indeed, dismissive outlook: 'It's easy for them to get a whole bunch of agencies to pitch for their business, use their ideas, then put it up for pitch again in three months [sic.] time'.[27]

However, it was the dotcoms' emphasis on speed that caused the greatest dissention among agencies. Having long enjoyed the luxury of creating and producing campaigns over weeks, even months, advertising agencies resented the dotcoms' truncated sense of time. 'They want to be on-air immediately, so the campaigns end up very ordinary', complained Boehm. Not surprisingly, this lack of creativity greatly irked those in the agency creative departments. Andrew Sexton, creative director at Spinach Advertising, illustrated such frustrations when he complained that:

> I haven't seen any great dot-com TV ads, which is surprising when you con-
> sider how much they're spending as a category. So why haven't I seen a great
> one? Maybe it's because they're all out there trying to grab attention and
> nothing else. They're not trying to sell me the product or a brand; they're try-
> ing to sell the advertising itself. Someday soon, they or their agencies (who
> should know better) will realise that it's not enough to have people just know
> your ads. People also have to feel something for your brand.[28]

While the expectation that dotcoms would use television again seemed to recon-firm the agency's inability to look beyond the 30-second television commercial, Sexton's assertion that advertising had a clear function, irrespective of medium, nevertheless offered a valuable reminder amid the dotcom hype. Sexton was not alone in calling dotcom advertising to task. In 1999, the UK magazine *Marketing* similarly noted that '[t]ough questions need to be asked of internet companies … Dot.com businesses can expect to be exposed to much fiercer interrogation of their ideas, development plans, content and brand values. … The challenge for new media business is to build their brands'.[29] If advertising agencies were to play a serious role in addressing such issues, they would need to invest more serious time, money, and effort in upgrading their digital expertise.

Inside the gold rush

By 1999 many of the large multinationals realised that they could no longer ignore the internet and that they needed to take action if they were to capitalise on the Dotcom Boom. Foote, Cone & Belding (FCB) was one of them. At its annual worldwide conference in 1999, FCB invited one of the heads of its newly acquired direct marketing agency, the Hacker Group, to address delegates. The speaker invited them to think more seriously about the 'three Ds'—data, digital, and direct marketing. Colin Wilson-Brown, the CEO of FCB's Australian offices, recalls attending this conference and being impressed by the speaker, who was 'hired as head of direct, but had effectively headed the three Ds based in New York and he was a centrepiece of their annual conference. … And I mean, I sat there thinking

"This is fantastic'".[30] Returning to Australia, an inspired Wilson-Brown duly set about establishing something along similar lines: 'we created a new department which was essentially the three Ds of data, digital and direct marketing'. Although there was already some demand from clients for such service, he recalls that the agency could stimulate more. In addition, 'we thought it would also be … a differentiator for the agency, you know, in new business growth and that sort of thing'.[31] In terms of the new medium itself, Wilson-Brown was clear: 'I mean, I didn't understand anything about it all'—and he was certainly not the only head of a large agency with this view. However, his 'thirst for knowledge and … respect for the way the industry was going' would see him actively pursue his digital plans.[32]

Wilson-Brown's plans for FCB's entry into the digital space would start modestly and would take inspiration from the way that British agencies had responded to the arrival of television. Matt Donovan recalls Wilson-Brown telling him how 'it started by putting one guy, back in those days, in charge of it and learning all about it, and then overtime that one person became the creative department'.[33] Donovan would be that man at FCB. With an interest in the internet and experience of working on IT accounts, Donavan was asked 'to become the agency's internet guy'.[34] This informal role meant that Donovan would be sent to FCB's San Francisco offices: 'They had a number of dotcom clients and were leading the way on this new era of online media and so I went over there to learn what they were doing for a few months'. Upon his return, he and Louise Brockbank (who had been recruited from overseas to head the agency's direct marketing operations) established FCBi, the agency's digital arm. However, Donovan still struggled 'because he wasn't an expert, nobody really let him take charge. But he was the guy who landed up being assigned with, "oh right, we need to do email stuff, so off you go," and that sort of stuff'.[35] This situation would change when Mike Zeederberg arrived in 2000.

Zeederberg's IT career had commenced in 1996 when he built a website for a London-based law firm. His entry into advertising was by accident, and 'with no background in digital, or marketing, or anything else' he found himself leading a digital start-up aligned to Batey Ads in Singapore in 1997.[36] After creating CD ROMs and award-winning websites for major brands like Visa and Mercedes, Zeederberg became more interested in the strategic side: 'And so, it sort of evolved into more of an account planning role very quickly, picking up a lot of the "where does digital fit into the overall marketing space?" And importantly, "where does that fit in inside an agency?"—as opposed to just being a sort of, techy delivery-type person'.[37] This was followed by another stint in London, this time with Brand, a direct marketing agency. 'Everybody needed stuff, everybody wanted stuff, and we were producing websites, and email marketing campaigns, and all sorts of stuff around that space', he recalls, noting that the agency grew from 3 people to 35 in the space of 18 months. While Zeederberg's team was riding the Dotcom Boom, it was also facing new challenges. He and his team were now 'hiring anybody that knew what the letters HTML meant. … we were struggling to find people. … we were competing with all the dot com start-ups. So, why work in an agency when you could go and work for a dotcom start-up that's burning through a million bucks a month and going to be the next big thing?'[38] Eventually, Zeederberg came to the attention of Wilson-Brown (via Donovan). Wilson-Brown considered him to be the right man for the job, telling him: 'given that you started up sort of the digital side of ad agencies a couple of times now already, it'd be great for you to come and start up this thing called FCBi. They're setting it up all over the world, so every office needs an FCBi element to it in the agency space'.[39]

Shortly after Zeederberg joined FCBi, Imogen Hewitt came on board. Unlike the others, she was a media person, working in FCB's media department as a planner/buyer. Hewitt was motivated by sense that 'you could see that there was something on the horizon with the introduction of the internet' and that 'interactive' media, as it was still known, seemed 'to be changing things pretty quickly'.[40] As a media person, she was also driven by an abiding interest in the internet's impact on media consumption and its capacity to connect advertising with audiences: 'And if this is the channel or the technology they're moving into, then it would be interesting to see how we go about utilising that for the purposes of getting advertising messages in front of them in an efficient and new kind of way'.[41]

Despite their investment and the growing popularity of the internet, the FCBi team struggled to gain traction among their colleagues across the agency. 'We were very definitely peripheral', observes Zeederberg, 'Nowhere near being the main game'.[42] The issues were not lost on Wilson-Brown, who points to the problematic attitudes residing in two key departments:

> The creative people in the main didn't understand it at all. They didn't understand the people. They wondered, initially what those people doing there because they speak in tongues … So that was complicated. The media department didn't understand it either. I mean, they were much more interested, because they could see that there were new channels that they needed to understand, but … they'd never seen direct marketing as a channel, for example. It's interesting that media people never saw direct marketing as a channel … it wasn't something they needed to be involved in at all…[43]

FCBi staff recall that the creative department's attitude stemmed from a number of sources. A key part of the creative department's antagonism towards FCBi stemmed from its creative director, who, according to Zeederberg 'really didn't want to know what we were doing, [and] wasn't that interested in anything we were going about'.[44] The agency's structural hierarchies helped reinforce the creative director's view. Recalling how 'you would come in and put forward a creative brief, and go away, and three days later they [the creative department] would deign to invite you back into their office to show you the creative concept', Zeederberg details the way in which FCBi was excluded from creative process and therefore had little scope of leading it. Of course, FCBi's standing within the agency also reflected the state of the medium that they were using. Hewitt thus notes: 'I don't recall having conversations with our creative teams about them being massively enthusiastic about what they were going to put in a really small space on a computer somewhere'. Not only were banners small, 'there wasn't a great deal of insight as yet into what would make that banner work. You know, "did someone click it?", [laughs] was about as far as you got'.[45] However, Hewitt also gives another important insight into the reasons for the media department's reticence to enter the digital space. Rather than seeing it as 'a new mass medium', she felt that she was 'dealing with an extension of CRM [customer relationship marketing] or an extension of direct mailers because it was small and it felt like you could pinpoint particular, I guess, contexts that people were in'.[46]

However, the challenges confronting the FCBi team inspired new approaches to developing and producing online campaigns. Zeederberg recounts how the team moved away from the linear model of creating campaigns towards 'a collaborative, brainstorm, workshop-type approach' as 'we started realising quite early on that you needed that mix of channel understanding, media understanding, creative messaging understanding, and planning, and customer insights'.[47] As FCB was one of the few agencies that had retained its media department, FCBi redoubled its efforts to bring the media team on board—and with Hewitt on board, it eventually managed to gain traction in this space.

Despite the challenges, or indeed in spite of them, FCBi began to produce innovative campaigns that were different in style and content. Its successful campaign for Nike football boots, which claimed that they offered unfair advantages over competitors, used a guerrilla viral-like approach. '[W]e actually at one point at one point set up a website which was an anti-Nike protest. Playing on the whole Nike and child labour, and that sort of stuff', notes Zeederberg, adding 'how the hell we managed to get it through anybody, I don't know'.[48] While FCBi's role in creating the website was eventually outed in the press, its unorthodox approach nevertheless generated industry chatter.[49] Donovan recounts the growth of the operation, noting how they created 'about 40 websites in the space of about a year', which enabled them to win 'big, digital advertising accounts', including 'AOL which became, at that time, FCB's biggest revenue advertising client'.[50]

Success in the digital space coupled with the Dotcom Boom suggested that FCBi had a strong future. However, such dreams would be dashed within months of the operations commencement. Zeederberg attributes the demise of FCBi to two factors: the globalisation of the advertising industry and the collapse of the Dotcom Boom. Zeederberg thus explains that 'FCBi at the time was owned by Publicis, and then they got bought by True North. At a holding company level, FCB ... traded hands. And one of the first directions that came out of the acquisition was, "this internet thing is a complete waste of time and money, shut down FCBi."'[51] While FCBi 'had managed to break even in the first seven months when we thought that was only going to happen in the first two years' and the (expensive) new staff 'were paying their way', the operation's weak staff-to-revenue ratio saw the new regional director calling for FCBi's closure.[52] And as the full impact of the Dotcom Crash became more apparent, FCBi had zero chance of survival. After 18 months, FCBi was 'reabsorbed' back into FCB in October 2001—the agency's press release cited a 'soft online market' as the cause.[53]

Looking back over the rise and fall of FCBi, Wilson-Brown remains disappointed with his bosses' actual commitment to going online: 'but at the end of the day, they were just paying lip service ... it wasn't changing the culture of the worldwide network in any way at all ... the focus was on the numbers and we closed the department down'.[54] In light of FCBi's achievements and, indeed, the developments that subsequently occurred in the digital space, Wilson-Brown also expresses regret for not defending the progressive project he helped devise: 'I'm sorry in a way I didn't argue more strongly, because ... absolutely what we were doing was the right thing to be doing. Well, at that point we were ahead of the curve as well, you know, and they never caught up after that [Laughs]'. [55]

The crash

'First it was tulips, then it was treasures from the South Seas, now it's technology stocks. Will this bubble burst, too?', asked the *Sydney Morning Herald* in March 1999. While it noted that '[t]he mania is not quite as pronounced in Australia, where the pickings are limited', the report nevertheless detailed the way in which 'enthusiasm has spread to Australia', spearheaded by mining companies. [56] Of these, the best known was an online marketer of adult products, adultshop.com. Shares commenced at 20 cents in August 1999 before reaching a high of $1.72 some four months later. 'How can a purveyor of marital aids and adult videos, even one of the world's largest, be worth that kind of money?', ruminated the *Age*, 'Only through the Internet, which has created a hysteria without precedent. Every day the predictions grow louder that the .com bubble will burst'. [57]

Such questions about the bubble were, of course, echoed globally and, of course, within advertising circles. Reporting on the dotcoms' rush to advertise during the American Super Bowl, the British journal *Marketing* noted that '[t]he UK is anticipating a similar frenzy of dot.com advertising' before sounding a clear warning: 'For many companies it will be a waste of money as unfamiliar brands get lost in the dot.com clutter and crash and burn. Many of these web crashes will happen in 2000—so make a note in your e-diaries'. [58] *AdNews* expressed similar concerns about the dotcoms as well as the advertising industry's vulnerabilities:

> It's obvious that a lot of dot-coms don't have the marketing expertise to take them down the path of creating a strong, trusted brand. And ad agencies seem so overwhelmed by the technological changes that they've forgotten what they're good at—creating advertising to support the values and long term strategy of a brand. Some industry pundits are predicting that, out of every 100 dot-coms that exist today, only one will survive. The lack of marketing expertise means they don't understand their market. [59]

So when the bubble began to deflate in April 2000, many were not surprised.

The Dotcom Boom stalled when American investors sought to rid themselves of overpriced stocks for companies that had yet to do anything. 'At the beginning of the year the markets were prepared to believe anything, provided it ended with .com. Now the cash has run out, and almost every e-commerce company from the largest to the smallest is feeling the squeeze', observed Dan Sabbagh in the UK's *Daily Telegraph*. [60] On the dotcom rise and fall more generally, Sabbagh mused: 'A two-year economic experiment that has unleashed more entrepreneurial activity than anything else for half a century is coming to an end, not with a bang but a whimper. Like the railways, suddenly nothing seems to work'. [61] Over the course of 2000 and 2001, the Dotcom Bubble steadily deflated.

The impact of the collapse varied. In the United States, where investment in the dotcoms was heaviest, the fall was felt hardest with investors left out of pocket and thousands left out of work. While Australia's relatively low investment meant that the impact was more muted in comparison to the US, the reverberations were neverthe-less felt. Online advertising agency DoubleClick closed its local media company (a decision made by its US parent company) while online audience measurement firm Red Sheriff relocated its staff from Australia to Hong Kong in a cost cutting move.[62] Online advertising figures for 2000 similarly illustrate the scale of difference between the Australia and the US. For that year, online advertising expenditure in Australia reached $72 million, an increase of almost 81 per cent over the 1999 figure. Significantly, this amount equates to $AU10 per capita, a drop in the ocean when compared to the $US400 per capita being spent on online advertising in the US'.[63]

The uneven impact was also discernible across Australia's advertising sector. Among the creative agencies, the impact could be seen in the reduction of staff in the digital departments. FCBi was not the only victim, Euro RSCG dismissed staff members from its digital division in early 2000, although it still lay claim to having 'the largest interactive division in Australia'.[64] Zeederberg, who went across to the Euro RSCG after FCBi folded, found that Australian clients had been spooked by the crash: 'The first year was horrible because every client stopped spending through the dotcom crash. I was told I had a revenue line of … about 4 million [dollars] … that actually turned out to be about 1.2 million'.[65] In addition to cut-ting staff, Euro RSCG threw itself into pitching: 'Everything that we could possibly get our hands on, we were pitching and going for to try and backfill the revenue as the dotcom clients—Ninemsn was one of their big clients. And they also just stopped spending'.[66] Of course, not everyone in the industry found themselves struggling. For many, the crash was irrelevant. Dominic Pearman, the head of an independent media agency, had little major recollection of the collapse. Asked if he remembered the collapse of the Dotcom Boom, Pearman replied: 'Not with any clarity, you know … I mean, obviously I remember it in terms of being in the news, but I don't remember it affecting my life as a media planner or buying digital'.[67]

As it became apparent that the Dotcom Boom had run its course, the advertis-ing industry, along with countless others, began to look ahead. 'The question on everyone's lips is: which of the new economy companies are going to live and which will die?', asked *AdNews*, noting that 'as many as 90% of Internet companies will either fold or merge in what has been called a "brutal", "long-overdue" and "rapid" shake-out'.[68] Condemning the failed dotcoms for their lack of business and marketing knowledge, *AdNews* predicted a brighter future for dotcoms with sustainable business models and 'an integrated marketing strategy to develop a strong brand presence'.[69] The aim now was to readjust and move on.

For the advertising industry, the key issue was client spending—both the amount and the media. In 2000, the total advertising expenditure on online display advertising was $80.2 million, a year later it had fallen to $60.7 million.[70] '[M]any traditional advertisers who were actually gearing up to fly online have been scared off by the "dot-bomb" publicity', observed Saul Sabath of the Western Australian-based online service provider Chrome Global.[71] Looking at the significantly larger reduction in online display advertising in the US, *Advertising Age* reported on the new attitude sweeping the industry: 'When dot-coms awoke at the end of spring to find their coffers nearly empty, many pulled the plug on marketing. ... Prudence replaced aggressive, pull-out-all-the-stops extravagance as a badge of honor'. However, the report also noted this dramatic downturn needed to be viewed in context, citing Charlene Li, senior analyst at Forrester Research: 'a lot of these dotcoms were wasting their marketing dollars ... So by cutting their marketing dollars, it didn't have any impact on revenue because the advertising wasn't doing anything in the first place'.[72] Despite becoming the CEO of Emitch, a major online media agency, at a time when 'the dot-com collapse has left many marketers apprehensive about the current value of online advertising', Janette Kendall similarly noted that Australian dotcoms were operating in a more prudent way: 'We are actually now seeing a shift from the dot-com frenzy to a much more sensible and sustainable approach ... People are beginning to see that good marketing is all about basic principles and communication, with online being just another way to communicate your message'.[73]

Stating that 'Dot-com advertisers will have to act like real, grownup companies in assessing how much to spend on offline media', *Advertising Age* noted in October 2000 that 'it's a somewhat different story online. Spending by Internet companies on Net ads has been growing consistently ... the big believers in online advertising turn out to be the Web divisions of traditional companies'.[74] In Australia, the drop in online display advertising did not mean that the medium was dead—far from it. [75] Adultshop, which had made a name for itself using various media including outdoor during the boom, decreased its advertising budget post-crash and restricted its marketing efforts to online in order to be 'more tuned to targeting specific audiences'.[76] Its Big Boy Briefs campaign in May 2001 was one of the first 'televiral' campaigns. Links to the commercial were 'initially sent to the Adultshop.com worldwide online subscriber list to forward the clip to their friends'.[77] While the principal objective was to enhance branding and publicity for 'low media outlay', it also seized the opportunity to use 'registrations on the landing page as product development market research'.[78] With some 2,500 to 9,500 hits a day in its first months, the campaign demonstrated the medium's capacity to reach target audiences. Various other retailers and banks similarly shifted their marketing expenditure on email campaigns and enhancing website functionality along with other 'below-the-line' activities.[79]

Looking back over the Dotcom Boom and bust, Jeff Perlman and Chris Jones of Euro RSCG Interactive mused: 'Has the whole dot-com thing failed? Is interactive dead? We don't think so. But reality has finally begun to settle in on an industry that thought reality wasn't relevant to them'.[80] While they reiterated the new mantra extolling the need for 'responsible business practices' and business plans using 'solid market research and real-world experience', their key point was that advertisers, and the advertising industry more generally, needed to develop a deeper understanding of the internet and its future role in advertising and marketing:

> It will be essential that they continue to recognise the interactive environment as a tool that can be leveraged for successful business, but not isolated from the broader marketplace. The integration of the tools and environments available

across this broader marketplace will ensure their ability to provide genuine benefits to their target audiences. It's been a bumpy ride, but those wearing seatbelts are still on the road to building real businesses.[81]

The new digital reality

Although the Dotcom Boom was brief, it would have a significant impact on the advertising business, particularly the agencies. In the aftermath, many simply dismissed it. Ricci Meldrum, an account director at Clemenger BBDO in Melbourne, thus recalls 'the older people in the agency that were a bit naysayers about all this digital stuff who adopted a "See, I told you" attitude towards the internet and the digital platforms in general'.[82] However, this was not necessarily shared by everyone in the agency. Meldrum notes that the agency's younger generation were unfazed by recent developments and maintained their faith in the new medium: 'it's going to take off'.[83] The youthful vision proved correct. Over the next five years, it would become clear that the future of advertising, and the agencies responsible for it, would be inextricably linked to the digital medium. However, it would be a gradual realisation rather than a sudden one, and while it demanded agencies take action rather than pay lip service, their actual embrace was not wholehearted.

In the immediate post-Dotcom Boom era, agencies struggled with negative client perceptions of the internet. '[A]nything with internet was completely on the nose and persona non grata and you kept away from it', recalls media strategist Phil Hayden, 'advertisers didn't want to touch it'.[84] When Clemenger BBDO announced its joint venture with Agency.com in 2001, agency CEO Robert Morgan sought to assure clients that were sceptical of the new medium that its decision was not another ill-conceived dotcom scheme. Noting that the internet was an important medium, Morgan sought to instil confidence in the agency's actions by explaining the new operation would bring 'a well-managed, well-resourced, technically competent company to work with the top companies in Australia' in the digital space.[85] Significantly, he actively distanced the initiative from the Dotcom Boom. Morgan thus emphasised that 'experienced staff' would be employed rather than '"some 25-year-old propeller head"—a reference to the headwear worn by some IT entrepreneurs during Internet boom'.[86]

With the images of the Dotcom collapse and young 'propeller heads' still fresh in their minds, clients remained highly wary of spending their marketing budgets online. Advertising agencies readily took aim at the (nameless) conservative clients that were unwilling or simply unable to comprehend the internet as a medium and the ways that it differed from other advertising outlets. Speaking in 2001, Laura Peck, the managing director of a newly established agency specialising in online advertising, argued that '[m]arketers are scared at present ... It's a combination of reticence and lack of education'. She notes that many marketers that ventured into the medium had little idea of what they were doing and unrealistic expectations: 'they do it badly, then blame the Net'.[87] Starcom's managing director John Sintras sought to change client attitudes by asking them to look in the mirror and consider 'what's happening in your own home life'. Such calls fell on deaf ears. In a speech, Peter Widdows, the managing director of Heinz Australia, explained that 'with most boards in Australia, if you said to them "iPod nano" they'd think you were talking about a re-run of *Mork and Mindy* … they're so far removed from the reality of what people are doing in their daily lives. Use of the internet, SMS, use of any emerging media—most of them actually don't know what they're talking about'.[88] Despite his best efforts, Sintras was dumbstruck by their inability see what was happening around them as well as the impact that it was having on their business:

> But do you know what they said to me? I still remember the meeting today and this was … the circulations directors and the CFOs of the big publishers that are no longer big. "Prove to us why we should invest this money," … "How's it going to grow our revenue?" All of them to a fault, to the last one. It's not about growing your revenue, this is actually about survival and defending your existing revenue and they just laughed at me. They just didn't believe it. … Most people didn't believe it was going to be big. Most people did not believe it was going that transformational. Most people were reluctant and late to the party and sort of did it kicking and screaming.[89]

Recognising the growing importance of the internet did not necessarily mean embracing it. As such, there remained an ongoing disconnect between promises of marketing online and the marketer's actual strategies. Mike Zeederberg thus recounts the frustration of being 'dragged into every single pitch' for mainstream accounts: 'We would then go in and present a whole bunch of digital stuff. The clients would then say, "we love the ideas, we love the fact that you guys can do digital … and that's why we gave you the account." And then they wouldn't do any digital'.[90]

Others felt that the clients' attitude reflected deeper structural problems. Rick Osborn, a former managing director of George Patterson, argued that the clients' moves to wrest 'control of their brands from the agencies' had effectively reduced the agency to being 'just another supplier along with direct marketers, event marketers, interactive marketers, sales promoters, PR agencies and independent marketing consultants'. With each 'supplier' advocating different and, indeed, divergent approaches to the marketing problems, many marketers not only struggled to develop a coherent approach across media and marketing platforms, let alone a deep and nuanced understanding of them.[91]

Stating that '[c]lients have always been well behind … consumers the whole time', Sintras contends that it is the agency's task 'to show clients the reality of what's happening in the world and to get them to catch up'. As the memories of the the Dotcom Boom began to recede around 2004, agencies were able to gain some traction with their clients on the topic of online advertising. Mike Zeederberg thus recalls how marketers' views went from 'we love the fact that you can do it, but we don't really know how to do it' to '"Right, this is actually a real thing." We've now got 50, 60% percent of the Australian population using online. We should be investing in it'.[92]

Reassessing the medium

As marketers displayed more serious interest in going online, the creative and media agencies similarly moved to improve their capacity to service their clients' digital needs. While many had publicly boasted of their ability to capitalise on the new medium, agency staff recollections some twenty years later suggest that the reality was somewhat different. Nicole Taylor, who had worked in account service departments at George Patterson and Young & Rubicam over this period, recalls the lack of real knowledge surrounding the medium: 'I don't think anyone truly understood [it]. Not clients and probably not even agencies'.[93] The range of agency initiatives and activities in relation to the digital space appeared to confirm this assessment.

Within the agencies, the internet continued to occupy an ambivalent space, albeit one that was beginning to change. Tom Moult identifies the shift in attitude that was beginning to sweep through the agency. Within the agency's internal hierarchies, the 'glamour boys' were still located in the creative department (which were still dominated by men) and they continued to dismiss those who were involved in the creation of television commercials. Thus despite its growth, direct marketing was still condescendingly labelled 'shit that folds'. Moult recalls that the creative department initially dismissed those working in the digital space: 'I remember internet, for a short while, was called shit that glows [laughter] because it was a, sort of, nerdy, weird thing'.[94] DDB Australia's chief executive officer Jhonnie Blampied paints a similar picture: 'All above the line, sexy, sexy, sexy and all below the line, boring, dull'.[95] Blampied adds that the lumping of digital with the unglamorous 'below the line' approaches also compounded another issue that had restricted its initial development: 'because it [online] was in its infancy, they didn't have the money to invest in growing it'.[96] This would change when audiences and clients moved *en masse* into the digital space. As digital began to attract more money in the mid-2000s, the status afforded to it in the agency ranks quickly improved. However, as planner Gavin MacMillan reveals, their growing commitment to digital did not necessarily reflect practice. He recalls an all-staff meeting at DDB in Melbourne, where it was announced that 'digital was now at the front of the bus'.[97] While this declaration sought to inspire staff and establish the agency's digital credentials, Macmillan and his colleagues were left unimpressed and somewhat bemused: 'it was just a statement with absolutely no backup to it. And so, nothing was done structurally process-wise. It was a charge in, say it, show a case study from something overseas and then everyone off to the pub and carry on as we always were'.[98]

The agencies' ambivalence towards digital media was reflected in their own websites. In 2006, *AdNews* ran a feature on agency websites. The results were underwhelming yet revealing, with the report finding that many agencies had poorly built websites, while others had sites that were 'under construction'. Agencies sought to defend their websites by arguing that they did not want to give clients the impression that they were spending too much time, money, and effort their own business. Scoffing at this explanation, *AdNews*' editor Dave Clutterbuck argued that 'agencies are a business and, despite what some creatives seem to believe, their reason for being is to make money. It would take a particularly short-sighted client to complain about that'.[99] In terms of the message being conveyed by agency websites, Clutterbuck declared: 'It's not too hard to work out that crappy website equals crappy agency in the eyes of said prospective talent if this is the only point of contact between the job market and the ad agency'.[100] Revisiting the topic three months later, *AdNews* found that little had changed. Such inaction, it argued, effectively exposed the agencies' real commitment to digital media: 'The generally poor state of ad agency websites in Australia exposes all this talk of integration and digital expertise as so much hot air'.[101] Reiterating his earlier point, Clutterbuck considered an inferior website to be an indication of the agency's level of understanding of the internet as an advertising and communication medium: 'Next time your ad agency gives you advice on your online strategy, check out their website. If it's under construction, bland, boring, hard to use or not regularly updated … you know what to expect from their advice'.[102]

The large agencies' slow embrace of the internet also reflected their mode of operation. As noted in Chapter 5, the lucrative commissions paid by established media in comparison to digital media meant that larger agencies had initially been reluctant to consider digital platforms. However, the growing popularity of the medium had forced a rethink, as agencies realised that they could not afford to dismiss the internet. As Rick Osborn noted, the larger agencies now found themselves falling behind and their livelihood depended on their capacity 'to win back lost share of client business and relationships'.[103] Their new strategy for many large agencies was simple and, as Blampied, was based on established practices:

> [A]gencies were really good at following once things have been discovered. So once people worked out all the kinks, then they will invest and buy the company that does that … they didn't actually invest in their tools, their knowledge. They bought PBT, they treated the business like bankers, not like entrepreneurs and they bought profit before tax. They buy companies that were already successful.[104]

Reports in the trade press appear to confirm this explanation. In 2003, STW Communications established STW Digital, which brought together seven separate digital operations under the one umbrella.[105] By 2005, *AdNews* was commenting that '[t]he big end of town may have been a bit slow on the uptake, but sooner or later, they'll have … bought best of breed and be beating the niche players at their own game'.[106] It cited Clemenger BBDO's continued efforts to acquire successful digital agencies as an example of this shift. Significantly, this acquisition process also offers insight into broader developments affecting state of advertising and the advertising industry. As agencies such as Clemenger diversified across multiple marketing and communications fields (which now included digital), the status of advertising within the networks appeared to deteriorate. With only 50 per cent of the Clemenger Group's income in 2006 being derived from its traditional advertising base, the future for advertising (and, indeed, those responsible for it) looked less certain than ever before.[107]

The agents (of change) start to figure it out

'The ad agency business has changed significantly over the past decade, everyone knows that', observed Rick Osborn in a 2002 opinion piece on the changes sweeping through agencies, 'What a lot of industry managers don't realise, however, is how much some of the big agencies have reengineered themselves after a decade of experimentation and evolution'.[108] His view was premised on the rise of the marketer and the emergence of the media agency. As demonstrated in Chapters 2 and 3, these developments certainly placed great pressure on the traditional agency operations. Tellingly, Osborn failed to reference the internet and its impact on the agency—but given the advertising industry's lack of progress in this space up to this point in time, this omission is hardly surprising. However, agencies were increasingly feeling the impact of developments in the digital space. Looking back, Nicole Taylor recalls: 'Probably 2000 to 2005 as the real transformation. You know, everyone kind of figuring it out'.[109] Their responses not only illustrate the way in which media convergence, as a process, was exerting a growing influence over their actions, they also illustrate the degree to which the industry was itself becoming an active driver of this process.[110]

The agencies' cautious response to the digital was hardly unique. Like so many other businesses, they simply did not know what they needed to know—the medium was too new, and experience was too rare a commodity. Nevertheless, the growing pressure to be active, let alone a leader, in the digital space meant that agencies needed to invest in building up their online capabilities. Only a few agencies could afford to buy out agencies with digital expertise; the majority looked to recruit individuals with digital skills. Michael McEwen, who worked in the account service department at Y&R and Clemenger BBDO, thus recalls the challenges faced by the agencies:

> [I]t's a little bit like "well who do you get?" And so anyone that comes in and says "well I'm digital and I know these things"—you don't know if they know it or you don't because you've got no way of assessing it. So, you're essentially taking a punt on someone's skillset ... until everyone else catches up, then you manage to work out who's top shelf and who isn't.[111]

As the number of digital-savvy staff in agencies increased, they began to exert a growing influence on agency operations. Nicole Taylor outlines the new ways of thinking they brought to the agency, as well as the unintended impacts:

> [A]ll of a sudden this ... different type of breed came into your agency ... [which] were more aligned with the direct, ... one-to-one end of the spectrum when it came to culture and talent, as opposed to the brand end of the spectrum ... And it started this gradual divide around ... "old school" and "new school" kind of thinking.

The young digital talent, Taylor adds: 'were pre-occupied with clicks and accountability and they talked the language and could offer clients something that the other agencies couldn't'. However, with the money and momentum moving in the new school's favour, advertising agencies began to reconsider their operations and structures.

Within the creative agencies, it was the creative department that seemed to struggle most with the digital medium. For many creatives, the advertising was not about selling but rather devising their next award-winning television commercial.

Their deep understanding of broadcast media and mass communication did not translate well to the internet, where audiences ceased 'to be isolated individuals' and connected 'with others to learn and to share opinions and passions'.[112] Interactivity via hyperlinks was similarly disrupting copywriters' efforts to craft holistic appeals. From a management perspective, the creative department's attitude towards digital media and their obvious limitations were extremely troubling, and they moved to excise them. 'Rather than embracing the potential of the written word', reported *AdNews*, various 'agencies are dramatically cutting the amount of money and time they spend on it'.[113] It also noted that agencies were willing to employ cheaper freelancers rather than maintain their creative teams.

While many creatives found it difficult to embrace the internet, others were able to see new opportunities. One of Australia's first creative breakthroughs online was the 2005 'Big Ad' commercial for Carlton Draught beer, which was developed by George Patterson Partners in Melbourne (creative director James McGrath, copywriter Ant Keogh, art director Grant Rutherford, agency producer Pip Heming, and group communications director Paul McMillan). The advertisement shows two opposing armies advancing towards each other, singing (to the tune of Carmina Burana) "It's a big ad, very big ad, it's a big ad we're in … This ad better sell some bloody beer." Aerial shots reveal the separate armies to be a face and hand and a glass of Carlton Draught beer. A parody of the 1989 British Airways' 'Face' commercial as much as the more recent *Lord of the Rings* movie trilogy, the humorous commercial would go on to win several awards for creativity and popularity, including a Gold Lion.[114] While the creative idea and production were integral to the campaign's success, Paul McMillan recalls that there were also other important factors underpinning it. Firstly, the agency had built a long and deep relationship with its client. This meant that the client had the confidence to support a campaign that bluntly told audiences it wanted to sell beer: 'It was one of the hardest things to sell because it was ironic, it was at a time when, culturally, the Simpsons had been in play for about ten years and it was very Simpsons-like'.[115] The second key factor raised by McMillan was the campaign's delivery. While it had been created as a television commercial, the team's excitement when sharing early versions online sparked a rethink: 'It was a moment where we actually went … "Maybe we should release this and get everybody really excited and … and get PR and energy off of the back of that"'.[116] The decision to launch the campaign with the hope that it would become a viral hit was impulsive and therefore risky. This risk was compounded by its reliance on new technology to automatically play the clip. However, McMillan notes that medium provided an opportunity to take a punt:

> I remember pushing the button to release that thing. And we didn't know what we were doing … at that time, there was no risk in doing that. It was like, well, just put it out there and if nobody does anything with it or shares it, then there's no problem. And if they do, then great. It was like a free kind of add-on. Because it was always going to run on television down the track. … It was a moment when we were brave enough to just try some stuff, and with a little bit of a background as to what we thought might work. But it was much more instinctively in the industry, in that sort of, wouldn't it be cool if our friends all saw this on their emails before anybody else did. You know? And then from there the rest is history.[117]

The gamble paid off—within two weeks the campaign had been viewed over a million times across 132 countries.[118] Other marketers and clients were inspired to do something similar.[119] However, McMillan is adamant that the campaign's innovations counted for little without creative thinking: '[T]hat's why the idea needed to be super powerful'.[120]

Although the internet presented an additional media outlet for media agencies (and the remaining few advertising agency media departments), media planners and buyers recall that its impact was still negligible and that the Dotcom Boom (and bust) counted for little. Jane Walshe, who had been working as planner and buyer in media agencies in Los Angeles before moving to Australia in 2003, explains that things continued as they were up until 2008: 'To be honest, I don't remember there being much change at all until the onslaught of digital and the requirement for agencies to have digital department and specialists and digital social'.[121] The media agencies' slow entry into the digital space shared certain similarities with that of the creative agencies, but also some differences. For media planner and buyer Simon Lawson, this inertia reflected a greater awareness of the actual state of the medium: 'Everything up until that point for digital was almost—I don't know—make-believe. There was potential, but it wasn't really working'.[122] Traditional media outlets still dominated the media scene, and the media agencies saw little incentive to change things. To this end, clients also played a key role. As Phil Hayden notes, media agencies needed to take the lead in educating their clients:

> I remember us clueing up on the internet and then trying to get clients to say, "You should move a bit of money from magazines to just to doing this little email thing," instead of trying to get responses in magazines and things like that. Some of them didn't want to know and some of them would try. So like anything, it had an incredibly slow start …[123]

However, Hayden remembers a shift in attitude around 2007, when large multinationals such as Unilever and Procter and Gamble began to spend significant proportions of their marketing and advertising budgets on digital advertising.[124] Fearful of being left behind, others began to do the same.

The shift in client attitudes coupled with the realisation that the future of media was online led larger media agencies to reconsider their outlook.[125] 'I think the multinationals realized that there was money to be made in digital, so they then started putting on large digital departments', recounts Dominic Pearman, founder of media agency Pearman Australia, 'And we as an independent, we got our digital department probably about, I don't know, five or so years after the large multinationals had big digital departments'.[126] The difference between the giant multinationals and independent local operations such as Pearman's was simple—access to funds. Jane Walshe thus outlines the scale of the large media agencies' investment when they decided to embrace digital:

> Definitely the bigger agencies that had the budget and/or the backing of holding groups, and also the holding groups were able to invest in small start-up specialist agencies, like search, social, content, they were able to acquire

those agencies and teams and then sit them in with their regular people, whereas the independent agencies just didn't have the money to do that. They might have had the nimbleness, but they didn't necessarily have the money.[127]

As with the creative agencies, the news of digital departments and the staff employed in them were viewed with suspicion. At Starcom, John Sintras explains that 'they started by being the weirdo nerdy people that nobody understood and nobody wanted to be a part of, and obviously they didn't exist as a discipline'.[128] Their insights and approaches encouraged media agencies to rethink their services in light of the broader changes sweeping through the industry. One response was the embrace of the concept of channel planning. This simple sounding concept quickly became a broad and nebulous catch-all term that enabled media agencies to present themselves as being up to speed in the digital age. An *AdNews* report identified no less than five definitions, including: 'Making sense of the explosion of (old and new) media channels in the context of increasingly fragmented consumer audiences', 'Integrating an above-the-line communications strategy with internal and external stakeholder marketing objectives', and 'Acting as a link or bridge between the media and creative process'.[129] Some, however, wondered whether this concept was in fact anything new. For Mike Daniels, Clemenger BBDO's strategic planner, channel planning was simply an updated version of what account planners had been doing in traditional advertising agencies: 'The shift … from the term "media planner" to … "channel planner" simply indicates the realisation of a commercial imperative by media shops. …They used to plan media, and now that traditional media is less dominant they know they need to plan channels'.[130]

Observing that '[c]hannel planning has certainly got everyone talking', *AdNews* wondered whether the debate might enhance 'good old-fashioned teamwork' within the industry.[131] This musing on the differing interpretations of channel planning and its possible outcomes offers a revealing glimpse into some of the tensions that had been building between media and creative agencies since the 1990s. While the advertising industry had initially seen the media's split from the creative side as a logical development of two distinct and separate disciplines, more recent developments revealed that the two were in fact entwined and were becoming more so over time. This was reflected in the agencies' battle to take the lead on a client's campaign. As Simon Lawson explains, both sides felt that they possessed the unique insights into the consumer and were therefore in a position to decide how the campaign should run:

> Well, the reality was, was that the approach that Mitchells had was far more harmonious with creative agencies because they didn't seek to uncover the consumer insight. They just did the channels, and the creative agencies did that. Where the friction arises [is] when you are doing it like Starcom, and like we all do now … suddenly you have got two agencies who are, you know, looking at the consumer and how the consumer is behaving, and what's the biggest challenge for this brief, and how can we arrive at a core idea that governs how we behave in media.[132]

Within this tussle, the media agencies possessed a structural advantage. Account director Nick Garrett notes the disparity lay in the fact that media agencies held the master portfolio: '[Y]ou might have three creative agencies on a roster working with different brands'.[133] This meant that 'the media agency started to drive [or] to have a more strategic role'.

Clients expected both sides to collaborate, but the differences often descended into conflict. Lawson thus recalls having 'stand-up arguments with creative agencies 30 minutes before a meeting where both of you are saying, you know, back down, or whatever'.[134] The internet created yet another battleground. Media research director John Grono thus identifies the way in which the direct sales generated through internet advertising exacerbated these divisions: '[it] has little to do with brand building. And to explain the mentality of this time, you had the creative agency saying it's all about the ad, and you had the media agency saying … a hell of a lot [is] about where we spend that money'.[135] While he similarly remembered the 'friction' and even 'loathing' between the two sides, he also points out that there was often 'cooperation' which resulted in creative and, indeed, effective campaigns.

The idea that media and creative needed to enhance collaboration would gain momentum as it became apparent to all parties that the internet was revolutionising advertising and advertising practices. Clients, noted Martin Sorrell, CEO of WPP, the British multinational communications holding company, were being particularly vocal in bringing the media back together with creative. A report thus noted that Sorrell had 'no intention of rebundling media and creative but if clients want it—and that's the trigger for Sorrell rather than a strategic push by his creative shops—then he says it will happen'.[136] And while it sounded a complete reversal on the media's separation from creative, agency leaders did not necessarily see themselves reverting to the past. They were keen to keep clients onside, but many were still unsure how this could be done. 'We have to build a new breed of super planners if you like, who are multi-dexterous and know a bit about all these things', asserted Clemenger BBDO's CEO Rob Morgan, 'It will take time but there's no other way of doing it'.[137] James Greet, CEO of media agency OMD, expressed similar sentiments: 'Until we've created an individual who can sit across both media and creative, we just have to find a way to work together. It's not rocket science'.[138]

Recollections on both media and creative sides reveal that the need to upskill in the digital space not only served to blur the lines between media and creative, it also prompted the agencies to review their practices more generally and to place greater emphasis on collaboration. Both processes illustrated the degree to which ideas of media convergence were informing everyday practices within the sector. In outlining how Starcom's embrace of digital media saw it evolve from being a useful add-on to core business for the media agency, John Sintras also reveals the pervasiveness of media convergence:

> There was more cross pollination. We started deliberately forcing ourselves to train people that were TV buyers into screen buyers and to help everybody understand what interactivity was and how it applied to everything we do, and to help strategists understand what investors did, and investors understand

what strategists did. There was a whole work and training program around that to try and get a more holistic [perceptive] … that was consumer centric.[139]

At the creative agencies, the arrival of staff with digital skills underscored just how weak their grasp of the internet had been. Not surprisingly, Clemenger BBDO group account director Ricci Meldrum likens it to a clash of cultures:

> [T]hey [digital specialists] spoke a language that we didn't necessarily under-stand and they would talk about things like wireframes and they would talk about things like the front-end development and the back-end development and creatives that had been in the industry or account services that had been in the industry didn't necessarily understand how to go about that and pro-ducers that were in the agencies didn't know how to do that necessarily.[140]

However, Meldrum also notes that the new digital specialists also had their own shortcomings, as they 'didn't know how to create ideas and didn't know how to tell stories'. Collaboration thus became essential, as both sides recognised the contribu-tion that others could make to the overall campaign and the inherent strengths of convergence. Another change in the creative agencies wrought by digital was the need to rethink the traditional division between above the line and below the line forms of advertising. Nick Garrett thus details the way in which his agency, Tequila, toyed with this division with a view to developing a more cohesive and collabora-tive result:

> Tequila was below the line for TBWA, but we all worked for TBWA and we all worked for Tequila and we all had two business cards, depending on what client and what day of the week, we could do anything. And it was a Trojan horse. … everyone understands that growth is coming from integration and creative opportunities, and once we realise that the below the line space, classic promo up, digital up, anything up, was creatively interesting, the light bulb goes off.[141]

One of the agencies that had fully embraced collaboration across the different departments was Euro RSCG. Under the direction of David Jones, it was already operating as a fully integrated agency with one bottom line by 2002. As the agen-cy's planner, Matt Donovan, recalls, 'they had media, they had interactive, they had traditional advertising, they had direct marketing, they had a database function, they had internal employer branding … they were going the opposite way to the rest of the industry'.[142] As the planner, Donovan recalls that his job was to 'create a way of doing strategy that could unite the disciplines and make them more power-ful together so that we could go to clients with a fully integrated solution as opposed to winning an advertising client and then trying to add another disci-pline'.[143] The success of this model led David Jones to apply it internationally as he moved on from Sydney and progressively worked his way up to the top of Havas Worldwide.

Looking back on the development of both creative and media agencies over the first decade of the twenty-first century, John Sintras offers a succinct summary: 'It's been the journey from "Madmen", where it's all about a suit and a creative, all the way through to this ecosystem of weird and wonderful people with specialisations from a huge cross section of disciplines sort of coming together'.[144] Such comments reveal that Euro RSCG's model, together with the other initiatives and collaborative and practices outlined earlier, were not attempts to return to the 'good old days' or to recreate the past—they were in fact pragmatic responses to the broader process of convergence sweeping the media sector.

★★★

As the digital dawn finally broke, it was clear that the advertising industry had irrevocably changed. Specifically, it was the advertising agency—now known as the creative agency—that had undergone the most radical transformation. Over the first years of the new century, it had to re-examine and re-invent its structures, operations, and practices in order to remain relevant in the new digital age. Far from embracing the new medium in full, the agency had been something of a conscript, forced into the digital space when it became clear that this was where the consumers wanted to be. Of course, the Dotcom Boom provided a lucrative incentive to engage more deeply with new media. While the agency's efforts to move online reflect its pragmatism, its ongoing ambivalence nevertheless betrays its deeper indifference to the medium, a point that was neatly illustrated in the rise and fall of FCBi. Ironically, it was the crash of the Dotcom Boom that compelled the agencies—both creative and media—to pay more serious attention to the internet and to recalibrate their services and operations accordingly. This process not only underscored the agencies' pragmatism, it would also offer further insights into the structural, financial, and cultural factors that had underpinned the agency's ambivalence towards the internet. With the popularity of the internet continuing to grow, it was pragmatism again that would drive the agencies to review and revitalise their capacity to service their clients' needs.

Although the advertising agencies managed to make it through the early days of the digital age, they had suffered enormous losses in the process: they had lost money; they had lost status; they had lost power. They had entered the digital age on the back foot and had struggled to make any advances thereafter. They were beginning to see the how the internet worked and how it affected them, yet their understanding was still shallow. Diminished in size, stature, and scope, they had nevertheless survived the digital dawn and would live to see the new digital day.

Notes

1 Al Ries and Laura Ries, *The Fall of Advertising and the Rise of PR* (New York: Harper Business, 2004), p. xxi.
2 Ibid., p. xvi.
3 Sergio Zyman and Armin A. Brott, *The End of Advertising as We Know* It (New York: Wiley, 2002). ProQuest Ebook Central, http://ebookcentral.proquest.com/lib/rmit/detail.action?docID=141424.
4 Euro RSCG Partnership, 'How to spot an Agency that's faking Its Way around the Internet', *AdNews*, July 16, 1999, T2.

5 Ibid.
6 Jhonnie Blampied, interview by author, July 31, 2019.
7 Michael Godwin, interview by author, November 27, 2018.
8 Elaine Leong, Michael Ewing, Leyland Pitt, 'Australian Marketing Managers' Perceptions of the Internet: A Quasi-longitudinal Perspective', *European Journal of Marketing* 37, no. 3/4 (2003): 566.
9 Matthew Crain, 'The Revolution will be Commercialized: Finance, Public Policy, and the Construction of Internet Advertising', PhD Dissertation, University of Illinois at Urbana-Champaign, 2013, 74.
10 Richard Siklos, Linda Himelstein, Ronald Glover and Catherine Yang, 'Dot.Com or Bust', *Business Week*, September 13, 1999, 78.
11 Matthew Crain, 'The Revolution will be Commercialized', 108.
12 Ibid., p. 140.
13 Chris White-Smith, 'Exposing the Hypocrisy of Dot-com Advertising', *Marketing Week*, April 6, 2000, 18.
14 Ibid., 108.
15 'Online Ad Spend Grows 200% in Year', *AdNews*, March 24, 2000, https://www.adnews.com.au/yafNews/814B6BC7-EF1A-417B-A1B52D86957FC276.
16 Andrew Hornery, 'Adland Fears the Dot-Com Dip', *Sydney Morning Herald*, April 20, 2000, 31.
17 Ibid.
18 Phil Hayden, interview by author, July 10, 2020.
19 Leithen Francis, 'Dot-Coms Tie Up Outdoor Sites', *AdNews*, April 20, 2000, https://www.adnews.com.au/yafNews/3CB93E73-EB05-4BED-915676A7FE320DC8.
20 Ibid.
21 Ibid.
22 Maria Ligerakis, 'A Frank Look at Dot.com Media', *B&T Weekly*, May 26, 2000, 6.
23 Evan Mistilis, 'Dot-Coms want Fast Response, *AdNews*, March 10, 2000, 1.
24 Bruce Baldwin, 'Is that a Creative Execution in Your Pocket?', *AdNews*, March 24, 2000, https://www.adnews.com.au/yafNews/37F5594A-9C1D-46EC-A5F25CD2 6816EC91.
25 Tom Moult, interview by author, May 11, 2020.
26 Evan Mistilis, 'Dot-Coms exploit Eager Ad Industry', *AdNews*, 25 February 25, 2000, 6.
27 Ibid.
28 Andrew Sexton, 'Where Are all the Great Dot-com Ads?', *AdNews*, April 20, 2000, https://www.adnews.com.au/yafNews/11D8F1BC-7FA0-4BC2-95BE32A 90DA13391.
29 Conor Dignam, 'Dot.com Bubble is Set to Burst in Less Happy New E-Year', *Marketing*, December 9, 1999, 17.
30 Colin Wilson-Brown, interview by author, May 6, 2020.
31 Ibid.
32 Ibid.
33 Matt Donovan, interview by author, May 29, 2020.
34 Ibid.
35 Mike Zeederberg, interview by author, May 8, 2020.
36 Ibid.
37 Ibid.
38 Ibid.
39 Ibid.
40 Imogen Hewitt, interview by author, June 1, 2020.
41 Ibid.
42 Mike Zeederberg.
43 Colin Wilson-Brown, interview by author, May 6, 2020.
44 Mike Zeederberg.
45 Imogen Hewitt.

46 Ibid.
47 Mike Zeederberg.
48 Ibid.
49 Todd Lappin and Bruce Grierson, 'The Year in Ideas: A to Z; Corporate Jujitsu', *New York Times*, 9 December 2001, https://www.nytimes.com/2001/12/09/magazine/the-year-in-ideas-a-to-z-corporate-jujitsu.html.
50 Matt Donovan, interview by author, May 29, 2020.
51 Mike Zeederberg.
52 Ibid.
53 Kris Ashton, 'Staff Shuffle as FCBi Closes', *AdNews*, October 26, 2001, https://www.adnews.com.au/yafNews/A24AB952-1DCD-460C-80C3E1479ED47D82.
54 Colin Wilson-Brown, interview by author, May 6, 2020.
55 Ibid.
56 Vita Palestrant, 'Another Blooming Mania', *Sydney Morning Herald*, March 24, 1999, Money Section, 1.
57 David Elias, Mark Button and James Button, 'Dot Com or Dot Con?', *The Age*, March 15, 2000, 10.
58 Conor Dignam, 'Dot.com Bubble is set to burst in Less Happy New E-Year', *Marketing*, December 9, 1999, 17.
59 Sam Tannous, 'Editor's Letter', *AdNews*, 20 April 2000, https://www.adnews.com.au/yafNews/17E0A011-388B-436B-BD05F3CC65885B10.
60 Dan Sabbagh, 'Pile-up on the Road to Riches', *Daily Telegraph*, 25 Nov. 2000, *Gale OneFile: News*, https://link.gale.com/apps/doc/A67301119/STND?u=unimelb&sid=STND&xid=4b90ecc5. Accessed 9 Aug. 2020.
61 Ibid.
62 Kris Ashton, 'DoubleClick closes, Red Sheriff shrinks', *AdNews*, 16 March 2001, https://www.adnews.com.au/yafNews/21AAACE4-530F-4400-87ECBDB28D6B6506.
63 'Net fails to score 1% of Total Ad Spend', *AdNews*, 3 February 2001, https://www.adnews.com.au/yafNews/4F610B53-BD6E-460B-BA268A763D151F8B.
64 Danielle Veldre, 'Aussie Dot Coms get Lean and Mean', *B&T Weekly*, 27 April 2001, p.10
65 Mike Zeederberg.
66 Ibid.
67 Dominic Pearman, interview by author, May 18, 2020.
68 Sam Tannous, 'Editor's Letter', *AdNews*, May 5, 2000, 8.
69 Ibid.
70 'Light at the End of the Tunnel', *AdNews*, February 15, 2002, https://www.adnews.com.au/yafNews/D165EA0B-5A7A-444D-A8518EAEA724FAD9.
71 Andrea Sophocleous, 'WA Dot-coms kick back and tune in after Crash', *AdNews*, October 26, 2001, https://www.adnews.com.au/yafNews/F2C5BE73-A286-4ED5-9D85BA04C89344CD.
72 Jennifer Gilbert, 'Running on Empty', *Advertising Age*, Nov 6, 2000, S2.
73 Jane Schou-Clarke, 'CEO has Online Confidence', *AdNews*, August 6, 2001, https://www.adnews.com.au/yafNews/09E156FE-7CC6-4783-ADAAFCF09AB82201.
74 'The Net Gain in Dot-com Fall', *Advertising Age*, October 2, 2000, 34.
75 Vanessa McQuarrie, 'Dot Coms not Spendthrifts', *B&T Weekly*, August 4, 2000, 2.
76 Andrea Sophocleous, 'WA Dot-coms Kick Back and Tune in After Crash', *AdNews*, October 26, 2001, https://www.adnews.com.au/yafNews/F2C5BE73-A286-4ED5-9D85BA04C89344CD.
77 Jeni Goodsall, 'Televiral Ads are Catching on Adultshop', *AdNews*, May 25, 2001, https://www.adnews.com.au/yafNews/8F101AE2-BFE0-4D2A-919C33BAAF42F9D9.
78 Ibid.
79 'Light at the End of the Tunnel', *AdNews*, February 15, 2002, https://www.adnews.com.au/yafNews/D165EA0B-5A7A-444D-A8518EAEA724FAD9.

80 Jeff Perlman & Chis Jones, 'Heard Around the Pub', *AdNews*, February 2, 2001, https://www.adnews.com.au/yafNews/13680034-041A-4866-891BB0254824FF52.

81 Ibid.

82 Ricci Meldrum, interview by author, May 24, 2019.

83 Ibid.

84 Phil Hayden, interview by author, July 10, 2020.

85 Danielle Veldre, 'Clems goes Online … Again', *B&T Weekly*, June 8, 2001, 32.

86 Ibid.

87 Kate Lyons, 'Why Online is the Hardest Sell', *B&T Weekly*, March 23, 2001, e8.

88 Will Sinclair, 'Boards "Clueless" on Online', *B&T Weekly*, September 23, 2005, 7.

89 John Sintras, interview by author, May 25, 2020.

90 Mike Zeederberg.

91 Rick Osborn, 'The Changing Face of Ad Agencies', *AdNews*, March 1, 2002, 20.

92 Mike Zeederberg.

93 Nicole Taylor, interview with author, February 1, 2019.

94 Tom Moult.

95 Jhonnie Blampied.

96 Ibid.

97 Gavin MacMillan, interview with author, February 8, 2019.

98 Ibid.

99 Dave Clutterbuck 'Wonderless Websites', *AdNews*, May 19, 2006, 10.

100 Ibid.

101 Dave Clutterbuck, 'Still Under Construction', *AdNews*, August 11, 2006, 24–5.

102 Ibid.

103 Rick Osborn, 'The Changing Face of Ad Agencies', *AdNews*, March 1, 2002, 20.

104 Jhonnie Blampied.

105 Danielle Long, 'STW does Digital', *AdNews*, March 14, 2003, https://www.adnews.com.au/yafNews/94816052-5CA4-403D-8B515D75035B44DC.

106 Dave Clutterbuck, 'Crocodile Fears', *AdNews*, February 24, 2005, 8.

107 Matthew Eaton, 'Ad Agencies at the Epicentre', *AdNews*, March 24, 2006, 4.

108 Rick Osborn, 'The Changing Face of Ad Agencies', *AdNews*, March 1, 2002, 20.

109 Nicole Taylor, interview by author, February 1, 2019.

110 Henry Jenkins, 'The Cultural Logic of Media Convergence', *International Journal of Cultural Studies* 7, no. 1 (2004): 34.

111 Michael McEwen, interview by author, November 20, 2018.

112 'Who Killed the Copywriter: The Internet or Agencies', *AdNews*, November 22, 2002, https://www.adnews.com.au/yafNews/58B561C8-75C2-48FC-92473793AA6B5A09.

113 Ibid.

114 'Big Ad Cleans Up at AWARD', *AdNews*, November 4, 2005, https://www.adnews.com.au/yafNews/7AFC095B-8E83-487C-BA4242F3AF7008C7. 'Carlton Draught 'Big Ad' Number One', *Campaign Brief*, 6 November 2005, https://campaignbrief.com/carlton-draught-big-ad-number/. Lynchy, 'GPY&R's Carlton Draught 'Big Ad' voted Best Beer Commercial of Last 15 Years', 28 July 2011, Campaign Brief, https://campaignbrief.com/gpyrs-carlton-draught-big-ad-v/.

115 Paul McMillan, interview by author, March 18, 2019.

116 Ibid.

117 Ibid.

118 'Big Ad Hits One Millionth Viewer', *AdNews*, July 29, 2005, https://www.adnews.com.au/yafNews/AEE89642-2A9F-452D-8319318E4A1BB7A9.

119 'Clients Catch the Viral Bug', *AdNews*, August 12, 2005, https://www.adnews.com.au/yafNews/FD723513-E8FF-4884-94C2009F21DE9051.

120 Paul McMillan.

121 Jane Walshe, interview by author, October 17, 2018.

122 Simon Lawson, interview by author, June 14, 2019.
123 Phil Hayden, interview with author, July 10, 2020.
124 Ibid.
125 'Evolution or Revolution', *B&T Weekly*, June 16, 2006, 6.
126 Dominic Pearman.
127 Jane Walshe.
128 John Sintras.
129 Matt Perry, 'Channel Planning: What's That Then?', *AdNews*, September 8, 2006, 19.
130 Mike Daniels, 'Channel Planning: New Word, Old Job', *AdNews*, October 7, 2005, 21.
131 Victoria Lea, 'Mutton or Lamb?', *AdNews*, September 22, 2006, 12.
132 Simon Lawson.
133 Nick Garrett, interview by author, December 14, 2018.
134 Simon Lawson.
135 John Grono, interview by author, June 19, 2020.
136 'Unscrambling the Egg', *AdNews*, October 8, 2004, https://www.adnews.com.au/yafNews/5A5E9125-8B78-4066-96988C27189A3C3D.
137 'Mutton or Lamb', *AdNews*, September 22, 2006, https://www.adnews.com.au/yaf-News/DD376238-8F33-4E2A-9C0FEA71FA322775.
138 Ibid.
139 John Sintras.
140 Ricci Meldrum.
141 Nick Garrett, interview by author, December 14, 2018.
142 Matt Donovan, interview by author, May 29, 2020.
143 Ibid.
144 John Sintras.

CODA

Perpetual uncertainty in the new digital age

But search engines were the thing that you had to get your head around. And nobody really did, and nobody really knew what they were … if you wanted to find out things, you could go into Google and you could start typing things up and things would emerge. Which was a very great link—a great link to e-commerce and direct and that sort of stuff. I don't think I had a sense at that stage though, of how the revenue model or advertising model would work for Google. … I didn't suddenly see Google as a big threat or—I found it fantastic.[1]

★★★

Google don't offer commissions or rebate, they're a conglomerate, they're a giant, there's no wiggle room, there's no flexibility, there's no partnerships in a way that we had with … TV networks or radio networks or heads of media channels. And so now … there's a Google spend … and the only way you could really make money is off a management fee. The problem with that management fee is that it's stock standard—it sits at 20 per cent. And that 20 per cent management fee, it doesn't really shift. In other words, it's okay when you're working on a $AU10 million budget, [as] that management fee is workable, but the truth is who has a $AU10 million budget in this day and age in Australia?[2]

★★★

In 2010, Google accounted for 17 per cent of all digital spend, and today it accounts for 36 per cent. Facebook has gone from 2 per cent to 13 per cent, so they now get a 49 per cent for every dollar spent on digital advertising.[3]

★★★

Now News Limited and free to air television stations are just left a bit in Google and Facebook's wake, aren't they?[4]

★★★

The digital dawn broke around 2007 with the emergence of Facebook and the iPhone, and the transformation of Google from mere search tool to major advertising medium. As the opening quotes illustrate, Google's impact on the advertising industry since the breaking of the digital dawn has been nothing short of revolutionary. However, as the previous chapters in this book have collectively shown, Google's emergence as an advertising behemoth was not entirely of its own making. It would in fact capitalise on many of the profound changes and developments within the advertising industry that had been in train since the early 1990s, as well as the advertising industry's own inertia in the digital space.

The growing popularity of the internet was integral to Google's rise. Offering relevant results quickly and in an easily digestible format, Google not only appealed to established internet users but also the new audiences looking to 'surf the net'. Audiences across the globe were actively choosing "to google", abandoning 'traditional' media outlets in the process. And by outmuscling its competition in the search engine space, Google emerged as the something of a posterchild of the neoliberal age as it transformed from a mere search aggregator to a gatekeeper of information. This consolidation of power sat at odds with the fragmentation of traditional media and audiences. Far from being threatened by fragmentation, Google's capacity to tailor information to meet its audience's individual histories and specific interests enabled it to capitalise on it. With fragmentation undermining traditional media's core strength—its mass appeal—Google pressed home its advantage and successfully transformed itself into the major commercial advertising platform of the digital age.

As audiences embraced Google, advertisers and marketers recognised that they needed to adapt. A growing proportion of their advertising expenditure would now be directed at Google. However, their interest in medium was also driven by other intrinsic factors with a longer history. Since the early 1990s, marketers had been developing a more sophisticated understanding of advertising and were no longer content to leave it to their agency to handle. Accountability had become marketers' new mantra as they sought to maximise the returns on their advertising expenditure. Lowering the costs of advertising was an obvious way of reducing outlay while mitigating risk. Not surprisingly, the lower costs of advertising on Google in comparison to producing a commercial for television resonated with marketers and advertisers. Google's capacity to target and reach niche markets in comparison to television's shotgun approach was similarly well received by marketers and advertisers looking to improve the effectiveness of their work. Significantly, advertising in the modern marketing mix had ceased to occupy the central position. As marketers reconsidered the role of advertising in their overall marketing campaigns, they began to reduce their advertising expenditure. Advertising dollars would thus be redirected at the cheapest and most effective medium—and Google would profit handsomely from it.

The rise of Google as an advertising platform occurred without any reference to the advertising agencies. Google's approach served to reflect and reinforce the advertising industry's weakened status. Over the 1990s and early 2000s, the advertising agency business had seen its size, scope, and sway continuously erode. As noted, clients had become more knowledgeable about marketing and more demanding of their agency. Decreasing advertising budgets not only reflected the way in which advertising had become just another tool in the marketing mix, they also illustrated the value that marketers now ascribed to advertising. The emergence of the media agency, yet another response to client needs, further undermined the power of the advertising agency. Advertising agencies not only lost their most profitable department, they would also find themselves in direct competition with them—in the media buying space and, later, in the strategic development space. While the fragmentation of the media had worked to the advantage of media agencies, Google's dominance, along with its efficient and adaptable advertising program Adwords, wrested power away from the media agencies. Unfortunately for the creative agencies, Adwords would also do little to help their cause—creativity on Google ran a distant second to being the first name that audiences saw when scrolling through the answers to their search query.

Although the advertising agencies were not directly responsible for the developments that had seen them lose ground to advertisers, media agencies, and consumers, it would be incorrect to view them as innocent victims of happenchance. Their actions and, indeed, inactions would also play directly into Google's hands. Like so many other industries and businesses, advertising agencies failed to recognise the degree to which the internet would impact their work. At one level, their ambivalent view of the internet was understandable. They could see that the internet would be an important communication medium and that its capacity to stimulate neoliberal concepts and values also sat well with its own outlooks and interests. Such hopes were counterbalanced by experience. The internet was initially a niche medium and very few industries and businesses were able to predict with any precision how it would actually affect their operations. Advertising agencies could also argue that their actions were in fact reflections of their clients' needs, or lack thereof. However, these arguments should not detract from fact that the advertising agencies were responsible for failing to take the internet seriously. There was a lot of talk about the internet, but there was little in the way of real action. Decreasing advertising expenditure and the loss of media commissions had certainly reduced the amount of time, effort, and funds that agencies could devote to improving their digital capacities and credentials. The reality was that they were still too comfortable with the existing structures and operations of the advertising industry (even if they had recently ceded ground to clients and media agencies). Consequently, advertising agencies were simply unwilling to move on from the stability of the past and to embrace the uncertain future. Charged with keeping their businesses afloat amidst a turbulent and unpredictable sea of change, agency managers and senior staff reasoned it was best to stick with what they knew for certain (i.e., how to advertise on television and other mass media) and to wait for the internet to find its place within the marketing mix. The agencies' conservative 'wait and see' approach might have saved money in the short term, but it meant that they would be on the backfoot when the digital dawn broke. For Google, the advertising agency was not only irrelevant, it was obsolete.

Of course, the rise of Google, along with Facebook and social media, did not spell the end of the advertising agency—creative or media. They still exist, albeit in a reduced size, scope, and profitability when compared to their predecessors. Agencies may have been slow and reluctant entrants into the digital age, but they were remarkably resilient. Once it became clear that digital media was eclipsing all other media and would continue to expand, advertising agencies repositioned digital at the core of their operations. Advertising thus became fully digital—from conceptualisation to execution. However, this born-again devotion to digital did not necessarily see the advertising industry reassert its dominance in the marketing and media sectors. Nor did it regain its brash confidence. The rapid evolution of the digital landscape post-2006 had meant that advertising agencies and the advertising industry more generally would remain in an age of ongoing uncertainty, particularly in the face of new giants such as Google and Facebook. However, there was one certainty—the advertising agency's 'golden days' were well and truly behind them, never to return.

Notes

1 Tony Hale, interview by author, May 13, 2020.
2 Michael Abdel, interview by author, July 19, 2019.
3 Dominic Pearman, interview by author, May 18, 2020.
4 Phil Hayden, interview by author, July 10, 2020.

Index

Note: Page numbers in **bold** indicate tables.

Printed in the United States
by Baker & Taylor Publisher Services